SCOTLAND '74

SCOTLAND '74

A WORLD CUP STORY

RICHARD GORDON

BLACK & WHITE PUBLISHING

First published 2014
by Black & White Publishing Ltd
29 Ocean Drive, Edinburgh EH6 6JL

1 3 5 7 9 10 8 6 4 2   14 15 16 17

ISBN   978 1 84502 749 0

A CIP catalogue record for this book is available from the British Library.

Typeset by RefineCatch Limited, Bungay, Suffolk
Printed and bound by Grafica Veneta S.p.A.

This book is dedicated to my son, Oliver, who has a strange fascination for football teams wearing dark-blue strips.

And to my daughters, Ella and Maddie, who have no interest in football, but make me smile. A lot.

CONTENTS

FOREWORD
BY
GORDON STRACHAN OBE

Like most, if not all, Scottish football fans, the national team has always been of great importance to me.

As a young lad growing up in Edinburgh I had my own football heroes and they were the Hibs players at that time: Peter Cormack, Pat Stanton, Colin Stein. They were on my doorstep, but when I first saw Scotland on the TV, I suddenly had new heroes and they somehow seemed bigger legends because they were on the telly.

The first game I remember watching was '67 at Wembley, the 3–2 win over England. Most of all I remember the excitement in the house and the rush outside afterwards to recreate it, everybody arguing over who got to be Bobby Lennox; who got to be Jim McCalliog.

You're hooked then, and it grows, because there were hardly any games on the TV then, but you did usually get some coverage of the Scotland matches, and every one of them seemed to be a magical occasion. I always remember Tommy Gemmell getting sent off for kicking Helmut Haller up the backside . . . Moments like that stick with you!

The next step was to see the team live and my first Scotland game was the 0–0 draw with England in 1970. There were 137,000 at Hampden that day. I remember Brian Labone was centre-half for England, Billy Dickson of Kilmarnock was left-back for Scotland,

and Willie Carr played. But I was only thirteen at the time and it's fair to say I didn't see much of the match. We were down to the right of the dugouts, everyone crammed in, and I'd see the ball in the air on occasion, people going up for headers, but that was about it.

It was an experience, a memory, but the real magic was watching these guys on the TV, because that way I could really see and appreciate those great players. Most exciting of all was the qualifier against Czechoslovakia, the goals from Jim Holton and Joe Jordan, and the realisation that we were heading for the World Cup finals.

I vividly recall the excitement that generated, and what made it even more special was that by then I was starting out on my own football career with Dundee, and a number of the guys at Dens looked to have a real chance to be part of the squad.

We had good players then – Gordon Wallace, John Duncan, Bobby Robinson, Jocky Scott, and the only one who ended up actually going to Germany, the goalie Thomson Allan – and it added to the buzz because I was playing with these guys, training with them. I remember they were lifted by the thought of playing in the World Cup and it was great for all of us, because nothing much happened in Dundee at that time. It was a big thing!

I wouldn't say it inspired me, because I've never been the sort to look that far ahead, I just float about and see what happens, but it did add even more to the World Cup, and to my personal interest in those '74 finals. I remember Peter Lorimer scoring the goal against Zaire; the confusion over the second one, wondering if it was going to be allowed; I remember Denis Law playing, that was a big thing for me because my dad used to talk about him all the time; Billy Bremner's miss against Brazil; and, of course, going out in typically heartbreaking fashion.

It was a great adventure, and I was lucky enough to enjoy my own taste of the World Cup finals, playing in the 1982 and '86 tournaments. I'm not one to remember incidents, games, even goals, but I still bump into people from across the world that I played against in those matches – aye, that was me, I've changed a bit, but aye, that was me – and I do recall some of the light-hearted moments. Of the six World Cup games I played, I was called in for drug-testing after four of them and they were hilarious, players having to be helped drunk into taxis afterwards because they'd had to drink so much beer before they could give a sample. The whole Scotland team was desperate to get called in for a doping test! After one of them I ended up in a bar in Torremolinos with John Robertson – how that happened I'll never know! Imagine that these days: it'd be all over Twitter.

The main feelings I had at the time were for my family back home, knowing how proud they'd be seeing me playing for Scotland at the World Cup, knowing my dad would have been jumping around the golf club with his mates when I scored against Germany.

Those are the special memories, and it would be great to play my part in bringing similar moments to the present-day Scotland fans, but it's so much harder to reach the World Cup or European Championship finals now. That '74 team essentially had a play-off against Czechoslovakia to qualify, and that would be lovely, but it's a different ball game now: football has changed beyond all recognition.

The 1974 squad did what it had to, and it's a group of players I have great fondness for. As I've mentioned, some of my heroes were in there – Peter Cormack, John Blackley, Erich Schaedler – great players. Jimmy Johnstone was another of my heroes and it was sad that he never got to play in West Germany.

It's difficult to assess one era against another, and we certainly didn't look after ourselves quite as well back then as players do these days, but with the right training and conditioning, some of those guys would be top players in this day and age, that's for sure.

I realise that for many younger fans you'll be reading about names which, in some cases, you might not have heard very much about before, but for the older supporter this will be a chance to relive some of the most memorable moments in the history of the

Scottish international team, to recall great players, great games. To wonder, once again, what might have been . . .

It was a special time for the national side, and what that squad achieved deserves to be remembered and celebrated.

Gordon Strachan OBE
Scotland National Coach
February 2014

INTRODUCTION

The Scottish national football team's relationship with the World Cup has long been a fractious one. Emotions engendered by our involvement in the competition have ranged from early scepticism to embarrassment, with a mixture of elation, frustration and bitter disappointment thrown in along the way.

Scotland's 'love affair' with the World Cup did not begin in earnest until 1954. The tournament itself began in 1930 and the first event was staged in Uruguay with just four European countries – Belgium, France, Romania and Yugoslavia – in attendance. The Scots missed out on that, and the two subsequent finals, as the national association, along with those of England, Northern Ireland and Wales, had withdrawn from FIFA, partly over a reluctance to compete against countries with which Britain had recently been at war, and partly to rail against what was seen as an unwelcome and growing foreign influence on the game.

The associations returned to the international fold after the conclusion of World War II, and Scotland would have debuted at the 1950 tournament but for the intransigence of the Scottish FA. FIFA designated the 1949–50 Home Championship as Group 1 of the World Cup qualifying competition, allotting two places in Brazil for the table-toppers and runners-up. The SFA, led at the time by its all-powerful secretary, George Graham, announced haughtily it would only accept the invitation should the Scots win the group.

The campaign began on October 1st 1949 with Scotland demolishing Ireland, as the football team was at the time known, 8–2 at Windsor Park in Belfast, Henry Morris of East Fife carving out a little bit of history for himself as he scored a hat-trick on what would be his one and only appearance for his country.

England won 4–1 in Cardiff a fortnight later, and the following month the Scots also disposed of the Welsh, John McPhail and Alec Linwood (winning the only cap of his career) netting in a routine 2–0 victory. England inflicted further damage on the Irish on November 16th, a 9–2 hammering setting up a Scotland v England title showdown. That game took place towards the end of the season, and on April 15th 1950, the English emerged triumphant at Hampden, Roy Bentley's goal securing a 1–0 win for the visitors. The Scottish FA stood firm, despite pleas from some leading players, and refused to send a team to the finals.

There were identical circumstances in '54, but this time Scotland did take up the offer despite again finishing second in the Home Championship. A 3–1 win in Belfast was followed by a 3–3 draw at home to Wales, but a win for Northern Ireland in Wrexham ensured the Scots a top-two finish, the runners-up spot confirmed by a 4–2 Hampden defeat to England in which Willie Ormond scored at the end to make the result a little more flattering.

So Scotland were set for their first appearance at a World Cup final. It was to be a half-hearted attempt, however, despite the appointment of Andy Beattie as the first-ever national team manager on a part-time basis. Until February 1954 all Scotland teams had been chosen by a selection committee; the introduction of a professional figurehead must have been seen as a progressive step, but the SFA seemed determined to put every obstacle in Beattie's way. Rather than the squad of twenty-two players permitted by FIFA, the manager was allowed to list just thirteen for the trip to Switzerland. Among the travelling party were two men who would later follow Beattie into the post: Ormond and Tommy Docherty.

But when Scotland's tournament kicked off on June 16th, Beattie was no longer in charge. Frustrated by the amateurish preparation and a lack of support from the SFA, the Huddersfield Town boss had quit, leaving trainer Alec Dowdalls to mastermind our campaign. The 1–0 defeat to Austria in Zurich was perhaps as good as the Scots might have hoped for in the circumstances, and there was sympathy from travelling journalists, the *Glasgow Herald* headline branding Scotland 'unlucky' and the Austrians 'mediocre'. That match report concludes with a remarkable summing-up, particularly given the disarray surrounding the squad. It reads: 'Scotland's name, thanks to the efforts of the team manager, trainer, and players, and those in authority who have seen fit to encourage them, stands higher than it has done for years and years.'

That name was about to take a battering.

In a unique format in which the groups consisted of two seeded and two unseeded teams, only four matches were played, with the leading pair in the seedings kept apart. That left the rudderless Scots with just one match to play, against the reigning champions Uruguay. In searing temperatures, and with a 43,000 crowd inside the St Jakob Stadium in Basel, Scotland slumped to the heaviest defeat in the history of the national team. They lost 7–0, the Scottish performance described by the *Glasgow Herald*'s football correspondent as 'a shambles of indecision and faintheartedness'. One of the players, George Hamilton, was quoted as saying, 'I'd rather be at home playing golf.'

In attempting to qualify for the 1958 tournament, the Scots had continental opposition for the first time, drawn in UEFA Group 9 alongside Switzerland and Spain, and it was the latter who provided the opposition in the opening encounter at Hampden on May 8th 1957. The star-studded visitors drew a crowd of 88,890 and twice took the lead, but Scotland showed great determination in fighting back to a 4–2 victory, helped in no small part by a hat-trick from

Blackpool's Jackie Mudie. The striker was also on target eleven days later as the Scots again came from behind, this time in a 2–1 success in Basel. The springtime fixture list was completed with a 4–1 humbling in Madrid, but with the Spanish having earlier been held to a 2–2 draw by the Swiss, Scotland knew a win against Switzerland that November would tie up the group. They did so, 3–2, thanks to goals from Archie Robertson, Mudie and Alex Scott, surviving along the way a nervous last few minutes.

The selection committee had been revived in the wake of Andy Beattie's departure, but the SFA turned to the Manchester United manager Matt Busby to guide the team through the World Cup finals on a caretaker basis. Those plans were thrown into disarray when, on February 6th 1958, Busby almost lost his life in the Munich air disaster. As he recovered from the multiple injuries incurred in the tragedy, trainer Dawson Walker assumed managerial duties, Busby taking over again in time for the trip to Sweden.

Drawn in Group 2, the Scots picked up their first-ever World Cup finals point in a 1–1 draw with Yugoslavia, Jimmy Murray scoring the equaliser in Västerås, but that was to be the only highlight of the '58 tournament. Over the next week Scotland lost 3–2 to Paraguay and 2–1 to France, finishing bottom of the table. Sammy Baird's consolation goal against the French would be the last scored by a Scotsman at a World Cup final for sixteen years.

Andy Beattie returned for another brief spell as national team manager, but by the time qualifying for the 1962 finals got underway, the team was under the command of the highly respected Ian McColl, who was nevertheless a surprise choice to take over, having just retired as a long-serving player with Rangers.

Group 8 consisted of three teams, and the Republic of Ireland were swept aside as Scotland won 4–1 at Hampden and 3–0 in Dublin in back-to-back internationals in May '61. The team were given a rude awakening a week later, however, as a rampant Czechoslovakia thrashed the Scots 4–0. Scotland's final qualifier was on Tuesday, September 26th and attracted a relatively small crowd of 51,590 to the slopes of Hampden Park. The Czechs twice went ahead, Ian St John and Denis Law equalising for the home side, before Law was set up by John White to slip home the winning goal just seven minutes from the end. Czechoslovakia duly disposed of the Irish in their double-header to match the Scottish points total, but despite having a vastly superior goal average, as was generally the deciding factor in those days, had to settle for a play-off at a neutral venue.

That match went ahead on November 29th 1961 at the Heysel Stadium in Brussels, but only after the Scottish FA had overcome a wrangle with Torino over their star striker, Denis Law. The Turin club only gave permission for Law to play after the SFA had agreed to insure him for £100,000. Everything had apparently been settled, but Italian officials turned up unannounced on the eve of the game demanding certain clauses be inserted for specific injuries. Association secretary Willie Allan refused, claiming the policy they wanted was one 'no British broker would accept'. In the end the Scots won the day, and also a dispute with the Czechs over which ball should be used for the match.

When it finally got underway Scotland took a first-half lead through St John. Jirí Hledík equalised in the seventieth minute, only for the Liverpool striker to immediately restore Scotland's advantage, but McColl's side could not hold on and Adolf Scherer levelled the match with a drive from the edge of the box. Denis Law shot just over in the final minute, John White struck the junction of post and crossbar early in extra time; and then the Czechs took over, Pospíchal and Kvasnák plundering the goals that earned a 4–2 victory and left the Scots on the World Cup sidelines.

Law's performance was berated by the newspapers, the *Daily Express* headline blaring 'DENIS LEAVES HIS MENACE IN TURIN', while the player himself explained, 'I was fit, but I just didn't get into it.'

Ian Ure and Pat Crerand were the only Scots to receive pass marks, with McColl giving this damning verdict: 'We were shocking.

It just wasn't our day. When we got in front we should have taken command, but we were let down by the four men we counted on so much, the inside forwards and the wing-halfs.'

Willie Allan offered only a succinct 'disappointing' to reporters.

The 1966 finals would be staged in England, and the Scots were determined not to be left on the outside looking in as the party got underway south of the border.

Seventy-four countries entered the qualifying campaign in the hope of securing one of fourteen spots available; hosts England and holders Brazil were exempt from the process. There were nine places available from UEFA, with thirty-two countries – including Israel and Syria – being split into groups of threes and fours. Scotland pitched in alongside Italy, Poland and Finland.

The campaign began with a routine 3–1 win over the Finns at Hampden on October 21st 1964, and the following May the Scots secured a 1–1 draw against the Poles. By then, Jock Stein – recently installed as Celtic manager – had taken over the national team on a caretaker basis, Ian McColl having resigned the week before the trip to Warsaw to become boss of Sunderland. Four days later Stein's side had to come from behind in Helsinki, Davie Wilson and John Greig securing a hard-fought 2–1 victory.

Italy had matched the Scottish points total in the early part of the campaign, but Poland were struggling when they arrived in Glasgow just a fortnight after losing to Finland. Another defeat would kill off their qualification hopes. Newspaper reports on the morning of the match expressed surprise over the Scots' team selection, with Billy Bremner, 'a player never far away from the centre of any available storm', earning just his second cap and Rangers winger Willie Johnston called up for the first time, to the exclusion of Celtic's John Hughes. Also dropped were Dave MacKay and Jim Baxter.

A crowd of 107,555 assembled on the Hampden terracing and had to endure a nervous start, home goalkeeper Bill Brown having to pull off three saves in the opening five minutes. Those nerves were soon settled, however, when Billy McNeill prodded the ball into the net after a slip by Brown's Polish counterpart Konrad Kornek. The Scots failed to build on that lead, though, Law and Henderson spurning clear chances while the Swedish referee Hans Carlsson waved away two genuine claims for a home penalty. Scotland were made to pay for that as the Poles scored twice in the closing six minutes, Pol and Sadek breaching the home rearguard as Poland became the first continental visitors to win a competitive match at the national stadium. It would be another two decades before Scotland next lost a World Cup tie at Hampden.

The *Glasgow Herald* declared our World Cup ambitions as 'shattered, probably for good . . .' and their correspondent Raymond Jacobs was to be proved correct, but not before the Scots, typically, revived the nation's hopes with a memorable success over Italy the following month.

With Jock Stein still operating on a part-time basis, the selection committee was again picking the side and sweeping changes were made for the visit of the Italians on November 9th 1965. Only four players retained their places from the Polish defeat, with debuts handed to Old Firm pair Bobby Murdoch and Ronnie McKinnon. Denis Law was among those left out, his place taken by Neil Martin, who had just been sold by Hibernian to Sunderland for the not inconsiderable sum of £45,000.

Scotland won 1–0, with John Greig, playing at right-back on the night, surging forward to drive home the only goal two minutes from the end. It was a match of few chances, as Martin and Alan Gilzean were well marshalled by the visiting defence, but the victory meant the Scots travelled to Naples a month later with qualification still in their own hands. A win would secure a place at the 1966 finals; a draw would mean a play-off at a neutral venue for a second successive campaign.

As it was, an injury-ravaged Scotland were beaten, heavily beaten, at the San Paolo Stadium as the Italians, backed by a fervent 68,873 crowd, dominated the match. The Scots were without Law,

Baxter and Henderson among others and had listed Liverpool centre-half Ron Yeats as a forward, although Italian pressure dictated he spent much of the ninety minutes helping his beleaguered rearguard. Goals from Pascutti, Facchetti and Mora secured a 3–0 victory and sent the Azzurri to the finals. There they would lose to North Korea, fail to progress from their group and be forced to return home in disgrace.

The 1970 qualification process saw eight places available to UEFA members, with Scotland drawn in Group 7 alongside Cyprus, Austria and the ever-powerful West Germany. The Scots were now under the control of our first-ever full-time manager, Bobby Brown, who had begun his reign by beating England 3–2 at Wembley in 1967, handing the world champions their first defeat since lifting the Jules Rimet Trophy the previous summer.

Confidence and expectations were high when the national side began its bid to finally reclaim a place at the top table of world football. The campaign got underway with a home match against Austria on November 6th 1968.

Two days previously Brown had taken his squad to the BBC studios at Queen Margaret Drive in Glasgow to watch 'a film show' of the Austrians' previous tie, a 2–0 home defeat to the Germans, and he told reporters that viewing had allowed him to point out various aspects of the visitors' play, which he believed would help his side. That was not immediately apparent, as within three minutes the Bayern Munich striker August Starek had fired Austria into a shock lead with a 35-yard shot that caught Ronnie Simpson unawares. Scotland were soon level, however, Denis Law scoring with a trademark header from Charlie Cooke's cross, and they eventually won the game 2–1, Billy Bremner scrambling home the deciding goal from close range. With the front page of the *Glasgow Herald* bringing news of Richard Nixon's election as US president, football fans had to turn to page twelve to read about the national team's performance, the headline informing them: 'SCOTS SCRAPE THROUGH WITH POOR DISPLAY'.

The second group match was away to Cyprus, the squad enduring a turbulent flight in which 'their aircraft was pitched up and down like the big dipper in the Kelvin Hall' according to one travelling journalist, but the players had clearly recovered by kick-off time and romped to a 5–0 victory, Alan Gilzean and Bobby Murdoch each scoring twice, with Colin Stein grabbing the other, all before half-time. The Germans had only scraped a 1–0 win in Nicosia the previous month, having to rely on a last-minute Gerd Müller goal to snatch the points, and it was clear the next game, a Hampden meeting of the pair on April 16th 1969, would be crucial in determining which country would be heading to Mexico.

A squad of seventeen players assembled at Largs 'for pre-match training under the guidance of Mr Bobby Brown, the Scottish team manager, and Mr Tom McNiven, the Hibernian trainer', with Celtic winger Jimmy Johnstone earning a recall. When the team was announced on the eve of the match it read, in the traditional formation of the time: Lawrence; Gemmell and McCreadie; Murdoch, McKinnon and Greig; Johnstone and Bremner; Law, Gilzean and Lennox. Suggestions that West Germany would be coming to defend in depth were quashed by Brown: 'The last thing we should think is that they are coming here to stonewall. We thought that about the Austrians and were caught out in the early part of the game.'

The Germans had never lost a qualifying match and knew a draw would make them favourites to qualify. With many supporters still queuing to enter the stadium because of 'chaotic traffic conditions', the game kicked off at 8 p.m. The Scots twice came close to opening the scoring, Law forcing Wolter into 'a magnificent save' and Gilzean heading inches wide. The German goalkeeper then denied Murdoch, Johnstone and Gilzean as the home side dominated, but it was the visitors who took an undeserved lead, Müller picking up a Franz Beckenbauer free kick, swivelling around McKinnon and beating Lawrence at his left-hand post. Sepp Maier replaced the injured Wolter at the interval and the Bayern keeper replicated his stricken team-mate's heroics, keeping Scotland at bay until five minutes from the end, when Murdoch sparked celebrations among the 90,000-strong crowd by firing high into the net after an exchange with Charlie Cooke. The 1–1 draw left the Scots top of the table on goal difference, but with three home games to come West Germany were now clear favourites.

The Germans won the first of those the following month against Austria, Müller again on target late in the match, and a week later Scotland thrashed Cyprus 8–0 at Hampden, Colin Stein scoring four goals. He remains, to this day, the last player to score a hat-trick for the national side. Gerd Müller emulated Stein a few days later as West Germany beat the hapless Cypriots 12–0 in Essen.

The decider would be played at Hamburg's Volksparkstadion on October 22nd 1969. Bobby Brown's plans were thrown into disarray when Eddie McCreadie, John Hughes and Bobby Lennox were all forced to withdraw because of injuries sustained the previous weekend. The player the West Germans most feared, Jimmy Johnstone, was available, however, and coach Helmut Schoen admitted he had made plans to try to stop the Celtic winger, who he believed 'could be the man to ruin German hopes of going to Mexico in 1970', according to Willie Waddell in the *Daily Express*.

Brown, as was the practice then, named his team the day before the game, listing Hugh Curran for his international debut, but the in-form Wolves striker was struck down by a bout of flu and had to call for the SFA doctor at 2 a.m. Colin Stein was drafted in despite a less than impressive start to the season with his club side, Rangers. The shock news was broken to fans back home by John MacKenzie in the *Express*: 'COLIN STEIN – off-form, out-of-touch Colin Stein – was hauled out of the shadows in this dismal, fog-enshrouded city today, to become a surprised central figure in Scotland's World Cup plans.'

The report described Bobby Brown as being 'amazingly calm' given the circumstances, and the striker was backed all the way by his Rangers team-mate John Greig: 'This is a big chance for Colin to show them he should have been there in the first place. I am certain he will take it.'

Fears the match might have to be postponed because of the heavy fog were allayed when the weather cleared. The 71,000 inside the ground were stunned into silence when the Scots took an early lead, Johnstone – despite Schoen's master plan – finding the space he needed to score after Maier had spilled a thirty-yard shot from Eddie Gray. Fichtel equalised just before half-time and the home team took the lead on the hour mark, albeit in controversial circumstances. Uwe Seeler seemed clearly to foul Billy McNeill as the pair contested an aerial challenge that left the Celtic defender grounded and clutching his face. As the Scots appealed for a free kick, Müller crashed the ball into the net. Alan Gilzean soon restored parity, heading in a McKinnon free kick, but it was not to be Scotland's night. They hit the woodwork three times and were caught out as the Germans counter-attacked rapidly, Libuda outpacing the visiting defence to latch on to Maier's through ball and beat Jim Herriot. The game ended in bad-tempered fashion and with the Scots down to ten men, Tommy Gemmell becoming just the fourth Scotland player ever to be red-carded in an international match after a retaliatory kick at Helmut Haller, which, according to reports, almost sparked a pitch invasion. The 3–2 victory clinched a place at the 1970 finals for West Germany, a tournament from which they would finally bow out in one of the all-time classic encounters, a 4–3 extra-time defeat to Italy in the semi-finals.

There were to be no such heroics for Bobby Brown's team, and the unsavoury conclusion to the game saw it feature prominently on the front page of the *Daily Express*, with a photograph of a disconsolate Gemmell under the heading 'TOMMY STARTS THE LONG WALK'.

Swiss official Gilbert Drosz was panned for his leniency until the late sending-off, and Brown was an unhappy and frustrated man when he faced up to reporters soon after the final whistle: 'Our players were the victims of a grossly weak referee. McNeill was punched in the face and left lying on the ground while the Germans scored their second goal. The referee sent Gemmell off, but ignored the shocking foul that tempted him to retaliate. It was a shocking display.'

A distraught Gemmell would say only, 'I am absolutely sick,' while Helmut Schoen, ever the diplomat, said, 'The Scots played better than they did at Hampden. It was a very tough game.'

MacKenzie's verdict was that Scotland 'went out with their heads held high, beaten by the breaks and an atrocious referee . . . These brave Scots have nothing to be ashamed of.'

Scottish dreams of going to Mexico had been dashed, denying the players the opportunity to collect the £600-per-man bonus on offer for reaching the finals, and the fixture list was rounded off a fortnight later with a 2–0 defeat in Austria that was greeted by the *Glasgow Herald* headline 'DISMAL DISPLAY ENDS SCOTS CAMPAIGN'.

For the third successive tournament Scotland had failed to qualify for the World Cup finals, the disappointment heightened by the fact that the squad at that time boasted a litany of world-class players. Throughout the 1960s the national team could call on talents such as Jim Baxter, Alan Gilzean, Billy Bremner, Jimmy Johnstone, Dave MacKay, Ian St John, Willie Henderson and Denis Law. All were recognised across the globe; many featured week-in, week-out for the top clubs in England; others were mainstays of Celtic's 'Lisbon Lions' or the Rangers team that reached the European Cup Winners' Cup final in 1967. And yet, for some reason, they were never quite able to effectively make that talent count when it came to World Cup qualifying campaigns.

The majority of the stars of the sixties would never play at a finals tournament, but a few did finally get the opportunity, albeit at the tail end of their careers, when the biggest show in town descended on West Germany in 1974.

1

CALL FOR THE DOC

The 1970 World Cup finals is widely regarded to have been the best and most memorable in the history of the event. After the more physical contests in 1962 and '66, the Mexico tournament was lit up by exciting, attacking football with eventual winners Brazil leading the way. Coach Mário Zagallo had already won the World Cup twice as a player and became the first man to double up, helped in no small measure by a squad littered with genuine world-class talents. Gérson, Jairzinho, Tostão and Rivelino all made their mark, as did the undisputed best player in the world at the time, Pelé.

Brazil coasted through the tournament, winning all six matches, but those finals were also notable for a number of other factors. It saw, in Morocco, the first African side to qualify in thirty-six years; it saw a thrilling Peru side led by Teófilo Cubillas (who would later haunt Scotland in the '78 finals); and it saw a new West Germany team boasting the talents of Franz Beckenbauer and Gerd Müller. Müller would win the golden boot with his individual haul of ten goals, which included hat-tricks in successive matches against Bulgaria and Peru.

The Germans came from 2–0 down against England in the quarter-finals, winning 3–2 in extra time and driven on heroically by the stricken Beckenbauer, his dislocated right arm in a sling, before falling to Italy in that memorable semi.

Brazil won the final, crushing Italy 4–1 in an imperious display capped off by captain Carlos Alberto's stunning drive low into the corner of the net, but four years on they would be a very different side, and West Germany, with the home advantage, were among the favourites to lift the famous trophy.

As hosts they did not have to enter the qualifying process, but Scotland did, and the Scots were among thirty-two European countries hoping to battle their way through. Eight automatic places were up for grabs, with a ninth facing a play-off against a qualifier from CONMEBOL, the South American zone.

On January 6th 1971, at the annual congress staged that year in Athens, FIFA announced a change in the format for the '74 finals. The sixteen qualifiers would, as usual, be split into four initial groups, but thereafter, in place of the regular knockout phase, there would be two further groups, with the winners of each contesting the final itself. It was also revealed the countries would be playing for a new trophy, the FIFA World Cup, to replace the Jules Rimet Trophy, which would be retained by Brazil to mark their third success in the competition.

When the draw for the qualifying campaign was made the following year, Scotland were pulled out alongside Denmark and Czechoslovakia in Group 8, but by the time the games got underway Bobby Brown had been sacked.

He had soldiered on for eighteen months, but the national team was struggling. There were narrow wins over Northern Ireland and Denmark, but then followed a seven-match run without a victory, including a dismal showing at the 1971 Home Championship that produced a single point from a 0–0 draw with Wales. A defeat in Copenhagen that June ended Scottish hopes of reaching the final stages of the European Championship, and five days later, in what was to be Brown's last game in charge, Scotland went down 1–0 to Russia in a friendly.

Six weeks later, the SFA's International Committee convened at their Park Gardens headquarters in Glasgow with the national press in no doubt as to the likely outcome. The *Glasgow Herald* suggested the Association 'can no longer dodge the issue', pointing to the dismal run of results as damning evidence. The manager himself attended the meeting, giving his report on the trip to Denmark and Russia, before being shown from the committee room to allow more serious matters to be discussed. Two hours later he was recalled and told he had been fired from his £80-a-week job. As he exited, Brown paused to tell reporters, 'I have been removed from the office of Scotland team manager. I have asked the secretary of the SFA to put the terms of my release in writing and until I have received this I have no more to say. I would like to add that I would wish my successor in a job that is complex and not easy, very good fortune. I hope he, more readily, is able to gain release of players.'

And with that Brown 'ran down the steps to a car and was driven home by his daughter to Helensburgh, where he has varied business interests'. His latter comment was a nod to ongoing issues the SFA was having with English clubs over the release of 'Anglos' for some international matches, a problem that was sparking much debate among the football press, with some journalists calling for those players to be overlooked entirely in favour of home-based Scots. Given that such a move would have at the time deprived the national team of talents like Billy Bremner and Denis Law, it was hardly likely to be one favoured by Brown's eventual replacement.

The SFA secretary Willie Allan issued a statement confirming the departure and announcing, 'Steps have been taken with regard to the appointment of a successor.' Early speculation saw the St Johnstone manager Willie Ormond installed as favourite, while there were also mentions made of Aberdeen's Jimmy Bonthrone and Bobby Seith of Hearts, both of whom had worked with the SFA in the past. Falkirk boss Willie Cunningham was rated 'a good outsider'.

Committee members had told journalists to expect a speedy appointment, but the SFA rarely did anything speedily in the early

1970s, and more than a fortnight later came the news the post would now be advertised. It had been confirmed it would remain a full-time position, a decision that would rule out the leading successful club managers such as Jock Stein and Eddie Turnbull, even at the increased annual salary of £5,000, which it was believed the Association was prepared to pay to secure the right man.

That process seems to have borne little fruit, as in late August 1971 the SFA made its first tentative approach to Cunningham, sounding out the Northern Irishman about his interest in the job. On September 3rd the Falkirk manager had a lunchtime meeting in Glasgow with an SFA delegation led by president Hugh Nelson and International Committee chairman Jimmy Aitken where he was officially offered the post. The Brockville club immediately countered with an improved salary offer in a bid to hold on to the forty-year-old.

Cunningham asked for the weekend to mull over his options, and by the Monday morning the SFA was considering his demands, which included complete freedom in team matters and a contract extending beyond the 1974 World Cup finals. It was also being reported that such was their determination to secure his services a salary offer of £7,000 was now on the table.

Throughout the process Cunningham had made no public comment, but he ended his silence on the evening of Tuesday, September 7th at a hastily arranged news conference at Brockville, where he read from a prepared statement: 'After having gone through the past ten days, which have been quite a strain, and after very careful consideration, I have decided my duty is to remain with Falkirk FC so that I can continue to take the club to the highest attainable standard in football.'

Within eighteen months he had left Falkirk to take over at St Mirren. His time there was to be short-lived, and when he retired from the game soon after the World Cup finals at which he might have enjoyed the highlight of his career, Cunningham revealed he had recommended his replacement to the Love Street directors: the then East Stirlingshire boss Alex Ferguson, who had embarked upon what would become a glittering career in management and which would later include a brief spell in the job Cunningham had turned his back on.

His decision to reject the Scotland national team post was said to have 'shocked SFA officials who offered him unprecedented terms', and the following morning's newspapers carried reports that the final salary offer had in fact reached £7,500. Writing in the *Glasgow Herald*, Jim Parkinson pondered, 'Where do the SFA go from here?' before noting, 'A pile of written applications has been thrown into the waste paper basket and Mr Cunningham has rejected the post . . . whoever takes over will be an embarrassing second choice.'

By the time the stunned members of the International Committee reconvened three days later, various names were being bandied about, among them the controversial Manchester City coach Malcolm Allison. It was felt likely the SFA would go for a safer option, with Jimmy Bonthrone being tipped as a probable caretaker manager, but over that weekend the Association announced it had appointed the Hull City assistant manager Tommy Docherty on a temporary basis. A colourful and outspoken character, Docherty had played twenty-five times for his country, including in the ill-fated 1954 World Cup finals campaign, before setting out on a nomadic managerial adventure in which the Scotland job was already his seventh appointment. It was a deal that left the English Second Division side in the unique position of having two international managers on its books, as Docherty's superior Terry Neill was at that stage part-time boss of Northern Ireland.

Docherty was quick to play down suggestions he was on trial for a permanent contract, claiming, 'I will be in charge for two matches, no more no less,' but with his first game, a European Championship (or Nations Cup as the competition was then better known) qualifier at home to Portugal, just a month away, he had work to do. The match was meaningless in terms of the group – earlier results had already eliminated the Scots – but it was being viewed as a chance to build for the future and a serious challenge for the forthcoming World Cup finals in West Germany.

Docherty, in time-honoured fashion, was quick to offer headline-making quotes eagerly devoured by the football writers: 'It is my opinion that outside of Brazil there is no stronger a squad of players in the world than the Scots' was one of his first utterings after being appointed. All he had to do was gather those players, select the right ones, and start to reverse the recent slide of the national team.

When he announced his squad for the Portugal tie, Docherty, unexpectedly perhaps, ruffled a few feathers with the inclusion in the sixteen-strong pool of two English-born players, Hibernian's Alex Cropley and the Arsenal goalkeeper Bob Wilson. That move had been made possible by the recent introduction of the ruling that footballers could represent the country of their parents. Also included for the first time were the Sheffield United full-back Eddie Colquhoun and the Arsenal midfielder George Graham. The listing of nine Anglo-Scots was picked up on by reporters, but Docherty batted that away, explaining that for geographical reasons these were the players he was most familiar with. He pledged that home-based young players like George Connelly, Kenny Dalglish and Arthur Graham would soon be given their chance.

A respectable crowd of 58,612 turned up to see Docherty get off to a winning start. The next morning's newspaper reports tell of superb performances by debutants Cropley and Graham; Colquhoun and Pat Stanton were described as defensive pillars; and there was praise too for Sandy Jardine, who put the shackles on the legendary Eusébio, rendering him so ineffective on his fiftieth appearance for his country that he was substituted at half-time. By that stage Docherty's new-look Scots had already taken the lead, John O'Hare heading in a Graham cross. The home support was stunned when Rui Rodrigues curled in a free-kick equaliser that left Wilson rooted to the spot, but that parity lasted barely two minutes, Archie Gemmill restoring Scotland's advantage. There was some debate over the goal: the Portuguese claimed the midfielder had handled the ball and proceeded to 'jostle the Polish referee all over the field'.

The 2–1 win delighted SFA officials, who, nevertheless, made it clear they would not be rushed into making a permanent appointment, while Docherty declared himself 'thrilled to bits . . . That was a great display for a team together for the first time.'

His second match in charge was also at home, although this time at Aberdeen's Pittodrie Stadium, and again Docherty brought in some new faces, with the Dons' Steve Murray, Dundee defender Jim Steele and nineteen-year-old Partick Thistle goalkeeper Alan Rough – the subject of a £50,000 transfer bid by Docherty's Hull City – all being drafted into the squad alongside a man who would become a virtual ever-present for the next decade and a half: Kenny Dalglish. The Celtic and Liverpool legend would go on to amass a record tally of 102 caps for his country, but in the late autumn of 1971 there was still some debate as to what his best position might be. On the day he was announced as a member of the Scotland squad, his club manager, Jock Stein, listed him at wing-half for a European Cup tie against the Maltese side Sliema Wanderers, prompting the press to ask the question 'defender or attacker?' Dalglish seemed unconcerned at the time: 'I could not care less so long as I'm playing for Celtic and Scotland. It's all the same to me. Football's a game you play from eleven different positions. You can only do your best.'

Dalglish was given his Scots baptism two minutes into the second half of the encounter with group winners Belgium, and according to match reports attracted much praise from the 36,500 crowd. His contribution was certainly noted by the *Glasgow Herald* reporter: 'Intelligently he kept the Scots moving with a smooth, fluent rhythm in the second half, and he could be around the international scene for years to come' was his prescient observation. The game again resulted in a narrow victory for Docherty's side, John O'Hare heading in the only goal after some Jimmy Johnstone trickery, and there was now a growing clamour for the manager to be installed on a full-time basis.

On Monday, November 15th 1971 the *Daily Express* back page was headlined: 'DOC'S DAY: THERE MUST BE NO MORE DITHERING . . .' Within hours of the newspaper hitting the streets, the SFA had met and quickly offered Docherty the job. He countered with a series of demands, including 'authority over all team matters . . . selection, travel and hotel arrangements, and opponents for non-competitive games' among them, and the Association, mindful of the embarrassment felt at the time of Willie Cunningham's snub, was in no position to bargain. With a four-year contract worth £30,000 – a huge sum at the time – a company car and an unlimited travel allowance, Park Gardens chiefs were confident he would sign up, and it was with some relief that Jimmy Aitken was able to issue a statement that read, 'I am happy to announce that a satisfactory conclusion has been reached and that Mr Docherty will take up his post on Monday.' Such an appointment these days would lead to massive spreads and pull-outs in the national newspapers, but the *Glasgow Herald* took a somewhat more subdued approach to its coverage in 1971, confining itself to three short paragraphs on the front page.

Peter Lorimer was at that time out of the picture, banned by the Association for declining a late call-up to join the summer tour to Denmark and Russia, but he remembers being delighted 'The Doc' had been confirmed in the post; Scotland, he felt, now had the right man at the helm: 'He was the kind of man we needed. Bobby Brown was lovely, but he wasn't the strongest of characters, and with the Scottish team as it was, they took a bit of handling, they were a little bit wild at times. It needed a stronger man to come in and stamp his authority on them . . . Tommy came in and got some ground rules, got some discipline in the camp, and it all changed.'

There was, at the time, some jubilation over the appointment, with Aitken adding, 'I am absolutely thrilled . . . it's the best day I have ever had at the SFA. He has done much to relieve the despondency that was enveloping Scottish football at international level and gives hope for the future. I feel we are on the way to re-establishing the Scottish image.' The Association president Hugh Nelson beamed, 'Tommy Docherty has earned the right to be Scotland's team manager. I am very pleased with his appointment.' And the Celtic boss, Jock Stein, was equally pleased: 'It is fine to see Scotland make a definite move after the impact The Doc has made.'

Newspaper reporters wrote of a renewed optimism and enthusiasm for the national side, of young players being given their chance, of life being breathed into the game, of confidence being revived within the team. It was, in short, an appointment that no one seemed to dispute.

Deal done, Docherty headed north for his first official appointment as permanent Scotland manager, watching Aberdeen take on the might of Juventus in a UEFA Cup tie at Pittodrie. Before leaving Glasgow, he spoke of his delight at securing the post and his hopes for the future: 'My biggest ambition is to take Scotland to the World Cup finals in West Germany. I have signed a four-year contract with Scotland, and that means I will be with them for all that time, completely dedicated to restoring the football fortunes of my country. I have been overwhelmed with the congratulations and good wishes I have received about my appointment. We are one of the greatest football nations in the world. We have the talent, and I can see the competition for a place in the Scottish international team being terrific. In the past there has always been the problem about the release of Anglo-Scots. In future the top Anglos will be battling it out with the home Scots for a place in the team.'

And he made it clear he would not be a desk-bound manager, preferring to travel the country, on both sides of the border, watching players and building relationships: 'I will be going around the country, meeting the various managers and even taking part in their training sessions. I want to know all my possible players, in the way they train and off the field. My aim is to make Scotland a world soccer power.'

Tommy Docherty's first match in full control ended in defeat in Amsterdam, a late Barry Hulshoff header giving a strong Holland side a 2–1 win in a friendly encounter. George Graham had earlier equalised a Johan Cruyff opener, but in what perhaps served as a wake-up call, the Scots were deservedly beaten, their play on occasion described as 'mesmerised and sluggish' in comparison to the 'authoritative and accomplished' Dutch side.

Qualifying for the World Cup finals in West Germany was to begin in the autumn of 1972 and Docherty was determined his men would be ready. He had a friendly against Peru and the British Championship already in the diary, but the manager knew he needed more competitive action, and so on February 28th, after weeks of prevarication, the manager finally managed to persuade his reluctant employers to sign up for the Independence Cup, a mini World Cup to be staged that summer in Brazil.

The Scots would receive a guarantee of £10,000 for each match played, a financial consideration that presumably helped sway the SFA, but there were concerns as to the likely strength of the travelling party, with Celtic and Derby County both expressing early unwillingness to allow their players to make the close-season trip, a decision that would strip Docherty of key players such as Dalglish, Johnstone, Davie Hay, Gemmill and O'Hare. The Doc ultimately won the day with his argument that he had verbal assurances from leading club managers that would guarantee a squad of sufficient calibre to make the venture worthwhile.

Details of the event, arranged as part of the celebrations of Brazil's 150th year of independence, were finally confirmed two months later when it was revealed that the Scots would line up against the winners of a preliminary group (which turned out to be Yugoslavia), Czechoslovakia and the hosts.

Next up for Docherty and his team, though, was one of the surprise packages of the 1970 World Cup finals: Peru. The manager again took the opportunity to introduce fresh blood, handing first caps to Willie Donachie, Asa Hartford and Ally Hunter, the goalkeeper being one of just two home-based players (the other was John Brownlie, the Hibernian right-back) in a starting line-up bereft of any Old Firm representatives because of club commitments. The early enthusiasm generated by Docherty's appointment seemed to have waned, with just 21,000 spectators scattered around the Hampden slopes. Veteran striker Denis Law captained the team, rounding off a 2–0 win with a memorable effort. The opener had come from John O'Hare, yet another header, and was his fifth goal in just eleven international outings. Remarkably, the Derby County striker would play just two more games for his country before his Scotland career was brought to a halt. The Peruvians failed to shine as they had at Mexico 1970 and it was a routine win for the home side, setting them up nicely for the annual end-of-season encounters with the other home nations.

Docherty named his squad for those matches at the beginning of May and it had a more experienced look to it, with recalls for the Celtic captain Billy McNeill and Leeds United's Peter Lorimer, who had been in the international wilderness since opting to go on a coaching trip to South Africa the previous summer rather than join up with the national team in the dying embers of Bobby Brown's reign. It is a time Lorimer remembers vividly: 'It was a life suspension I got because I went there. It was the time of apartheid and the Scottish FA took exception to it. England didn't, Frannie Lee went; Ireland didn't, Johnny Giles went; but Scotland did. All we did was play in half a dozen charity games, do a bit of coaching and play a bit of golf, but I was banned and it looked like my international career was over until Tommy Docherty got in, and with the World Cup qualifying coming round he made it clear he wanted the best players available, and he got the ban lifted, which I was very grateful for. I hadn't even been picked by Bobby Brown for the tour to Denmark and Russia, but at the last minute there were some withdrawals and the call came. Don Revie [Peter's manager at Leeds] didn't want me going on it anyway because we'd had a long, hard season – he didn't mind me going to South

Africa because it was going to be relaxing, no training, no hard games, just getting a bit of sun. He rang up the SFA and said he didn't want me to travel, that I was going to South Africa just to have a break, but they took exception to it and my career was in ruins . . . until The Doc stepped in.'

The first game was against Northern Ireland at Hampden in what was technically a home fixture for the men in green but played in Glasgow because of the troubles across the Irish Sea. Lorimer recalls an incident in the build-up to the match that displayed the grip Docherty had on his men: 'We were going to the pictures and we called into some little pub in Largs just for a half. Little Jimmy [Johnstone] was at the bar ordering them, and there was a glass panel in the door and we could see there was The Doc and the trainer who'd obviously followed us . . . We were trying to signal to Jimmy and he thought we were waving at him, so he was smiling and waving back. The Doc came in and tapped him on the shoulder, and Jimmy – who was a funny little guy and always had an answer – turned round and without missing a beat said, "Oh, hello there, what are you having?" And of course Tommy says, "What am I having? Get the fuck out of here!" and that was the end of it. He sat us down later and told us that he knew how it had been in the past, but that's the end of it. The Doc did get us in line, he knew exactly how to deal with his players.'

The Scots recorded another victory – Docherty's fourth out of five – but again failed to impress, and had to rely on two late goals to secure the points. The first came four minutes from the end, Denis Law spectacularly hooking the ball into the net from a Lorimer cross for what was the thirtieth, and final, goal of his international career. Law then turned provider, setting up the Leeds man, a second-half substitute, to tuck away his first for the national side.

Peter Lorimer did not have to wait long for his second Scotland goal; in fact, it came just four days later in the next match of the tournament, against Wales. The Scots improved throughout the game but spurned a series of chances until the seventy-second minute, when Lou Macari's flick allowed his team-mate to crash the ball into the roof of the net in trademark fashion. There were just 21,332 fans there to enjoy the goal, the sparse attendance at least in part explained by a remarkable fixture clash: on the same night, Rangers were playing Dynamo Moscow in the European Cup Winners' Cup final, an unimaginable arrangement these days. Coverage of the Scotland match was somewhat overshadowed the following morning by the Ibrox side's first-ever European triumph, and more particularly by reports of the pitch invasion and fighting with baton-wielding Spanish policemen that followed the final whistle at the Nou Camp.

The Scottish players, meanwhile, were given a rest day at Largs and Seamill by their satisfied manager. England had surprisingly lost their midweek encounter with the Irish, which meant Docherty's side required just a draw against the old enemy at Hampden to become British champions. And he was in a relaxed frame of mind as he previewed the decider: 'Even if we lose, we still share the title. I think the Home International Championship must be used for bigger things . . . We must have it as a lead-up to Brazil and World Cup commitments. If we are to be successful then we must look higher.'

Docherty, a fiercely patriotic Scot, must have surprised many fans with that viewpoint. In the early 1970s the match against England was seen as the biggest on the international calendar. It was one of the few games shown live each year on television and drew massive audiences. And unlike in the two previous fixtures against Northern Ireland and Wales, Hampden Park would be full to capacity with noisy, fervent and, in many cases, inebriated supporters baying for English blood.

The crowd was officially announced as 119,325 and those inside the national stadium were, according to the *Glasgow Herald*, treated to 'a savage contest . . . crude action . . . maiming kicks, tough body-checking and tripping which could have resulted in broken bones or serious injury'. Such was the intensity of the play that Italian referee Sergio Gonella issued three yellow cards in the opening twenty minutes, to Billy McNeill, Asa Hartford and Alan Ball. Given the sort of tackling then permitted in the game, the trio must have perpetrated crippling fouls to be disciplined in that way so early in the encounter. Ball scored the only goal, bundling the ball into the net in the twenty-eighth minute, and there was a degree of criticism aimed at the manager for failing to put out a more defensive line-up in a bid to secure the solitary point required. Docherty was unrepentant: 'We must develop a Hampden mentality. We must always go out to win on our home ground. If you talk of settling for a draw in one game here you are letting yourself down. I could have played eleven defenders to get a draw, but that would not have been progress.'

His next job was to assemble a strong enough squad to cope with the rigours and demands of the trip to South America, and that was proving to be something of an onerous task. Clubs were not at that time compelled to release players, and although the SFA went on a charm offensive and attempted to call in favours, it soon became clear that Docherty was going to be travelling across the Atlantic minus a number of key figures.

Chelsea withdrew Charlie Cooke, and Sandy Jardine was withdrawn, as was Eddie Gray, by Leeds United. Hibernian said they would allow only one player to be selected – Pat Stanton was chosen, but later decided himself he did not want to go – then refused to bow to requests for John Brownlie to be added as a late call-up. And Celtic blocked any attempts to include George Connelly, Kenny Dalglish and Davie Hay.

Docherty tentatively listed a twenty-strong squad and then faced a nervous three-week wait while the players holidayed before turning up at Largs to begin training.

In the end, eighteen turned up, and after four days of preparations on the Ayrshire coast – Docherty claimed he had worked the players so hard they had crammed two weeks' worth of conditioning into those days – the group set off for Rio via London and Paris, arriving in Brazil at six o'clock the following morning. It was a less than relaxing journey and Martin Buchan recalls they were given a less than welcome call as they spilled off the aeroplane: 'I'll never forget it. It was quite a marathon trip in those days and we're coming down the steps, all tired and just wanting to get to the hotel . . . and there's a piper there – I think his name was Ronnie McKinnon, he'd been round the world playing at various embassies – and he's skirling away as we come down, and I remember Tommy Doc saying, "Aye, there's nothing like the sound of the pipes in the distance . . . preferably three hundred miles away!" Overall the ex-pats were very good to us, they were pleased to see the Scots lads there, but at that time in the morning, it was the last thing we needed.'

By then, the Brazil Independence Cup, or 'Minicopa' as the hosts had branded it, was well underway. An initial qualification phase, comprising three groups of five countries, had begun on June 11th and only three teams made it through to the final stages: Argentina, Portugal and Yugoslavia.

It was a measure of Scotland's standing back then that they were seeded – along with the hosts, Czechoslovakia, Uruguay and the Soviet Union – while the Argentines and Portuguese, and France, Colombia and Paraguay among others, all had to pre-qualify.

While there was newspaper coverage back home of the tour, it was relatively limited and the Scots had to battle for column inches with two other big sports stories: Rangers' two-year ban – later reduced to twelve months on appeal – from all European competitions following the pitch invasion by their fans at the Cup Winners' Cup final, and the controversial defeat of boxer Ken Buchanan at the hands, or rather fists, of Roberto Durán in their world championship showdown at Madison Square Garden.

It was reported, briefly, that the Scots spent a couple of days in Rio, training at the Cricket Club, before heading north to Belo Horizonte for their opening encounter with Yugoslavia.

The group had begun with a 0–0 draw between Brazil and

Czechoslovakia twenty-four hours earlier, the blank scoreline largely down to the heroics of Czech goalkeeper Ivo Viktor, and Docherty was keen to steal a march on his rivals.

With his defensive options limited, the Scotland manager had few decisions to make regarding his starting line-up. Incredibly, the right-back position was being fought for by two Partick Thistle players, John Hansen and Alex Forsyth, and it was the latter who got the nod, while Kilmarnock's Ally Hunter was chosen in goal ahead of the more experienced Bobby Clark of Aberdeen.

The side read: Hunter; Forsyth, Buchan, Colquhoun, Donachie; Graham, Bremner, Hartford; Morgan, Law and Macari.

It was to be a bad-tempered affair played in a sweltering 80 degrees, and the tournament had yet to excite the locals, with fewer than 3,500 turning out to watch. Those who did saw a series of early bruising challenges, with Argentine referee Ángel Coerezza struggling to control the players. Emotions bubbled over when a fight broke out between Willie Donachie and the Yugoslav midfielder Blagoje Paunovic, punches being thrown by both, but that seemed to settle the match down, and five minutes before the interval the Scots took the lead, Lou Macari firing home his first international goal after being set up by Willie Morgan.

Hansen replaced the injured Forsyth for the second half and the game was soon tied up, Dusan Bajevic beating Hunter to equalise. Within three minutes, however, Scotland were back in front thanks to the same combination, Morgan's cross being headed in by the diminutive Macari.

Tiring in the oppressive heat, the Scots looked to kill the game and were jeered for doing so, but they had a gilt-edged chance to clinch the victory with little over ten minutes left on the clock. Asa Hartford was bundled over in the box by two opposing defenders, but Willie Morgan's penalty was clutched just inside the post by keeper Meskovic.

As so often happens in football, Scotland were soon punished for their profligacy. Jovan Acimovic shot goalwards and as Hunter moved to cover his effort the ball cannoned off Martin Buchan's shoulder and arced into the net, leaving the Scottish goalkeeper stranded. It later emerged that the linesman at that end of the pitch had had his flag raised signalling for offside but was ignored by the referee, so simply put it down again and trotted back to the halfway line. Yugoslavia were more threatening in the closing minutes, but the exhausted Scots held on for a 2–2 draw.

The manager's thinly spread resources were being stretched to the limit. Alex Forsyth was struggling after being kicked on the knee just ten minutes into the game; Eddie Colquhoun had hauled himself out of his sickbed and played despite suffering a serious stomach upset; and even teenager George Anderson of Morton, who had been seriously in contention to feature in the opener, had been laid low by a throat infection.

Docherty declared himself frustrated by the outcome yet pleased by aspects of his side's play: 'I felt before the game that a draw would be a great result, though I wanted to win it. I thought the boys did a first-class job. Yet they were coming to me at the end apologising ... Willie Morgan sick at missing the penalty, Billy Bremner for a bad pass that let the Slavs through in the end. We may be thin in numbers, but what a bunch of lads this is.'

Despite his late error, Bremner was named man of the match by the local organisers and was presented, much to the Scots captain's surprise, with a 'magnificent television set' as his reward. Whether he ever managed to get it back to his Yorkshire home has not been recorded.

There was also praise for Donachie and Hartford, two of the youngsters The Doc had called up, and for Morgan, despite his failure to convert the potentially match-winning spot kick.

'I hit it well and to the right place,' he later explained, 'but did not allow for the longer, tougher grass here. And the goalkeeper certainly moved before I struck the ball.'

The manager and his players had little time to dwell on the game, as the Scots were in action again just three days later. The group headed 1,000 miles south to Porto Alegre for their second fixture, against Czechoslovakia, and despite the fatigue experienced by his men, the manager made just one change, replacing Hunter with Clark.

The Aberdeen goalkeeper was to be the man of the match, pulling off outstanding saves to deny Medvid, Hagara and, on three separate occasions, the Czech's star man Jaroslav Pollák. Asa Hartford might have scored for the Scots, and Billy Bremner shunned an opening from the edge of the box, but the best chance of the game fell to substitute Colin Stein with just seven minutes remaining. The Rangers striker was not long on the park, having replaced Denis Law, when Viktor inexplicably dropped the ball at his feet. With the goal gaping, the keeper somehow threw his body in front of Stein's effort and got lucky when Hartford smashed the rebound goalwards, only for the ball to deflect off a defender and wide for a corner.

It had, in truth, been a disappointing encounter, with the *Evening Times* reporting that both teams were booed from the pitch by the 6,000 crowd after their 0–0 draw. Law had struggled throughout and might, Docherty later accepted, have been substituted earlier, while Morgan, the star of the show against Yugoslavia, had failed to replicate his mazy dribbling against the tight marking of the Czech defence. John MacKenzie in the *Daily Express* summed it up as 'a lifeless, walking pace, practice game'. The one plus was that Scotland remained undefeated after two hard games in stifling conditions and were still in with a chance of reaching the final.

When Brazil beat Yugoslavia 3–0 in their second match, it was confirmed the Scots would have to win their final fixture when the pair went head to head back up the coast in Rio de Janeiro at the legendary Maracanã Stadium on July 5th.

The organising committee had invited all participating nations to stay on in Brazil and enjoy the remainder of the competition after their elimination. That offer led to a rift in the Scottish camp. Thirteen of the eighteen players in the squad requested it be taken up, their reasoning being that they would learn a lot by studying the other matches and get an insight into how other teams played. Both the third/fourth play-off and the final itself would be staged in a double-header at the Maracanã the following Sunday. Of the five who were keen to return home, Partick Thistle trio Denis McQuade, John Hansen and Alex Forsyth needed to get back in time for a club trip to Sweden; Willie Donachie wanted home to his new bride, the pair having married shortly before his departure for Brazil; and Ally Hunter, a part-timer with Kilmarnock, had to get back to work after being given special dispensation by his employers to go on the trip. The others might well have had genuine football-related reasons for wanting to extend their stay, but the SFA clearly believed the potential delights of Rio were an even greater attraction to a group of fit young men. They made it clear that the party would be flying home as soon as their interest in the competition was at an end.

The players had indeed been enjoying their time in the city, with one particularly famous landmark at the top of the list, according to Martin Buchan: 'We weren't too far from Copacabana Beach, so of course we'd go down and have a swim and enjoy the sun . . . and the sights! Before the Yugoslavia game I was out swimming, but it was a very steep beach and I got caught in the waves and got turned and landed hard on the beach and hurt my back. I was terrified; I never told anybody. My back was sore, but I didn't mention it to the physio because he'd have told the boss and that would have been it . . . No one would have been allowed to go to the beach. I wouldn't have been very popular if that had happened!'

Docherty admitted he had agreed the early departure with the International Committee before leaving on the trip, but was now urging a change of mind. His pleas, and those of his squad, which had been put to him in a meeting with captain Billy Bremner, were firmly rejected. The Doc, clearly frustrated by the bureaucrats, was right behind his men: 'This is a shattering blow to the boys who want to stay on. They have done a wonderful job for Scotland here.

They have given every ounce of effort over a three-week period after giving up so much of their personal lives to come here and learn. They have had no relaxation whatsoever, and they take this as a slap in the face.'

Bremner was angry and bewildered by the decision: 'Are we asking for so much . . . an extra forty-eight hours in which we could learn such a lot? Is there anywhere in football that one can learn so much about the game in such a short time?'

The man from the *Express*, John MacKenzie, put that to the chairman of the selectors, Jimmy Aitken, who was unrepentant: 'We are only following through on a decision made before we came out here at all. It was clearly laid down at a meeting that we should return as soon as we had been eliminated.'

As the controversy threatened to boil over, a squad meeting was held on the ninth floor of their luxury hotel in Rio. Immediately, the five who wanted to leave early said they would stick by the group decision. There seems little doubt the players were prepared to take on the SFA over the matter, the mood in the room described by one of them as 'militant'. Some were said to have been determined to ask for their air tickets and to make their own travel arrangements home. Tempers were only cooled when Denis Law – much respected by his colleagues – took to the floor.

'Right lads,' he began. 'We all want to stay and see this final, but nobody, and least of all the boss, is going to get into trouble because of our request. I move here and now that we go home, all of us together, when the boss says we go, even if it means missing the game we want to watch. OK?'

There was no cost involved in extending their stay, as the organisers were covering all expenses. The SFA representatives – pointing to Docherty's earlier agreement that the group would depart as soon as their tournament was over – simply decided not to alter their thinking, and the matter was at an end.

As it was, the players came agonisingly close to extending their stay by right.

Docherty had said ahead of the match, 'My young side have little chance of beating the masters . . .' but captain Billy Bremner was more bullish: 'We are going out to win. We've surprised a lot of people with our performances out here – so there's no reason we shouldn't beat Brazil. In our two other games we were unlucky to drop a point.'

Willie Morgan was simply relishing the opportunity to prove what he could do at one of the most iconic venues in the game and against the most glamorous of opposition: 'This is the game I came for. I gave up a lot for this trip and it was mainly because I wanted to play against Brazil. The Maracanã will be a classroom for me, and before I even get onto the field I know that the occasion and the atmosphere is going to lift my game.'

The Doc named an unchanged starting eleven and his side put in an outstanding defensive performance to blunt their hosts. Brief and grainy black and white 'highlights' of the match can be found online, but they give little real flavour of the match. Newspaper reports talk of Scotland 'running rings round the dumbfounded Brazilians' before half-time and give details of the chances the Scots created: Macari crashing a header over the bar in the thirty-second minute; Morgan shooting from twenty yards only for Leão to make the save; and Forsyth cutting in and firing a low shot towards the far post, which the keeper touched round for a corner. After the interval, Bobby Clark saved 'magnificently' from Dário before Gérson passed up a glaring opportunity.

Yugoslavia beat the Czechs 2–1 in the other match, Bajevic and Dzajic cancelling out a Katalinski own goal, and that result meant a draw in front of 150,000 noisy fans at the Maracanã would see Docherty's team progress on goal difference to battle it out for the bronze medals. With just ten minutes remaining they seemed set to do just that, only for the home side to shatter their hopes.

John MacKenzie, perched in the press box high in the stadium, marvelled at Scotland's display: 'It was a bitter blow to a Scottish team which had, for so long, looked like pulling off one of the finest results in Scottish soccer history . . .' he wrote, adding, 'Tommy Docherty's boys, written off before a ball was kicked in the tournament, had rocked the world champions with a display of skill and discipline which I have never seen matched by a Scottish team anywhere.'

The goal that finally broke Scotland's resistance came when substitute Dário collected the ball down the left channel five yards outside the penalty area. As Forsyth went to close him down, he whipped an angled cross over the heads of Buchan and Colquhoun, and with Clark rooted to his line the Scotland keeper was helpless . . . 'Gol Jairzinho! Jaaaairzinhoooo . . . Gol do Braaaasillllll! . . . Jairzinho . . . Gol do Brasil . . .' was the television commentator's typically excitable assessment of the conclusion to the move.

After the match, Docherty was scathing about the hosts' tactics: 'A good team does not use fouls to be able to win, and I was surprised that some Brazilian players used tactics for which the Brazilian eleven are not known.'

Bremner was victim-in-chief, left nursing a painful ankle injury following a particularly nasty challenge by Gérson, and the local papers backed up Docherty's claim, criticising their own team's crude tackling while praising the Scots for their 'fair play and spirited defence'.

Overall, the manager saw the exercise as a successful and worthwhile one, and had nothing but admiration for his side: 'I just can't say how proud I am of these boys – not only for their performance tonight, which was superb, but for their play and conduct since we came here. They were magnificent.'

His Brazilian counterpart, Mário Zagallo, agreed: 'Each team made four good scoring chances. We took one of them; the Scottish team did not. It could easily have been the other way, and I was very nervous during the game.'

And so, in a forerunner to what lay ahead in West Germany two years later, the Scots were out at the hands of Brazil and Yugoslavia, although in 1974 they would fashion an even crueller exit for themselves.

The hosts would go on to win their own tournament, Jairzinho scoring an eighty-ninth-minute winner against Portugal in the final, while the Slavs took third place thanks to a 4–2 beating of Argentina.

MacKenzie's verdict of the trip was a positive one. Under the *Daily Express* headline 'NOW WE ARE READY FOR MUNICH BID' he wrote, 'We return from this tournament that officialdom did not want as a team with a reputation.' He praised the squad, singling out Willie Donachie, Alex Forsyth and Eddie Colquhoun among his top performers, earmarking them as players who could be expected to make a significant impact during qualification and, hopefully, at the finals themselves. Ironically, none would feature during the competition in West Germany. Donachie made the squad, but was never stripped, while Forsyth and Colquhoun failed to be selected.

In the summer of '72, the World Cup finals remained no more than a dream, and Tommy Docherty would have to wait more than three months before getting his squad together to kick off their qualifying campaign, with a match against Denmark in Copenhagen.

It was a long and frustrating period for the manager, during which he attended matches both sides of the border to assess the talents at his disposal, and when he finally got the chance to announce his selection there was a first call-up for the country's top scorer. The Aberdeen striker Joe Harper had been in sparkling form, netting nineteen goals in eighteen games, and having scored forty-two for the Dons the previous season his repeated omissions from the national team had sparked much debate. Now, he was to get his chance. 'This is fantastic news,' he told the *Evening Times* from his Stonehaven home. 'I've been disappointed in the past when not chosen for Scotland squads . . . but this makes up for everything. It's terrific.'

Docherty also irked the traditionalists by listing two 'Englishmen', the Leeds goalkeeper David Harvey and midfielder Bruce Rioch, who played then for Aston Villa. Both had been born south of the border to Scottish parents but were now eligible for selection. It was a route the manager had gone down previously when 'capping' Bob Wilson and Alex Cropley, but it still rankled with some observers.

A number of those who had missed the South American jaunt were recalled – although Pat Stanton was ignored – and the squad, unusually, did not contain a single Rangers player. Those named were: Clark, Harvey; Brownlie, Donachie, Forsyth, Buchan, Colquhoun, Connelly; Bremner, Morgan, Graham, Hartford, Rioch; Lorimer, Dalglish, Macari, Bone and Harper. Four were placed on standby: Ally Hunter, Billy McNeill, Iain Phillip and John O'Hare.

Within a couple of days Rioch had withdrawn, but Docherty ignored his reserve list and drafted in Peter Marinello, the Arsenal winger.

The Scotland party flew out on Monday, October 16th on the first stage of what they hoped would be a journey which would take them all the way to Munich twenty months later. They set up camp in the luxury resort of Vedbæk, thirty miles outside Copenhagen, and got down to final preparations.

They did so without their regular 'trainer' Ronnie McKenzie, who was forced to stay at home by his full-time employers Falkirk because of an extensive injury list at Brockville that required his attention. The physio told reporters, 'I am bitterly disappointed, but I must accept the decision of the club.'

With the manager pledging the team would 'go for goals', much of the emphasis in training the following morning was on finishing, with overworked goalkeepers Bobby Clark and David Harvey facing a barrage of shots from strikers eager to get into the scoring groove.

The afternoon was spent 'relaxing in the sauna room and on the massage table', before a further evening session aimed at allowing the players to prepare for the likely conditions at kick-off time twenty-four hours later.

Meanwhile, back home news was emerging of a disagreement

between the four home football associations and their players. All four paid the same appearance fees – £60 for a full international and £30 for Under-23 games – and there was a significant gap in the new figures being offered and demanded. The players' representatives, pointing out there had been no increase since 1961, wanted £250 and £60, while the FAs were looking at £100 and £50. A spokesman said, 'In view of the serious financial positions of the football associations of Wales and Northern Ireland, and the agreement that international fees should be common to all countries, it was felt that an increase of such magnitude could not possibly be made.'

It was the universal fee that most angered those players down south, as Cliff Lloyd, secretary of the England Football Players' Association, explained: 'We want further discussion with the Football Association. Without any suggestion of aggressive action, we would like to point out that tying England fees to those of less prosperous countries is like saying Arsenal players must not be paid more than the professionals of Barnsley.'

It was not a matter to trouble Docherty as he set about finalising his starting line-up, and when he named his team there was some surprise expressed: Harper, despite his goal-scoring exploits, would have to make do with a place on the substitute bench; Jimmy Bone was instead picked to lead the line. The team that began the campaign read: Clark; Brownlie, Buchan, Colquhoun, Forsyth; Morgan, Bremner, Graham; Macari, Bone and Lorimer.

Docherty had remained true to his earlier assertion that his selection would be built around those who had travelled to Brazil during the summer; only three of the side – Brownlie, Bone and Lorimer – had missed out on the trip, and the Leeds man was one of two players highlighted by the manager in advance of the game: 'He is the man who can turn the key on this tight Danish defence. Lorimer's own brand of thunderbolt can loosen them up and even if he does not hit the target direct, he is going to cause all sorts of problems and open up many possibilities for the strikers.'

25

The other of his men The Doc singled out was the Manchester United winger Willie Morgan, a very different proposition for the home rearguard to try to contain: 'I know this Danish defence does not like a player who will take them on in a one-against-one situation. They tend to fall back . . . Morgan is on his home ground in a situation like that, breaking from midfield, taking the ball to a defender, and using it to advantage.'

More than anything, Docherty was determined to begin the campaign with the full two points on offer for a winning start: 'A draw is of no value to me whatever. It has to be victory, and preferably with a goal or two in hand.'

And he sent his players out with a stirring pre-match team-talk ringing in their ears: 'This is warfare. We blitz them . . . and we keep on blitzing them until they crumble. Go out there and hit them with every big shot you can throw at them.'

The game was televised live by both BBC Scotland and Scottish Television, and the viewers back home were treated to a sparkling display by the white-shirted Scots.

True to his pre-match pledge, right from the first whistle Docherty's side laid siege on the home goal, Therkildsen having to move smartly to touch a Peter Lorimer piledriver over his crossbar. The goalkeeper was, however, only delaying the inevitable and the opening goal came minutes later. Lorimer drove in a flat corner from the right and Lou Macari stooped to head home at the near post.

Within two minutes, the lead had been doubled. A corner on the left was played short to Lorimer, who swung a high cross to the far corner of the box. George Graham drove the ball back towards goal on the volley, and when it rebounded off the keeper Jimmy Bone was first to react, gleefully hammering home the second from just four yards out.

Scotland were on easy street, or so it seemed, but there was a shock for the visitors in the twenty-eighth minute when a long ball out of defence found Eigil Nielsen racing towards goal. The midfielder was upended by Martin Buchan, who was booked for conceding the foul, and Finn Laudrup, showing the skill he obviously passed on to his sons Michael and Brian, cleverly chipped the twenty-five-yard free kick over the wall and into Clark's top right-hand corner.

With the 31,200 crowd inside the Idraetsparken starting to believe a shock might be on the cards, the Scots wobbled, but driven on by captain Bremner – 'This must truly have been his finest hour' claimed the *Evening Times* – soon had a grip on the game once more, and would have extended their lead but for flag- and whistle-happy officials, and the woodwork. The Danes escaped time after time, but Scotland eventually put the game to bed with another quick-fire double late in the second half.

Lorimer – involved in every attacking move – fed the ball wide to Willie Morgan. The Manchester United winger teased two defenders on the angle of the box, then jinked between them. He played the ball into the box, Macari back-heeled it, and Joe Harper took a touch before blasting the ball high into the top corner with his left foot. Having replaced Bone, the Aberdeen striker had been on the park just two minutes: not a bad way to mark his international debut!

Denmark were now in disarray and it was 4–1 just sixty seconds later. Lorimer, inevitably, was again involved, gathering a chipped ball forward from Bremner and looping it to the edge of the box. Willie Morgan took a touch and laid it off for Harper, and his low-angled shot beat the keeper only to rebound from the far post. Lorimer again stepped in, steadied himself, then lofted a cross to the back post, where Morgan dived forward to head in the only goal he would score for his country.

Their spirit now deflated, the home side simply sat in and saw out the remainder of the match, a period utterly dominated by the Scots, who might have added further to their tally. As it was, a 4–1 victory away from home was seen as the perfect way to get the qualification process up and running.

The Doc was beaming with delight afterwards: 'It's embarrassing.

We've so much talent it's an embarrassment of riches . . . so many players, it isn't true – it's a matter of who to leave out.'

There have not been too many occasions in the history of the national team that the Scotland manager could make such a bold claim, but when you consider Docherty had been without, among others, Davie Hay, Sandy Jardine, Archie Gemmill, Eddie Gray, Jimmy Johnstone and George Connelly – who had been a late call-off because of flu – it was not perhaps as fanciful as it might seem these decades later.

The Danish media went overboard in its praise of the Scottish performance. The newspaper *Politiken* gushed, 'The Scots shone with their ability to vary both speed and play,' while the assessment of the *Berlingske Tidende* was, 'The Scots won by a big margin and were superior in many ways . . . they tackled splendidly and covered brilliantly.'

Back home, the *Evening Times* headline stated boldly: 'OUR BEST TEAM IN A LONG TIME'.

Peter Lorimer was, naturally, picked out by his manager following his man-of-the-match performance. Four decades on, a beaming smile stretches across the winger's craggy features as he recalls that night: 'They weren't a bad side, Denmark, especially over there, and we went to Copenhagen and we played really well, we were up for it. I think that was probably one of my best games for Scotland.'

Tommy Docherty was proud of his relationship with his players, of the bond that was developing, and he cited Joe Harper as an example of the mutual respect that existed within the camp: 'He had a beard, but obviously thought I wouldn't like it, so he shaved it off before turning up. I like that . . . I have been fortunate with the type of players, the type of lads, who have played for me. They are the best. I can say we can only go up from here.'

While Docherty was delighted with the striker, his club manager, Jimmy Bonthrone, was about to be less enamoured with him, as two days after the victory in Copenhagen, and with Harper yet to return to Pittodrie following his international adventure, the *Daily*

Express back-page headline read: 'JOE HARPER BOMBSHELL: Dons star will ask for move'.

He was gone less than two months later, signing for Everton for £180,000 in what must have seemed like a dream transfer at the time, but his goals dried up considerably, and little over a year later he was back in Scotland, having joined Hibernian. His World Cup dreams, at least for 1974, had evaporated.

With the Czechs not due to begin their campaign until the following May, Scotland had the ideal opportunity to lay down a marker with back-to-back beatings of the Danes. The Doc announced his squad for the return encounter on November 1st, and there was a surprise recall for Pat Stanton, shunned for the previous match after pulling out of the trip to Brazil. At the time, Docherty, upset that Stanton had not told him personally of his decision, had claimed the Hibernian captain would never play for him again. In today's media that would inevitably have been reported as a 'dramatic about-turn' by the manager; in those gentler times it was seen as a 'statesmanlike' move. Also in the squad, for the first time, was twenty-year-old Leeds United striker Joe Jordan, a rookie with just a handful of first-team appearances under his belt at that stage but a player Docherty believed might have an impact to make 'somewhere nearer Munich'. He was to be proved correct on that score; Jordan was destined to be at the heart of all the most dramatic and controversial Scottish World Cup adventures over the following decade.

Reports of the squad announcement also carried details of how fans could attend the match: 'The SFA have reserved stand tickets for the game on sale at prices ranging from £1 to £2, and all applications should be sent with the appropriate remittance and a stamped addressed envelope. For the Hampden terraces, admission will be by payment at the turnstiles.'

When the players reported for duty eleven days later, they were lucky to have their manager there to greet them in Glasgow ahead of the short trip to their Largs retreat. Forty-eight hours earlier

Docherty had remarkably emerged unscathed after his chauffeur-driven car 'had spun madly out of control on the M6'. In typical fashion, he made light of the accident, observing, 'With my luck we'll go on to win the World Cup.'

As the countdown to kick-off approached, The Doc continued to talk up his men, boosting their confidence, praising their abilities and doing everything he could to keep them onside. On the eve of the match he turned his attention to Joe Harper, comparing him favourably with the West German superstar Gerd Müller and confirming his place in the starting line-up. He also urged reporters to make sure the Danes knew Peter Lorimer would be starting: 'I want them to have a sleepless night before the match.'

Docherty made four changes from the side that had won so impressively in Copenhagen. Harper was, as promised, given his long-awaited first start in place of Bone, while David Harvey, Willie Donachie and Kenny Dalglish stepped in for Clark, Forsyth and Macari.

Denmark were at that time very much down the European football pecking order, described by the legendary football writer Ian Archer as 'nice people, but somewhat outside the mainstream of the modern game'. And yet Archer urged against complacency and arrogance in his match preview, offering the final thought: 'An early goal would be helpful, for it would ease the strain not only on the players, but also on the fans.'

And that was exactly what Scotland got. On a freezing night, and on a slippery, ice-bound surface, the home side were ahead within two minutes, George Graham setting up Kenny Dalglish for a six-yard tap-in. Lorimer and Harper each came close to adding to the lead, while at the other end the Scots goalkeeper Harvey enjoyed 'a quiet, almost unseen debut'. Lorimer did finally score just forty-five seconds into the second half to round off a routine 2–0 win, but his night was to end in shame, as he was sent off for retaliating in the wake of a crude Danish challenge: 'I was playing well at that time, and they had targeted me. I was getting plenty stick, they were getting plenty kicks in, and I just got up and pushed the guy away in disgust. I didn't punch him or anything like that, but the referee came over and sent us both off, much to my surprise. It was a bit of a blow, as I knew I'd miss the big one against Czechoslovakia.'

Docherty declared himself delighted to have got four points (it was two for a win in those days) in the bag before Czechoslovakia had even kicked a ball but could not disguise his disgust at the tactics employed by the visitors: 'Denmark did not come here to play football. They wanted Lorimer off the field from the start of the game – but eventually he was dismissed for nothing. This Danish side wasn't a patch on the team who we played in Copenhagen, either in terms of ability or in terms of sportsmanship.'

Despite his displeasure, Scotland were well placed for the second half of the World Cup qualifying campaign in the autumn of 1973. But by then Docherty would be long gone from the national team.

Manchester United had endured a torrid start to the English league season. Still coming to terms with the departure of European Cup-winning manager Sir Matt Busby from the managerial hot seat, and with the failure of Wilf McGuinness to cope with the demands of the role, the Old Trafford board had turned to the Leicester City boss Frank O'Farrell. He had made a superb start to his first season, guiding United well clear at the top of the table, but a lengthy run of defeats from January 1972, which coincided with another George Best walkout, saw the team plummet down the table, eventually finishing eighth for a second successive year. Worse was to follow. The 1972–73 campaign kicked off without a win in nine games. Despite a mini-revival, by mid-December United still found themselves deep in relegation trouble. On the 16th of that month they were thrashed 5–0 by Crystal Palace, and three days later O'Farrell was out after just eighteen months in the job. The following morning's newspapers had already installed Tommy Docherty as favourite to replace him.

The *Daily Express* gave over its entire front page to the story under the banner headline 'THE BOOT! O'Farrell sacked and Best quits', while on the back page readers were confronted with 'DOC IS THE BIG TIP: IT'S WORTH £15,000 A YEAR'.

John MacKenzie made it clear what he thought, warning the SFA should not be asking 'if we can afford to keep Docherty, but if we can possibly afford to let him go'. He urged the authorities to double The Doc's Scotland salary and to offer a substantial bonus for reaching the '74 finals, and he suggested that international management better suited the 'abrasive, hard-hitting little tough guy' than the club game, as he had less day-to-day contact with the world of officialdom, for which he had little time or respect.

If the Scottish Football Association did make any serious attempt to hold their manager to the three years remaining on his contract, it made no impact. Docherty's mind was made up the moment United Chairman Louis Edwards offered him the post: 'It is an honour for myself and Scottish football to be asked to United. In the words of the Mafia, they made me an offer I could not refuse.'

Three days after O'Farrell was axed, the newspaper headlines blared 'DOCHERTY JOINS MANCHESTER UNITED' and 'SHAKE ON IT DOC: United's £16,000 Christmas present'.

United had moved swiftly and the deal was done within hours of SFA secretary Willie Allan giving the English club permission to speak to him. Docherty initially suggested he might continue with Scotland on a part-time basis, saying, 'I would like to see the team through the World Cup qualifying rounds,' but that never seemed likely, and within a week the Association had officially terminated his contract.

Docherty failed to immediately arrest United's slide, having to wait until mid-February for his first league win, a narrow 2–1 success over Wolves, but he eventually propelled his new club to an eight-match unbeaten sequence, a run of results good enough to see them finish eighteenth out of the twenty-two First Division sides, and seven points clear of the drop. That was to prove merely a stay of execution, however, and the following year United slipped meekly out of the top flight. The directors kept faith in The Doc and he repaid them, surging to immediate promotion with an exciting new-look side packed with young talents such as Steve Coppell and Gordon Hill. United then finished third in the First Division, just four points behind champions Liverpool, but surprisingly lost in the FA Cup final to Second Division Southampton. That wrong was righted twelve months later at Wembley, Docherty leading his side to glory with a 2–1 victory over Liverpool, but within six weeks his career had blown up in his face. In June 1977 Tommy Docherty admitted he was having an affair with Mary Brown, the wife of club physiotherapist Laurie Brown, and he was sacked, bringing to an end a roller-coaster four and a half years at Old Trafford.

All that was in the future; back in the winter of 1972 the Scottish Football Association was once again searching for a new manager.

2

THE QUIET MAN TAKES OVER

Scottish football in the early 1970s was dominated by one man: a manager widely respected abroad for his success and the style in which his sides played football; a manager who won matches, who won trophies. Jock Stein's imposing shadow loomed large over the whole game. His young Celtic team had become the first British side to win the European Cup and had subsequently reached another final, losing out to Dutch side Feyenoord, and had gone on to rule the domestic game. Season 1972–73 would see Celtic clinch the eighth of their record-breaking nine-in-a-row Scottish titles. According to Ian Archer, writing in the Christmas Day issue of the *Glasgow Herald*, he was the only candidate to lead the national team: 'Scottish football possesses one man strong enough to carry the country into the final stages of the 1974 World Cup . . . Jock Stein should be asked as a matter of pressing urgency to take over the post deserted by Tommy Docherty last week. He is the best Scottish manager, and therefore should be given the best Scottish job. If he refuses, the outlook is bleak.'

Archer went on to suggest that only Bill Shankly and Eddie Turnbull among Scottish-born managers had sufficient pedigree to take on the role, before posing the question: 'Does Scotland's manager need to be a Scot?'

The SFA were saying nothing on that subject. Despite two

International Committee meetings having been held in short order, there was no public comment from the authorities regarding any of the potential candidates.

The day after quitting Scotland, Docherty had tipped either Partick Thistle manager Davie McParland or the fiery Dave MacKay, then with Nottingham Forest, as his successor. There were also mentions in the press for Aberdeen manager Jimmy Bonthrone, East Fife boss Pat Quinn and Jim McLean, then in the early days of what would become a stellar managerial career with Dundee United. But none of them would get the job.

There had, in actual fact, been little in the way of speculation in the daily newspapers until Friday, January 5th, when the St Johnstone boss Willie Ormond was described in the *Herald* as having 'suddenly emerged as the front runner'. The *Scottish Daily Express* took a similar line, revealing that Ormond's name would be the one put forward by 'several of the selectors'. Others thought to be in the frame were McParland and MacKay, Bobby Seith of Hearts (who had been linked with the job prior to Docherty's appointment) and the Birmingham City coach Willie Bell. It was hardly a list of candidates to meet Archer's, or the nation's, lofty hopes, and there was certainly no word of Stein having been approached, or even considered.

Further confirmation of Ormond's status as front runner came when the St Johnstone Chairman Alex Lamond admitted his man was on his way to Glasgow to meet with the SFA: 'He goes with the full approval of my board. He discussed the situation fully with me today. He has no contract with us, and if he accepts the job we will relieve him of his duties at Muirton immediately so that he can start in his new job without delay.'

The Scottish Football Association had declined to comment on the matter, but within hours of the papers hitting the news stands, Ormond had been appointed.

In a playing career that had started at Stenhousemuir in 1946, Willie Ormond became a Hibernian legend, part of the celebrated

'Famous Five' forward line alongside Bobby Johnstone, Lawrie Reilly, Gordon Smith and Eddie Turnbull. Ormond collected three League Championship winner's medals during his decade and a half in the capital, finally leaving in 1961 to wind down his time on the pitch with a year-long spell at home-town club Falkirk.

By then he had won six international caps, making his debut in a World Cup qualifier against England in April 1954, before playing in both matches in the finals. He would be in the international wilderness for almost five years before earning a surprise recall for a 1–0 defeat at Wembley, which was to be his last involvement with the national team, at least as a player.

Having spent a number of years as trainer with Falkirk, Ormond was unveiled as St Johnstone manager in 1967, and two years later led the Perth side to their first-ever League Cup final, which ended in a 1–0 defeat to Celtic. In 1970–71 Saints achieved their highest-ever league placing, third in the First Division, qualifying for a debut in the UEFA Cup. Saints recorded memorable victories over SV Hamburg and Vasas Budapest, before going out to FK Zeljeznicar Sarajevo.

By January 1973 he was obviously experiencing frustration in the job, and was ready to test himself at a higher level: 'I felt I had achieved all I could with St Johnstone, bearing in mind the limited resources there. After working in front of crowds of 3,500, I wanted to take the chance of moving into football with a big-time atmosphere. Even when we were third in the league there were only 6,000 there.'

Ormond had a reputation as a quiet man, and one of his first acts was to apologise in advance to journalists that he would not be supplying the ready-made line of quips and quotes regularly on offer from his predecessor. The forty-six-year-old was, however, quick to dismiss any notion that he might be an easy touch, particularly for the older, more experienced members of the squad, and felt he would quickly gain their trust: 'I can be hard. I can make players work like fury. But I think that, of all things, I am fair. I believe in treating players like men, and not boys.'

He also displayed a steely determination and confidence in his own ability at that first news conference, proclaiming, 'Tommy has already offered me his World Cup file, a magnificent dossier on football, and I am delighted to accept it. I do not see anything to stop us from qualifying. I want to take us to Munich . . . and believe we could go further than ever before. We have the players and my job is to find the blend. In talent, we rank with anywhere in the world.'

One month later Ormond carried out his first acts as national team manager, naming squads for Under-23 and full international matches against England the following midweek. Unsurprisingly, perhaps, he stuck pretty rigidly to Docherty's script, taking no chances with the list of players drawn up.

The younger team, consisting of future SFA Hall of Famers Alan Rough, Danny McGrain and Asa Hartford, went down 2–1 to their English counterparts at a snowbound Rugby Park, but Ormond had been given an insight into the lot of the international football manager during the build-up. His initial squad list was decimated by call-offs. A total of seven withdrew, leaving him at one stage with just thirteen players, two of whom were goalkeepers, and he had to draft in Aberdeen centre-half Willie Young on the eve of the game to make up the numbers. Given the circumstances the result was acceptable enough, but if Ormond thought the Under-23 match had given him a few headaches, he was about to suffer the mother of all migraines as attention focused on the Hampden showdown, a game arranged to help celebrate the Association's centenary.

Captain Billy Bremner was up for the challenge. He always relished taking on the English and was determined to keep confidence up ahead of more important contests that lay ahead: 'All the players want to give new boss Willie Ormond a good send-off. Team spirit is high, and we want to make this a stepping stone for our two World Cup clashes with Czechoslovakia.'

On the morning after Willie Ormond's appointment, Ian Archer had written, 'We must hope that he starts his career with a victory, preferably by about five goals.'

It did not quite work out that way. On a frozen surface at the national stadium, and on the coldest day of that winter, with temperatures in some parts of the country dipping as low as –12 degrees Celsius, the Scots were destroyed by a ruthless English team, Sir Alf Ramsey's side running out 5–0 winners.

The Scotland defending was, on the night, woeful; goalkeeper Bobby Clark and central defender Eddie Colquhoun would never again represent their country, while Martin Buchan would be on the international sidelines for thirteen months after ignoring an injury to take part: 'I had a bad ankle, a dodgy ankle, didn't do myself any favours, but I took a chance because I wanted to play against England. The pitch was frozen, the game should never have gone ahead, and if it hadn't been the centenary match it would have been called off. Still, at least I got a nice set of coasters from the SFA to mark the occasion – they're still kicking around the house somewhere.'

Another memory Buchan has is of the *Daily Record* on Friday, February 16th, the newspaper having clearly decided who had been culpable on the night and how they should be punished: 'There were five mugshots printed, and they must have scoured the archives to get the worst photographs of us they could find. There's Bobby Clark, Eddie Colquhoun, me, George Graham and John O'Hare. And then, in the size of letters normally only used when war has been declared, there's the headline "THESE MEN MUST GO".'

The actual headline read 'ORMOND WILL AXE FLOPS' – and Lou Macari, rather than John O'Hare, was the fifth of the scapegoats – but the story behind it was exactly as Buchan remembers. Alex 'Candid' Cameron was furious with what he had witnessed, and raged, 'The honeymoon is over between Scotland's international players and new manager Willie Ormond. He will axe several of the Hampden Horrors who flopped 5–0 to England. Heading the list, in my view, will be . . .' at which point he uses bold capital letters to name the culprits, before adding, 'They are worth £675,000, but by the time Willie Ormond picks his Home Internationals pool they will definitely be struggling for places.'

It was a performance and scoreline that had stunned the brave 48,470 souls who turned out to watch. Many of them had left long before the final whistle; those home fans who stayed on did so only to boo the team from the pitch or to chant sarcastically, 'We want six! We want six!'

The victory matched England's best ever on Scottish soil, previously recorded in 1888. As Archer noted drily in his match report, the earlier mauling had been so long ago that 'the motor car had yet to be invented'.

The *Daily Express* headlined its report 'FLOP OF THE CENTURY' while the *Record* went with 'CENTENARY SHAMBLES' as writer Hugh Taylor observed, 'The Scots started well and England looked worried . . . alas, ONLY FOR FIVE MINUTES. Peter Lorimer tried to clear, but only smashed the ball past keeper Bobby Clark. That was the beginning of the end . . .'

Ormond's summation was brief: 'We made too many mistakes. England adapted themselves better to the conditions and didn't try anything fancy. This was a terrible blow. Now there must be no panic. I must sleep on this – if I can sleep at all, that is – and get down to sorting things out.'

He was, however, offered some solace from his English counterpart, Ramsey, who noted, 'If it's any consolation to Willie, he might like to know that I started off my England career with a 5–2 defeat [against France in Paris].'

As he left Hampden that night, Ormond was unlikely to be taking comfort from anyone or anything. His dream job had got off to a nightmare start and he was aware the doubters were already expressing concern, suggesting the man from Muirton Park had been the wrong choice to replace the ebullient Docherty. It was up to him to prove them wrong, but he would have to wait: it would be three long months before the national team was in action again, at the 1973 British Championship.

Ormond named his squad at the end of April – one that leant more heavily on home-based players than those listed by Docherty during his time in charge – then flew off to Copenhagen to watch the Czechs kick off their World Cup campaign. His main group rivals tripped up at their first hurdle, having to come from behind to secure a 1–1 draw that left the Scots in pole position to qualify, but the manager was left bemused by the Czechs' approach to the game: 'Obviously it was a good result, but I can't remember when I last saw a team so physical and a side which got away with so much . . . When they come to Hampden we must not try to match them with this physical stuff. We have the players for the football and they must approach this tie remembering that skill still counts.'

With that encounter still four months away, Ormond was focusing on the Home Internationals. After gathering at their regular Largs base, the Scots party travelled to Chester for final preparations ahead of their opener against Wales, in Wrexham. Billy Bremner was left on the substitute's bench, rested after a demanding conclusion to Leeds United's campaign, Ormond handing the captain's armband to Pat Stanton, who would lead out a side boasting five new caps: Danny McGrain, Jim Holton and a Rangers trio of Peter McCloy, Derek Johnstone and Derek Parlane.

The conditions – a strong wind allied to a hard, bumpy pitch – meant the game was never going to be a classic, but the manager declared himself particularly pleased with the contributions of McGrain and Holton, who snuffed out the Welsh danger-man John Toshack. The 2–0 victory, thanks to a George Graham double, was described in the press as 'solid and surefooted'.

Preparations for the next match, at home to Northern Ireland, were relaxed and involved a trip to Ayr Races on the Tuesday afternoon, then onwards to BBC Scotland to watch England beat Wales 3–0 to record their second win in the tournament. The Scots were fully expected to do likewise, but Ormond was about to suffer a second Hampden embarrassment.

He had made just one change to his line-up, Colin Stein replacing his injured team-mate Parlane, but Ormond's side put in an abject performance that had the 39,018 repeatedly chanting, 'What a load of rubbish!' Martin O'Neill and Trevor Anderson had the visitors 2–0 up within seventeen minutes and they never looked like relinquishing their advantage, Dalglish plundering Scotland's only consolation effort a minute from time.

Within fourteen hours the Scotland squad had landed at Heathrow, and over the next couple of days an estimated 30,000 supporters made the pilgrimage south. British Rail laid on eleven 'football specials' and British European Airways had five flights, the larger Trident II aircraft being used to cope with the demand. The midweek defeat seemed to have done little to quell the optimism of the fans who invaded the English capital, the newspapers carrying the obligatory photographs of hordes of them 'taking over Trafalgar Square' and revelling in the fountains. The Saturday morning newspapers were somewhat more pessimistic, with the *Glasgow Herald* headline talking of a 'sense of foreboding', giving the Scots little or no chance of a first Wembley success since their memorable 3–2 victory in 1967.

Ormond's chances were lessened by an injury crisis that saw half a dozen players excluded from his thoughts. The expected defeat duly arrived, England winning 1–0 thanks to a Martin Peters goal, but, less expectedly, the Scots performed well and were desperately unlucky not to return home with a point, denied only by a stunning Peter Shilton save from a Kenny Dalglish volley. It was a third defeat in four matches for the new regime, but one that at least offered signs of improvement. That was just as well, as the manager now had only two more matches to get it right for the crucial World Cup showdown with the Czechs, a double-header of friendlies the following month against Switzerland and Brazil.

Ormond named a familiar squad for those encounters and received a welcome boost from the Scottish Football League when it announced it would be happy to postpone matches ahead of the Czechoslovakia tie in order to enhance Scotland's World Cup hopes. In the meantime, the Czechs were much improved in their return with Denmark, netting half a dozen goals after the interval to secure a 6–0 thrashing and set things up nicely for the Hampden head-to-head.

The players gathered on Monday, June 18th, a full six weeks after the end of the domestic season, and were put through their paces at the Inverclyde Recreation Centre, before flying to Zurich two days later. The hard work continued there as Ormond attempted to restore his troops to something approaching peak fitness, but he was wary of pushing them too hard: 'I told Hugh Allan, the trainer, to warm them up a bit . . . and then I had to stop him. He was doing his full sergeant major act.'

Either way, the preparations had little effect as the Scots put in a disappointing showing in the Wankdorf Stadium in Berne, going down 1–0 to the unheralded Swiss, the only goal a thirty-yard effort by Walter Munschin that Peter McCloy should have done better in trying to prevent.

The Everton winger John Connolly had been handed a debut – his one and only Scotland appearance – and he and Willie Morgan were charged with the responsibility of servicing the lone central striker, Derek Parlane, but it was a tactic that failed miserably.

The loss was a fourth in five games under Ormond and just three goals had been scored. The manager was under growing pressure and knew he had to find the answers.

'I was happy with the defence and the midfield and maybe we could have scored ourselves if the players had been a little sharper,' he told reporters, before adding, 'but it's hard to blame them when they've come back from their holidays to play for their country.'

The manager responded by making one significant change to the side for the next match, a second striker, Joe Jordan, being introduced in place of the unfortunate Connolly.

Brazil's preparations for their trip to Hampden had been going poorly. Their European tour began with a 2–0 defeat in Italy, and three days before meeting the Scots the world champions were beaten 1–0 by Sweden in Stockholm. Willie Ormond had attended that second game and returned home extolling the virtues of the richly talented Roberto Rivelino, one of the undoubted stars of the 1970 finals. His ability to score from long range with viciously swerving shots was the talk of world football at the time, and one unnamed member of the Scotland squad suggested to journalists this was because he had only four toes on his left foot, a disability that allowed him to 'corkscrew' the ball. It was a claim reported at the time, but not investigated, and there seems to be no evidence to substantiate it.

Of the team that had won the World Cup, Rivelino was one of just three players who travelled that summer, the others being Jairzinho and Clodoaldo, but coach Zagallo was determined to avoid a hat-trick of defeats on the south side of Glasgow. As the Brazilians flew into town, the Scots were training at Largs, a session which involved a full-scale practice match. With numbers limited, Ormond drafted in a group of players attending the SFA Coaching Course that was being held there, among them the Dundee striker Gordon Wallace and Aberdeen's Hungarian wizard Zoltán Varga, as unlikely a 'Scotland' player as one might imagine.

Brazil's first Hampden session drew crowds of schoolchildren to the stadium who were entertained by watching the South Americans 'open their training with ballet-type callisthenics, before getting to work with the ball'.

The *Glasgow Herald*'s reporting suggested the Brazilian preparations to be somewhat more refined and advanced than those of the Scots, and it was a theme picked up on by Ian Archer on the morning of the match, which followed a 'grand SFA dinner in Glasgow' as celebrations continued to mark the Association's centenary.

Archer was in no mood to wallow in the past, preferring to 'concentrate on the last decade, a period of decline that has seen Scotland sink, unmourned by outsiders, well into the second rank of European, let alone world, football'. He points to constant struggles and failures, particularly against continental opposition, and to a four-year spell, from 1968 until 1972, during which the Scots failed to record a single away win. He tries to equate the national team's failures with the successes of our club sides in Europe and the fact that most top English teams were at that time overloaded with Scottish players, and he concludes by laying the blame firmly with the SFA, 'a body which increasingly falls down . . . and which has little or no understanding of what is needed in modern football'. Archer goes on to note, 'The fact that Hampden's vast capacity will not be tested even by the presence of the finest footballers in the world should remind the SFA of the growing disaffection that threatens the traditional place of football in the fabric of Scottish society.'

It is a remarkable piece of writing, a damning assessment of the national game, and one which could have been written at virtually any time in the four decades since he sat down behind his typewriter, ever-present cigarette in hand, and bashed it out.

As it was, 78,171 spectators paid their money and went along to Hampden that afternoon to watch Brazil record a 1–0 win 'with embarrassing ease', the sides separated in terms of the scoreline by a Derek Johnstone own goal, but reports suggest a vast gulf in the respective talents of the two sides.

'We just weren't good enough,' admitted captain Billy Bremner.

There would have to be significant improvement when the Scots next took to the field on the night of Wednesday, September 26th 1973, with the nation's World Cup hopes and dreams very much on the line.

3

HAMPDEN SHOWDOWN

Season 1973–74 got underway at the start of August with a competition long since erased from the fixture calendar: the Drybrough Cup.

Sponsorship in football was very much in its infancy and the tournament was one of the first of its kind, with the Edinburgh brewers organising and financing the event itself. The format was simple enough, a knockout competition involving the four highest-scoring sides from each of the two divisions then in operation, with seeding ensuring the top-flight clubs were kept apart and given home advantage. Celtic had lost in each of the two previous finals, and would do so again as Hibernian took the honours for a second successive year. Then as now, fixture congestion was a hot topic, and in his programme notes ahead of a tie against Aberdeen, Jock Stein made clear his club's opposition: 'I am one of those who are not really enamoured of this kind of cup-tie football at this time of year.'

The tournament was staged once more (with Celtic at last ending their run of final defeats), then resurrected briefly at the turn of the decade, before being laid to rest.

The 1973 final was an entertaining affair, Hibernian winning 1–0, and prompted the *Glasgow Herald* to pose the question, 'Are

Ormond's travels really necessary?' following the manager's decision not to attend the match.

Ian Archer found it puzzling that Willie Ormond should eschew the chance to see at first hand at least half a dozen men who would be included in his World Cup squad. Indeed, Archer went further, suggesting the top players on show at Hampden should form the nucleus of the team that would take on Czechoslovakia.

The following weekend saw the League Cup kick off in its sectional format, group stages followed by a knockout competition which would be deemed overly unwieldy by clubs in the modern game, and it was not until Saturday, September 1st that the seventy-seventh season of the Scottish Football League got up and running.

Celtic began the campaign as favourites and would go on to clinch a record-breaking ninth title in a row, albeit pushed virtually all the way by Hibernian and Rangers, but in that early autumn of '73 domestic matters were not at the top of the footballing agenda; the main focus was on the fast-approaching showdown with the Czechs. The importance of the match was such that the SFL had already agreed to postpone key league fixtures to ensure the fitness of Ormond's home-based star men, but no such support was to be given by the Football League, which ran the English game. The body's secretary, Alan Hardaker, had already refused a request to bring forward a Leeds United v Manchester United match by twenty-four hours – apparently without even contacting the clubs involved – a decision that would leave Ormond hoping up to seven players emerged unscathed from what was always likely to be a hard-fought fixture.

The SFA's frustration was further heightened when Hardaker then spoke publicly about how the League would do all it could to aid England ahead of their World Cup ties.

Willie Ormond had continued his preparations by embarking on a tour of English grounds. He took in Liverpool's 2–0 win over Derby County, with the home side's Peter Cormack judged to have done his chances slightly more good than the County trio of John

McGovern, Archie Gemmill and John O'Hare, but overall Ormond left Anfield a disappointed man: 'I saw nothing here to help me for the Czech game. As far as the World Cup is concerned this was my only chance to see them and on the night they did not pass the test.'

He was given food for thought when watching Manchester City beat Coventry City the following night, a match in which veteran striker Denis Law reinforced his selection claims with an imperious performance. Another player who caught the manager's eye was the largely unknown Coventry winger Tommy Hutchison, who, Ormond let it be known, had propelled himself high up the list of 'possibles' due to his trickery and attacking skills. But it was thirty-three-year-old Law's display that had the manager purring with delight: 'He is the best I have seen. If he keeps up the same kind of form, I have to be interested in him.'

It was the news Denis Law had been desperate to hear. Earlier in the year, while still with Manchester United, he had rejected a transfer to Hearts after the clubs had agreed a fee, preferring to remain down south to try to press home his World Cup claims, and even four decades later he beams with delight, recalling the moment he realised he still had a chance of going to West Germany: 'It was very nice of Willie Ormond to say that and of course it was lovely to play at Hampden Park again. I would have to say I had feared my international career was over; don't forget I wasn't particularly fit, I had a cartilage problem, and things were not going well.'

That weekend, Ormond was at Elland Road to see Leeds, boasting a healthy Scots contingent, brush Birmingham City aside by three goals to nil. The star of the show was Peter Lorimer, who bagged a hat-trick but ironically was suspended for the Czech match as a result of his sending-off against Denmark the previous November. The following midweek the manager travelled south again, to watch Everton play hosts to Manchester United, before taking in the Rangers v Celtic clash at Ibrox.

Throughout his sojourns, Ormond was not only assessing form but also keeping his fingers well and truly crossed that his most

47

important players would avoid injury, a major concern for managers in the 1970s, when tackling was somewhat more robust than in the early part of the twenty-first century.

He was also relying on his own International Committee, the members of which had seemed likely to ban the Celtic defender George Connelly for walking out on the Scotland squad just before its departure for the summer friendly in Switzerland. As it was, at a hearing in mid-August, leniency was shown. SFA secretary Willie Allan issued a statement which accepted that 'the player was under considerable pressure because of his wife's condition ... [Mrs Connelly was pregnant at the time and the family was in the process of moving house.] No action should be taken because of this single, irrational act regarded as being out of character.' A relieved Willie Ormond made it clear the player would now feature in his plans.

Just a week before the Czechoslovakia tie, five Scottish clubs were heading into European action across the three competitions, with others involved in the cross-border Texaco Cup, so it was with some trepidation and no great certainty that Ormond, having delayed naming his squad for four days until after that first Old Firm encounter of the season, was able to list the following group for the match that had dominated the nation's thoughts for the best part of a year:

Goalkeepers: Harvey (Leeds United), Hunter (Celtic), Stewart (Kilmarnock)

Full-backs: Donachie (Manchester City), Jardine (Rangers), McGrain (Celtic), Schaedler (Hibernian)

Half-backs: Holton (Manchester United), Johnstone (Rangers), Forsyth (Rangers), Connelly (Celtic), Bremner (Leeds United), Hay (Celtic), Blackley (Hibernian)

Forwards: Dalglish (Celtic), Hutchison (Coventry City), Jordan (Leeds United), Law (Manchester City), Macari (Manchester United), Morgan (Manchester United), Smith (Newcastle United), Stein (Coventry City).

The only inclusion regarded as a surprise was that of the Newcastle winger Jimmy Smith, but it was a squad of players that once again left Ian Archer bemoaning the lack of genuine top-class talent available to the manager. 'This is a non-vintage period for Scottish football, and there was little sparkle in the names that filtered from Park Gardens yesterday,' he wrote the next morning, adding, 'Hardly another World Cup contender would announce a squad which contains seven players still to earn their first caps ... this is a squad longer on unfulfilled ambition than proven quality.' He concluded gloomily, 'The fear is that better-looking teams have failed to last in previous years over the same course and distance.'

Of the five Scottish clubs in European action, only Dundee lost, at home to FC Twente, but more importantly for Willie Ormond there were no fresh injury scares, his only concern being Derek Johnstone, who had picked up a leg knock against Celtic the previous weekend and who would ultimately miss out against the Czechs, breaking up his partnership with Jim Holton. Ormond had considered heading south on the Saturday prior to the tie to watch the Leeds United v Manchester United match but decided he would only ending up 'shuddering at every knock and tackle' as six of his men contested what was always likely to be a highly charged fixture. Instead, the Scotland boss joined a few thousand others in the more relaxing surroundings of Brockville Stadium to watch Falkirk and Motherwell play out a 1–1 draw.

Then he returned home to Musselburgh to sit and hope that the phone would not ring.

Thankfully for Ormond it remained silent, and the following lunchtime the squad members gathered at their usual meeting place at the North British Hotel on Glasgow's George Square before transferring to their Largs base.

Denis Law had been nursing a thigh problem for a few weeks and was awaiting the imminent birth of his fifth child, but nothing was going to prevent him from taking part in his country's biggest football occasion in years. The 'Lawman' held court while drinking copious amounts of tea, bullishly telling the assembled press, 'Look, if I were a Czech I would be worried. Do you think any team fancies playing at Hampden Park knowing that if they lose they are out of the World Cup? Of course not. They are the ones to worry, not us.'

The manager was in a similarly positive frame of mind: 'Mention the Czechs to my team – why should I? We'll play our game – there's nothing in their side to worry us at all.'

He did spend some time at Largs showing his squad film of recent Czechoslovakia matches, but did not dwell on the opposition, preferring instead to work with his players, to try to hone their talents and to concentrate on the tactics he wished to employ on the night. This was a time long before the general introduction of sports psychologists, but such was the mindset of that squad that one would not have been required in any case; every utterance from the Scottish camp was laced with positivity. No one spoke of defeat; no one spoke of failure. Ormond, ably backed by Law and the equally experienced national captain Billy Bremner, talked only of success, of fulfilling a nation's dreams, of winning at Hampden.

As Davie Hay looks back on the build-up to the big showdown, he recalls that quiet confidence, that utter determination, and believes there was every reason for the Scots to be in such a frame of mind: 'They were a top team, but when you had players like Billy Bremner and Denis Law – Denis was my boyhood hero – you were approaching the game thinking you could do it, and the old Hampden definitely had a way of lifting you. I always felt we would win it.'

The Czechs had suffered some delays en route to Glasgow: having departed Bratislava at 6 a.m., it took them more than twelve hours to reach their hotel, at which point coach Václav Jezek ordered his players back on to their team coach for a late-night training session at Hampden. It would be almost midnight when the exhausted players sat down to eat, before finally getting to their beds.

The travelling party was also stunned to learn of the apparent riches on offer to the Scots should they be successful. Czechoslovakia general secretary Jan Fadera told reporters, 'Our players know your men will receive a £2,000 car plus other bonuses to qualify for Munich. Honestly, they did not believe this was possible, but we will not be changing anything. We have told our men their £20 bonus stays, and they accept that. They still believe in the honour of the country.'

Such was Willie Ormond's belief in his side that the manager was happy to sit down with the media the day before the match and reveal the eleven men he had chosen for what Ian Archer had described as 'the most important game Scotland has ever played'. Ormond selected five from Celtic, one from Rangers and five from south of the border, handing out international baptisms of fire to new boys George Connelly and Tommy Hutchison. Those debutants were the big talking points. Connelly was a skilful, ball-playing 'sweeper', but fears were raised in the daily newspapers about his defensive abilities, while it was noted that Hutchison, despite having blossomed in recent months, was untested at international level, his only previous Hampden appearance having been for Alloa Athletic against Queen's Park in a Second Division fixture seven years earlier.

Otherwise, the line-up was as expected and gained a thumbs-up from the football writers, with the front line, taken to be Willie Morgan, Kenny Dalglish and Denis Law, described as 'a trio with that old-fashioned Scottish skill, a combination of grace, quickness and art'.

The team read: Hunter, Jardine, McGrain, Bremner, Holton, Connelly, Morgan, Hay, Law, Dalglish and Hutchison.

Ormond's parting shot to the assembled media was, 'Almost all these players are playing in their club positions and all I ask is that they reveal their club form for their country. It's up to them.'

It would be the one and only time those eleven players took to the field together to represent their country. But what memories they – and a twenty-one-year-old substitute – were about to provide.

This is how Ian Archer reported the match in the *Glasgow Herald*:

The first minutes were scandalous, but we kept the head. Hutchison dropped to the ground twice and here was bare-chested nationalism, played on a battlefield 100 yards in length. Panenka was the villain, a dreadful man, a good player. There was a foul every other second with overworked and worried trainers covering every yard. Denis Law replied with the retaliatory foul on Bendl that showed we were well served for the hand-to-hand stuff and the booking of Samek after only seven minutes brought about a slight, badly observed truce.

Slowly the Scots emerged with talent in the farthest corners of the pitch. Hutchison, ducking tackles and turning on rubber legs, stretched the Czechs on one side, Morgan's more sinuous approach helped on the other. So the chances started to appear.

After 14 minutes Bremner, hustling into the penalty area, met a Morgan cross and headed strongly towards the top of the net. Viktor, that marvellous goalkeeper, leaped upwards and made the first of three first-half saves that kept his side alive, our faith in the essential goodness of Czech football still burning.

Kuna went off after 20 minutes, the only victim of that early outbreak of viciousness, and Dobias replaced him. From a mid-European point of view that might have made all the difference.

After 26 minutes the game's best move again ended with a Viktor save. Hutchison crossed long to the far post, Law headed strongly back across an unbalanced defence, and Morgan, twisting viciously, hit a strong volley that the goalkeeper reached in a fraction of a second – all the time he had.

Then, after 32 minutes, there was silence. The Czechs, who had attacked sparsely, and without conviction, sauntered unconvincingly down the right wing. Nehoda hit a tame shot and Hunter, baffled by its lack of weight, dived uncertainly as it crossed his body. The ball ended in the net almost with apologies. It was a bad time to be a Scot.

It was certainly a bad time to be Ally Hunter. The inexplicable loss of such a poor goal, a goal that might have proved so costly, tainted his career. On the Scottish Television commentary, the legendary Arthur Montford exploded with pain: 'Disaster! Disaster for Scotland!' Hunter would not add to the fourth Scotland cap he was winning that night; he would not be included in the squad for the World Cup finals.

Archer continued: 'But that insistent spirit remained unbroken. Law hit a cunning free kick and Viktor saved again. The side was back on the rails and after 40 minutes it had re-established parity. Hutchison, with a corner on the left, aimed high on to the six-yard line where Scots queued up to jump. Law, the great distracter, took two men with him and Holton, that oak of a man, leaped upwards and placed the ball in the net.'

For such a patriot, Ian Archer's words seem understated, his description barely doing justice to such an important moment for the national team. On the television, Montford was not holding back, his elation evident as he yelled, 'Over it comes. Holton's there. And it's there! Holton scores!' The giant centre-half was helped by Viktor rushing from his goal in a vain attempt to punch the ball clear, but it was a towering and perfectly judged header by the Manchester United man which looped in over the head of a despairing Czech defender and dropped just under the bar and into the net. The noise from the Scotland fans was quite deafening as

Holton was swamped by his team-mates, with Bremner, Dalglish and Law leaping all over him.

The Scots were quickly on the attack again, looking for a second goal to utterly break the Czech resistance, as Archer noted in his report:

> That was not all in the first 45 minutes of unremitting action. A Hay shot was blocked by Dalglish as it headed for the net, Holton placed another header past Viktor, only to be called offside.
>
> So to an historic second half which started quietly with Panenka finally booked after 55 minutes for the latest foul on Bremner. The Czechs, now time-wasters, started the cool possession stuff.
>
> Too often Scotland's only answer to the insoluble problem of a packed defence was the high and hopeful ball into the penalty area. The flesh seemed willing, the tactics weak. For 10 minutes another World Cup attempt seemed to be over; new doldrums appeared to be round the corner.
>
> Then it happened, just 12 minutes after Ormond had replaced the tiring Dalglish with Jordan. 'Just push up . . .' he told him.
>
> Scotland's winning goal started typically. Law was obstructed inside the penalty area and the Norwegian referee – a man suitably from a permissive society – awarded an indirect free kick. Morgan played it short to Bremner, who bustled to the side of the defensive wall and shot strongly against the foot of a post. The ball bounced across the line and out.
>
> All was not lost. Morgan picked up the rebound, chipped it across, and Jordan, dropping forward, headed the ball into the net. For Scottish sporting man it remained the joy of a lifetime.

Arthur Montford, meanwhile, was giving voice to what the entire nation felt, cheering, 'Magnificent Scotland! Magnificent!'

Joe Jordan was just twenty-one years old and had never known anything quite like it. He was winning only his fourth international cap and had scored his first international goal. It would be one of the most memorable nights of the striker's career: 'A hundred thousand people at Hampden and Willie Ormond says, "On you go." We were playing against a really top team, '76 they'd go on to become champions of Europe, but we had the players and the pressure was building and building and eventually it came, and I got on the end of it and put it away. It was . . . it was a great feeling.'

There was one further opportunity for Scotland to put the result beyond doubt when, in the closing minutes, Denis Law broke clear, but was thwarted by the Czech goalkeeper. Again, it was reported in very different ways by the two observers quoted above, with Archer, apparently calmly, writing in the aftermath, 'Through the gaps they left Law ran alone through the middle but could not round Viktor and score a third goal,' while an emotional Montford, caught up in the heat of the moment, implored excitedly, 'Law's in the clear! Come on now, Denis, come on, Denis!' The keeper got a hand to the ball and nudged it to safety, denying the Manchester United striker the goal he so desired.

'I saw that later on the television. I think if I'd actually heard him I might have gone on a bit further,' laughs Law, 'but in actual fact, I was absolutely knackered!'

It mattered not, because within a few moments the Norwegian referee Henry Oberg had signalled the end of the contest.

As his final whistle sounded and a relieved Hampden erupted, Willie Ormond was carried shoulder high across the pitch by his jubilant players to the resounding chant of 'Munich, Munich here we come!' For more than fifteen minutes after the end of the game the crowds refused to leave the national stadium, with reports suggesting it was a full two hours before traffic jams eased throughout the South Side of Glasgow. The Scots had become the first European nation to qualify for the following summer's finals; the euphoria and celebrations continued well into the early hours as a decade and a half of frustration and bitter disappointment was drunk to the backs of supporters' minds.

Ormond was also euphoric and, despite his brave talk beforehand, somewhat stunned by what had just unfolded: 'I just can't believe it's happened. That last period seemed to be the longest quarter of an hour of my life. Every thirty seconds I checked my watch and the wait seemed never ending. I also lost my voice shouting at the lads . . . but it was a tremendous victory . . . my team just refused to give up and admit that they would get any other result than a victory.'

Even all these years later, Danny McGrain lets out a sigh as he looks back on that night, admitting it was one of the most stress-laden occasions he encountered in his long and successful career: 'Probably without knowing it, you've got that pressure. Some players carry it well, some can't carry it at all, some crack and can't perform because they're too worried about the "what ifs" . . . You're playing for Scotland, you're playing at Hampden, you've got all those supporters behind you and they all want to go to the World Cup as much as we do, and then they score a goal and that dream is diminishing before your eyes. Czechoslovakia couldn't believe they're one–nil up . . . as soon as we scored, big Jim Holton equalised, there was only going to be one winner, but we still had to get that second goal. There was pressure, internal pressure, we wanted it so much . . . and then Joe comes on for Kenny, throws his big head at it and that's it . . . but you're always fearful, what if they equalise? Thankfully they didn't, and afterwards the whole world breaks out at Hampden.'

Players often have trouble recalling certain emotions from particular games, especially those played out many years previously, but McGrain's feelings that night remain fresh in his mind: 'I just felt this big weight lift off my shoulders. How good is this? I hadn't been aware of just how much pressure I'd been under, not beforehand, not during the game, but I certainly realised at that point. Party time! We're going to the World Cup . . . We are going to the World Cup! I was twenty-three then, Kenny was twenty-two, Joe was just twenty-one . . . We'd grown up watching World Cups, dreaming about them . . . To think you'd be playing at a World Cup was just surreal.'

One of those youngsters, Joe Jordan, remembers it as being among the noisiest atmospheres he was to encounter throughout his glittering career, but on that occasion, he says, it went further than just the 'Hampden Roar': 'I was lucky, I played in an era when Hampden, especially for night games, was an impossible place to go to for an opposition . . . and after the game, Glasgow's a place I've never seen like it was that night. Scotland's a football nation . . . That night it was a nation united, and I saw it around the city, whether it was a bus driver, a guy walking down the street . . . It was there, it definitely caught the imagination. There was a great pride in being a Scot that night, without a doubt.'

Davie Hay looks back at that night with similar feelings, although he admits it was not until after the final whistle had sounded that the enormity of the occasion dawned on him: 'You know when you realise it? At the end, when you do the lap of honour. You go out there and do the job, and we were lifted by the crowd after going behind, but it's only at the end when you see and hear the reaction of the fans, that's when you understand how important it was and what it's meant to everybody . . . You know it by the reaction you get. The lap of honour almost becomes better than the game itself!'

The suspended Peter Lorimer had been determined not to miss out on the big night, so he had driven a group up from Yorkshire to at least watch the game from the Hampden stand. With the winger were his brother-in-law, Leeds team-mates Gordon McQueen and Eddie Gray, and another young Scot who was in the Elland Road reserves, Bobby Shields. They were to have a memorable night in more ways than one, as Lorimer recalls: 'In the excitement when Joe scored the winning goal, I must have thrown my keys up in the air.

We went down to see the players, it's all "well done" and everybody's happy, and when we finally got back to the car I says to the lads I've lost my keys, and of course they think I'm joking. We went back in, couldn't find them anywhere, so I call the AA, but they can't help because it's a French car, a Peugeot, and they don't have any keys to fit it. So, we went back to the North British Hotel and had a few drinks with the lads, we had a right good session, then we rung a taxi, and when it arrived the driver was absolutely pissed. He turned up in a funeral car, we needed a bigger one as there were five of us, and he asks where we're going and we say Leeds, and he goes, "Leeds?" Eventually we set off and he was all over the bloody road, but we didn't mind because we were merry as well. It was a good little trip. I can't remember what the fare was, it would have been a right few quid, but it was worth it. It didn't make any difference how much it cost, because we were going to the World Cup finals. I went into training the next morning, got a spare key from the garage, got the train back up to Glasgow, then drove home again.'

Having been reunited with his car, Lorimer's next concern might have been getting back into the side, but, such was his self-belief and level of performance at that stage, he was in no doubt he would be heading for West Germany: 'I was playing particularly well at the time and I was confident I'd get back in. I was just so disappointed to have missed playing in that game. But I certainly expected to get back into the squad and indeed I was very confident I would be playing when we got to the finals . . . although the competition, even in my own position, was so strong. I had Jimmy Johnstone, Willie Morgan and Tommy Hutchison, Eddie Gray, who was injured at the time, all great wingers, all desperate to get into the team, so it wasn't a foregone conclusion, I suppose.'

The Hibernian central defender John Blackley was just at the start of his international career. He had yet to make his debut, and he was another sitting in the old main stand that night, alongside the other unused squad members: 'What a night! All of a sudden we were going to the World Cup finals and it was great, great to be part of that. I got down to the dressing room quickly and it was just fantastic, everybody knowing what they'd achieved. The players were just so excited given what was ahead for them . . . If I had been playing it would just have been the best thing ever, but me going down in a shirt and a tie, a suit . . . while you joined in, and congratulated everybody, it was a wee bit more difficult for me to really feel a part of it.'

For veteran striker Denis Law, at the other end of his career, the match had offered up one last chance to represent his country on the biggest stage of them all, and he summed up the occasion in emphatic terms: 'It was the greatest moment of my sporting life.'

Of the 100,000 who had gathered on the slopes for the night of their lives, twenty-four were arrested for what an unnamed police officer described as 'minor offences', before adding, sympathetically, 'I think probably most of them had too many celebration toasts. On the whole they were a fairly manageable, happy crowd out to enjoy themselves.'

The next morning's headlines were predictable enough: 'SCOTLAND INTO WORLD CUP' and 'SCOTLAND BOOK THEIR TICKET FOR WORLD CUP FINALS' among them, as the nation recovered slowly from its collective hangover.

Even in those less commercially driven times there was already talk of the cash bonanza that awaited those players lucky enough to be selected for West Germany, with early estimates suggesting the promise of around £250,000 worth of contracts ready to be shared out.

Those riches would, of course, be welcomed by the squad, but overshadowing any financial gain was the chance to represent their country on the biggest stage of all, the chance to make history, the chance to become Scottish football legends.

Denis Law was, of course, already a legend and he had played his part despite his wife Diana being heavily pregnant and likely to give birth at any time: 'These days guys will say, "Sorry, I can't play, my good lady's expecting," but it was a different attitude in those days, wasn't it? Your country came first. We had four boys already . . . If it had been another boy it was going back!'

Four days after the Hampden showdown there was further cause for the striker to celebrate when he finally got the daughter he and his wife had longed for. Diana Law was born on September 30th 1973.

4

COUNTDOWN TO THE FINALS

Although Scotland had already tied up qualification for the finals, there was still the job of fulfilling the Group 8 fixture list, the concluding match being the return against the Czechs. Willie Ormond had initially drawn up a squad consisting of virtually the same players as had been chosen for the glorious occasion at Hampden but gradually saw names disappear from his list as Jim Holton, Billy Bremner and Jimmy Smith all withdrew because of injury. Their absence allowed Derek Johnstone, Willie Donachie and the Hearts striker Donald Ford the opportunity to press their claims for a place in West Germany.

As he addressed the media on the eve of the game at their hotel on the banks of the River Danube, Ormond eventually named a side showing four changes. David Harvey replaced the unfortunate Hunter in goal, Tom Forsyth and debutant John Blackley were drafted into the defence, and Hampden hero Joe Jordan was given a place in a potent-looking strike force alongside Law and Dalglish. Davie Hay was selected to captain his country for the first time.

Anticipating a robust approach from their hosts, the manager's main concern was for his men to avoid getting involved in any confrontations that might lead to a sending-off and a subsequent suspension from the opening games of the World Cup: 'In our pre-match talk I will tell the players that if I see anyone getting into any trouble then he will come off immediately – even if it means ending the match with eight men. I don't expect it to be a bloodbath, but we will look after ourselves, I assure you of that.'

The game had hardly caught the imagination of football fans in Bratislava, with just 13,668 scattered around the unusual three-sided Tehelné Pole Stadium, the atmosphere so muted that reporters could clearly hear Hay delivering instructions to his team-mates as he guided them through the ninety minutes. Ormond's pre-match fears were unfounded, and the referee's only major decision was to award a debatable early penalty from which Nehoda scored the decisive goal. Ford, a second-half substitute, and Blackley were deemed to have done their chances no harm with assured performances, but that apart it was a game that petered out, with the home side booed from the field as they exited the competition. The Scots, on the other hand, had plenty to look forward to: seven fixtures over the next eight months that would allow Willie Ormond to finalise the squad he hoped would bring joy to the nation at the finals.

Meanwhile, some 800 miles away, a much more frenzied occasion had also concluded in a scoreline that definitely would bring joy to Scottish football fans. A 1–1 draw with Poland at Wembley, in which the visiting goalkeeper Jan Tomaszewski had performed heroics, meant England were out: they would not be joining Scotland in Germany the following summer.

When the news reached the ears of the Scotland players it was greeted with much surprise and enthusiasm, particularly by those returning to dressing rooms south of the border. The Manchester United winger Willie Morgan declared his intention to return to work sporting his national team shirt: 'I will just wear it, that's all. I won't say a word. Well, it wouldn't be fair to rub it in, would it?'

That was a moment his Old Trafford colleague Denis Law thoroughly enjoyed, having the chance to get his own back after years of stick from his English team-mates: 'It was lovely going in the next day to training with United because they hadn't qualified

... that made it even better when I got to see Nobby [Stiles], Bobby [Charlton] and Alex Stepney and a few others.'

Football at that time was largely untouched by the commercial world. Few matches were allowed to be shown live on television, the jerseys worn by the players were untainted by the names and logos of sponsors, and what advertising there was around the perimeter of the stadiums was largely bought at knock-down prices by local firms. There were no agents to take 10 per cent of the still relatively small sums earned by the stars of the day, and those players had only limited opportunities to supplement their incomes through tie-ups with companies eager to exploit their fame.

All that would change considerably over the following decade or so, and on October 29th 1973, the Scottish FA, with some trepidation, it has to be imagined, first dipped its toe into the murky waters of commercialism when it placed an advertisement in the national newspapers for a 'sports business consultant'. The successful applicant would be expected to have the wherewithal to successfully 'exploit the financial possibilities of sponsorship for football, of the use of the association's name, etc., in regard to the World Cup, and generally explore the advertising market on behalf of the association'.

It was a remarkable, and unexpected, step by what was seen as a very conservative and cautious organisation and one that would ultimately lead to relatively few deals being struck as the finals campaign drew nearer. None of the players would be able to retire on the proceeds.

One of the first contracts struck was with car-makers Vauxhall, who offered up twenty-eight vehicles on a free loan for a year. They were to be distributed between players and officials, but there was to be much squabbling – some of it in public – before the SFA finally drew up a list of the beneficiaries. In the end, each of the players who had featured in the qualifiers against the Danes and the Czechs got one, as did Ormond, the squad's trainers Ronnie McKenzie and Hugh Allan, and the team doctor Dr John Fitzsimmons.

Unfortunately, the exact terms of the deal had not been made clear to the players and a number of them were under the misapprehension that the cars – in World Cup colours such as 'Russian Red' and 'Brazilian Gold', boasting radios and stereos, and monogrammed on the driver's door with the players' initials – were theirs to keep. As the saga rumbled on, the car-makers issued a statement from their Luton headquarters: 'We want to make it quite clear that at no time have we promised to give motor cars to Scotland's World Cup squad ... We have agreed to lend each member a car for a year. After that, if they wish, they may buy the car at market price.'

This came as a surprise to some of the squad, who were quick to confront their larger-than-life business manager, Bob Bain. The forty-two-year-old, a former clarinet player and warm-up comedian who worked from hotels in Glasgow and Switzerland and who spoke, according to the *Express*, with a clipped mid-Atlantic accent, was typically bullish in response: 'I would hope to meet the top Vauxhall people – and I mean *the* top people – to discuss this. There is no need for anyone to get steamed up about it.'

No such meeting took place and the terms of the contract remained unaltered.

At that point, the Scots were one of five nations to have qualified for the 1974 jamboree, Uruguay, Argentina, Poland and Italy having also secured their places alongside hosts West Germany and holders Brazil. It was becoming clear there would be a different look to the competition, with five of the 1970 finalists already eliminated and four others in serious danger of missing out.

One of those four, the Soviet Union, eventually staged a recovery and qualified for a two-legged Intercontinental play-off with Chile. The first game finished 0–0 in Moscow, with the return due to be staged at the Estadio Nacional in Santiago. Chile was at the time under military rule following a recent *coup d'état* and protestors against the Augusto Pinochet regime had been held captive and executed inside the stadium. The Soviets refused to play the match there, issuing a strongly worded statement claiming the stadium had been 'turned into a concentration camp, an arena of torture and execution for Chilean patriots ... Soviet sportsmen cannot for moral reasons play in a stadium stained with blood.' FIFA refused to stipulate an alternative venue, so the Chileans – who took to the pitch unopposed, much as Scotland would in Tallinn, Estonia, almost a quarter of a century later – were given a bye to the finals.

Alongside the Soviet Union, another much-fancied team made its exit, albeit in somewhat less controversial circumstances. Belgium lost out after concluding their campaign with a 0–0 draw in Amsterdam, which was enough to see the emerging Dutch side qualify for the first time since 1934. Some observers were already tipping that team – boasting talents such as Cruyff, Neeskens, Krol, Haan and Rensenbrink – as dark horses to win the tournament. Their prediction would very nearly come true.

Ninety-nine countries had begun the qualification process, and in the winter of 1973 the line-up was all but complete. In addition to the nine already mentioned (Scotland, Uruguay, Argentina, Poland, Italy, West Germany, Brazil, Chile and Holland), Sweden, East Germany, Bulgaria, Yugoslavia, Haiti, Zaire and Yugoslavia – who would beat Spain in a play-off – all made it.

The next milestone would be the draw, to be staged in Frankfurt on the 5th of January, which would determine the make-up of the four groups.

The first of the warm-up games for the Scots was an encounter with the World Cup hosts at Hampden in mid-November, the last of the SFA centenary matches, and Ormond made his intentions clear. Now free from suspension, Peter Lorimer was handed an instant recall, and the fit-again Billy Bremner and Jim Holton were also included.

When the West Germans touched down on Scottish soil, they did so without their top scorer Gerd Müller, injured while scoring a hat-trick for his Bayern side against Hamburg at the weekend, but boss

Helmut Schoen could still draw from a list of considerable talents, chief among them his imposing captain Franz Beckenbauer.

Bremner was reinstalled as Scots skipper, fresh from an outstanding display against Hibernian in the UEFA Cup, a match Willie Ormond had attended: 'I just had to rush down at the end and tell Don Revie [Leeds United manager] that it was one of the greatest personal performances I had ever seen. It was quite incredible, out of this world.'

Such was the Scot's standing in the global game at that time, at the end of the year Bremner was voted fifth in the magazine *France Football*'s European Footballer of the Year poll, behind legends Johan Cruyff, Dino Zoff, Müller and Beckenbauer. He gathered twenty-two votes; the England captain Bobby Moore amassed just two.

Holed up at their usual Largs base, the Scotland players were being prepared for the encounter with Schoen's side, but at a more leisurely pace than normal. 'They have all been undergoing a very heavy schedule these last weeks and there is no point in tiring them any further' was the manager's reasoning.

The West German boss was also holding court with reporters, playing down his team's ranking as favourites to lift the World Cup. He listed Brazil and Italy as obvious threats and also pointed to Poland and Holland as potential winners before turning his attention to the Scots: 'I am not forgetting Scotland and do not put them alongside the others just because we are here in Troon and want to be diplomatic. I would certainly rate them along with the sides we already fear . . . They are such good competitors . . . They keep going, and in the World Cup, with a match every three or four days, that is a priceless asset.'

When Ormond named his line-up it showed just two changes to the team that had beaten Czechoslovakia two months earlier. David Harvey was named as goalkeeper rather than the now discarded Ally Hunter, while skilful Newcastle United playmaker Jimmy Smith was given his first cap in place of the injured Davie

Hay, who was at that time also embroiled in a controversial contract stand-off with Celtic and being lined up for a transfer to Manchester United, a move that ultimately fell through.

The Germans, while not at full strength, looked strong, with Uli Hoeness leading the line, Günter Netzer in midfield and Berti Vogts – a man who would much later make a mark of sorts on the Scottish national team – in defence, in addition to talisman Beckenbauer.

The front-page headlines the following morning were dominated by the wedding of Princess Anne to Captain Mark Phillips, hundreds of millions of people having watched the ceremony live on television. A much smaller audience – 58,235 – had gathered at Hampden to watch Scotland play the European champions on a raw Glasgow night, and the general verdict seemed to be that the Scots had outplayed their visitors and shown superior skills but had been frustrated and had ultimately had to settle for a 1–1 draw, a scoreline that nevertheless extended the Germans' record of never having won at the stadium.

Scotland had snatched an early lead, Holton heading the ball into the net after Bremner had inadvertently blocked a net-bound Law effort. The flow of the game was almost entirely towards the West German goal, but time and again the home players failed to convert. They were handed a glaring opportunity when Beckenbauer tumbled Dalglish in the box, but Bremner's weak penalty – 'I just got caught in two minds,' he later admitted – was easily saved by second-half substitute Sepp Maier, and the visitors were quick to capitalise on their good fortune, Hoeness nodding in a late, if undeserved, equaliser.

Helmut Schoen admitted as much afterwards, reconfirming his belief that Scotland should be rated among the favourites to become world champions: 'We have known that for some time and the events at Hampden only confirmed our suspicions. It puzzles us that the Scots themselves do not regard themselves in the same way as the rest of the world sees them.'

It would be over four months before their next game, another encounter with Schoen's side in Frankfurt, but before then there was an even more important date to consider in West Germany.

It had already been announced that Britain's quota of 35,812 tickets for the finals had been sold out in advance, with more than half that number allocated to Scotland, although many more supporters would ultimately make the short trip over to follow the team. All these fans needed to know was who they would be watching, and where.

This was a time long before the official FIFA world rankings, so the seeding for draws tended to be made on an ad hoc basis, and early indications suggested that the holders and the hosts would be joined in the top pot by Italy and Uruguay, one unnamed official revealing, 'No other solution is likely to be acceptable as those are the only four nations in the finals which are previous winners of the cup.' The same source confirmed the other countries would be split into three 'graded' sections, with the Scots, given their woeful historical record in the competition, likely to be in either the third or fourth tiers.

Planning had begun well before the draw took place. Brazil already knew they would head one group and play their matches in Frankfurt and Gelsenkirchen, while West Germany would be based in Hamburg and West Berlin.

When official confirmation came, it brought the news that Scotland had avoided being dumped in the bottom pot. Instead, Sweden – despite having a superior World Cup record to both the Scots and East Germany – were inexplicably listed alongside minnows Zaire, Haiti and Australia. The East Germans were elevated for political reasons; no one could explain quite why Scotland had managed to avoid the ignominy of being rated as cannon fodder, although the indications were that Sir Stanley Rous, the Englishman who was then president of FIFA, had applied some pressure to the seeding committee.

It was a clear stroke of good fortune for Willie Ormond, his spirits not in the least dampened by seeing his team drawn in Group 2 with Brazil. Yugoslavia would beat Spain 1–0 in their play-off the following month to claim their place, with first-time qualifiers Zaire making up the section. Ormond had watched the draw live on the BBC in a no-frills broadcast that lasted just a quarter of an hour.

'I can see no reason at all why Scotland cannot qualify for the later stages. I am more than happy with the way things have turned out' was the manager's bullish assessment.

His team would kick off against the Africans in Dortmund on June 14th, then move to Frankfurt for the daunting task of taking on the defending champions. They would face a Brazil team shorn of some of the heroes of 1970 – among others, Pelé, Tostão and Gérson would all be missing – but one taking the defence of their crown very seriously. The Brazilian Football Confederation had already announced that the squad would gather in Rio at the beginning of March and spend three months together building up for the finals, with up to ten international matches being played during that time. They would be better prepared than any other side heading for West Germany. The Scots' last, and almost certainly decisive, match would be back in Frankfurt on June 22nd.

Scotland's achievement in reaching the finals had set the nation buzzing, with enthusiasm for the national team once again restored, and there was a call for further support from south of the border. Labour's former Minister of Sport Denis Howell went public with his demand for the Scots to be treated as England had been at the 1966 and '70 tournaments: 'I hope the clubs will be as generous in agreeing to release the players for build-up training as they would be in the case of England. Scotland is not a wealthy country from a football point of view and the government should ensure that they get all the facilities and assistance they feel they require in preparing for West Germany, where they will be representing the country as a whole.'

One manager had already made his position clear and it was hardly encouraging news for Willie Ormond. His predecessor Tommy Docherty was in the midst of what would ultimately be an unsuccessful battle to avoid the drop with Manchester United and he was quick to make it clear his club would come first: 'If we have important matches and still need the points I would not be prepared to release players from club duties to help Scotland. Hopefully that will not be the position, but I have to consider it.'

Meanwhile, a bizarre and unexpected story was emerging as First Division Dumbarton revealed they had been in contact with the Zaire Embassy in London and hoped to play the Africans at Boghead in a game that would act as a World Cup warm-up for their visitors and also as a finale to the club's centenary celebrations. Scottish FA regulations did not permit club sides to take on national teams, but Dumbarton's managing director Alex Jackson told reporters, 'The people at the embassy seem most hopeful and anxious that the game should take place. We will be having talks at the earliest opportunity with the SFA to resolve the position.'

But Dumbarton soon had competition. Hibernian Chairman Tom Hart announced he would be meeting a Zaire representative in the hope of fixing up a match with his club, while East of Scotland FA secretary Sandy Jack was also bidding to arrange a fixture against a Select XI.

It was the latter offer which was eventually accepted, with Hibs and Hearts players expected to make up the majority of the team, which it was arranged would face the tourists in early May. As it turned out, and despite lengthy discussions that also involved the Hearts director Bobby Parker, the game never actually took place, although there seems to be no historical record as to why the plans were shelved.

January 1974 was proving to be a busy time for the Scottish Football Association. In addition to preparing for the World Cup finals, plans were already underway for the 1976 European Nations Championship, with the Scots learning their qualification campaign would consist of group matches against Romania, Spain and Denmark.

More immediately, the SFA announced the Glasgow-based company International Image Consultants had won the contract to help reap the commercial rewards from the World Cup. The firm would also be expected to put together a long-term strategy for developing sponsorship in the game, with one of its first tasks to design a World Cup mascot that could be licensed for use on various products and prove a potentially lucrative money-spinner.

Two weeks later, IIC introduced the world to Roary Super Scot, a somewhat demented-looking lion brandishing the Saltire while balancing his right foot on what looked suspiciously like a rugby ball. Over the next few months all manner of memorabilia was produced as Roary became almost as familiar as the players themselves.

Those players were also on the lookout for more financial benefits, and the squad's own commercial manager Bob Bain announced he had struck a deal with Polydor Records for 'a single and an LP' to be written and produced by the highly successful duo of Bill Martin and Phil Coulter, pop music legends with a string of chart hits behind them. The pair had also worked with the England World Cup squad four years earlier, a collaboration that saw 'Back Home' enjoy three weeks at number one while the players toured Mexico.

They came up with an album entitled *Scotland Scotland*, which featured not only the national team but also an eclectic mix of some of the most successful Scottish acts around in the mid-1970s, including Lulu, the Bay City Rollers, Gallagher and Lyle, and Junior Campbell. The most remarkable track was a reworking of Rod Stewart's 'Angel', which featured the gravel-voiced singer bantering with Denis Law throughout, the track ending with Stewart – who was clearly having a ball – asking, 'Do I get paid now, or later on?'

Forty years on, Law has, perhaps wisely, decided he has no

recollection of that unique duet. 'I can't remember a thing about it
. . .' he contends, although his smile suggests he perhaps does, but
chooses not to admit it.

The album spawned the single 'Easy Easy', which was a new
entry at number 30 in the official UK charts on June 22nd, the very
day the team was playing Yugoslavia in the final group match. A
week later it peaked at number 20, sandwiched by the rereleased
'Young Girl' by Gary Puckett and the Union Gap and 10cc's 'Wall
Street Shuffle', before dropping back down to 32 and then out of the
listings altogether.

Those who bought the record clearly did so out of national pride
and to support the team. No one surely was drawn in by the singing
of Dalglish, McGrain, Jordan et al., and no one seduced by lyrics
such as:

> Yabba dabba doo, we support the boys in blue. And it's
> easy, easy
> Yabba dabba doo, we are gonna follow you. And it's
> easy, easy
> Yabba dabba day, we'll be with you all the way. Singing
> eeeeeeeeeasy
> Ring-a-ding-a-ding, there goes Willie on the wing. And
> it's easy, easy
> Ring-a-ding-a-ding, knock it over for the king. And it's
> easy, easy
> Ring-a-ding-a-dong, now we know we can't go wrong.
> And it's eeeeeeeeeasy . . .

Followed by:

> Eeny meeny mo, get the ball and have a go. And it's
> easy, easy
> Eeny meeny mo, we'll let everybody know that it's easy,
> easy . . .

What Willie Ormond thought of the recording does not seem to have been archived, but he had enough to keep him occupied in any case as he spent the early months of the year monitoring the potential members of his squad both on and off the pitch.

Having played in both qualifiers against Denmark, and having scored in Copenhagen, striker Joe Harper had dropped off the radar after a disappointing spell with Everton. At the end of January Hibernian brought him back north for a Scottish record transfer fee of £120,000 and Harper was hoping to gatecrash the World Cup party.

On the other hand, Celtic's stylish central defender George Connelly was in the process of playing – or rather not playing – his way out of the squad. Having gone missing for six days in November, Connelly had not featured in a match of any consequence since Scotland's draw with West Germany, and at the beginning of February the club accepted his written transfer request. Connelly was the reigning Scottish Football Writers' Association Player of the Year, but Jock Stein's patience had finally snapped. 'Now we will wait and see who comes in for him' was his terse response. It would be another two years, and various further walkouts, before the defender finally left the club. He returned to the side soon after, but injury eventually prevented him from boarding the plane for the finals.

Connelly's situation mirrored that of his friend and team-mate Davie Hay, who had endured a contract dispute with the club earlier in the season and had seemed set for a move to Manchester United, only for the transfer to fall through. An uneasy truce was eventually brokered and the midfielder restored to the Celtic first team, thus remaining an important member of Ormond's squad. He would ultimately leave after the World Cup to embark on a career in England with Chelsea.

There was also trouble across Glasgow for another of Ormond's hopefuls, versatile youngster Derek Johnstone, who had irked his irascible manager, Jock Wallace. The twenty-year-old had been dumped into the Rangers reserves for violating Wallace's personal code: 'And that is where he stays – unless he can prove that he has the right attitude to return to the first team.'

Leaving all that behind, Willie Ormond flew off to Frankfurt in mid-February to attend the play-off between Spain and Yugoslavia that would decide which of the countries would complete the Scots' World Cup group. The Spanish were underdogs, their domestic game at the time bereft of home-bred stars and reliant on imported talent such as Johan Cruyff and Günter Netzer to illuminate their league. With a crowd of 60,000 anticipated, and with the atrocities of the Munich Olympic Games still fresh in their minds, the German authorities drafted in an extra 500 police officers in a bid to ensure the occasion passed peacefully. As for the game, Ormond was quite clear what he hoped for: 'No doubt about it – I would like to see Spain win.'

The Scots boss was to be thwarted. Yugoslavia, playing a fluid 4–3–3 formation, won 1–0 thanks to an early goal by Josip Katalinski, but were dominant throughout against limp opposition, leading Ormond to reflect, 'I think we will cause them more trouble than Spain, who disappointed me.'

The manager's next appointment was to attend a somewhat more run-of-the-mill fixture, a Scottish Cup fourth-round encounter between Partick Thistle and Hearts at Firhill. The visitors won 4–1 and Ormond was given food for thought by a stellar performance from the Hearts striker Donald Ford, a largely peripheral figure on the international scene, who made the first goal, scored a hat-trick and was denied a fourth only by the woodwork. Given that the national team had netted just three goals in its last six matches, Ford had gone a long way towards demanding inclusion.

A number of younger players were also hoping to catch the manager's eye and they were given their opportunity in an Under-23 international at Pittodrie. The Scots beat their Welsh counterparts 3–0, with Bobby Robinson of Dundee and the Hibernian forward Alex Cropley deemed to have done most to improve their chances. In the end, only one of the squad made it to West Germany: the Kilmarnock goalkeeper Jim Stewart, who remained on the bench throughout the finals. Ormond had clearly decided long in advance on the majority of the players he would take to the World Cup – it would have taken something special to alter his thinking.

At the start of March Willie Ormond was off on his travels again, this time to Egypt for the Africa Cup of Nations, where he would get a first opportunity to cast his eyes over Zaire. The 'Leopards' kicked off their campaign with a 2–1 win over Guinea in front of 30,000 fans at the Ala'ab Stadium in Damanhur, Ndaye Mulamba scoring both goals, but the Scots manager saw little to trouble him: 'I thought Zaire were quite good in attack, all four could play a bit. But at the back they were loose, marking man to man and lacking pace. I did not see anything to give me a sleepless night. The pace was not everything I had expected, even allowing for the heat. I am sure we can take them.'

It was a theme picked up on by Zaire's Yugoslav coach Blagoje Vidinic when he spoke to Scottish reporters the following day: 'Four years ago when I was with Morocco in the World Cup we had good results [they led West Germany before going down narrowly, and drew 1–1 with Bulgaria], but that was because we had a good defence. You saw Zaire yesterday. They have a good attack, but the defence is poor. That makes the competition, the World Cup, very difficult.'

Two days later Vidinic's side were beaten 2–1 in Alexandria by Congo, and Ormond was even more emphatic in his assessment: 'I just want the people back home to know that we have nothing to worry about. We will beat Zaire.'

Despite Willie Ormond's scathing assessment, the Leopards were clearly a strong side on their own continent. They beat Mauritius 4–1 in their last group game, saw off Egypt 3–2 in the semi-finals and then, after a 2–2 draw, won 2–0 in the replay against Zambia to become African champions for the second time in six years. Mulamba ended the tournament with a record total of nine goals.

Meanwhile, back home there was some debate about whether Scotland should take to the field in Germany with 'God Save the Queen' ringing in the players' ears. The discussion was sparked further when Ormond offered the opinion that the team was not going to the World Cup to represent Britain, but purely as Scotland. Ian Archer explored the issue in his column for the *Glasgow Herald*, where he challenged the SFA president Hugh Nelson. Archer was adamant that Scotland needed its own national anthem, but the administrator's response was typical of the Association's intransigence: 'I am sure that the committee will not change its decision on the matter.' The writer felt strongly about the subject, but in his 'The Archer Angle' of February 5th conceded it might not matter in any case, suggesting that within twenty years the South American bloc within FIFA would have garnered enough support to prevent Scotland, and the other home nations, from competing as separate entities. He did contend, however, that playing 'God Save the Queen', seen across the globe as the English anthem, he felt, would further strengthen opposition to Scotland taking part in the competition.

As excitement mounted ahead of the finals, the domestic game was emerging from its own winter of discontent, in keeping with the rest of the country. The Conservative government had introduced a three-day week to conserve electricity, production of which had been severely curtailed by a national strike by coal miners. The measures were enforced at the start of 1974 and kept in place for over two months. It had meant earlier kick-offs, as football clubs were restricted in their use of floodlighting.

Alongside that, the 'top six' in the Scottish game – at the time Celtic, Rangers, Aberdeen, Hibernian, Heart of Midlothian and Dundee – had been trying to force through reconstruction plans that would eventually see the formation of the Premier Division the following summer. In the spring of '74 there remained much opposition from smaller clubs in the Scottish Football League, but most were won over, and on March 15th the SFL announced the package had been comprehensively voted in on a 29–8 majority. The clubs, however, decided 20–17 against rushing the proposals through for the upcoming season, League secretary Tommy Maule explaining, 'They wanted to know exactly what they would be playing for over a whole campaign.' Ferranti Thistle would later be elected to the SFL to even up the numbers, changing the club's name to Meadowbank Thistle. The new set-up introduced a ten-team top division where sides would play each other four times, which, although initially successful, would sporadically lead to further outbreaks of discontent over the next four decades. The game was split apart in the late 1990s, with a breakaway to form the Scottish Premier League, only for all member clubs to be reunited in the Scottish Professional Football League fifteen years later. The one constant throughout was the four-times-a-season fixture list, which continued to irk both supporters and those involved directly in the game.

Willie Ormond had enough to keep him occupied without concerning himself about the politics and administration of the game. During March he had to oversee Under-23 and League international matches against England (the Scottish League played regular games against select sides drawn from other League bodies until 1980), with his selections for both severely curtailed by injury and club commitments. Of more concern was the forthcoming full international in Frankfurt, and Ormond had been left reeling by the news that Leeds United were attempting to play a rearranged First Division match against Sheffield United on the same night the Scots would be taking on West Germany. The manager delayed naming his squad in the hope that clarification would arrive but eventually had to release a list of eighteen players minus the Elland Road contingent of Bremner, Lorimer, Harvey and Jordan. As it turned out, the league fixture never went ahead and the Leeds quartet was needlessly left at home.

Ormond, who was suffering health problems following his recent trip to Egypt, was also without a host of other leading names, injury depriving him of Jim Holton, Danny McGrain, John Blackley and Jimmy Smith, among others. When Smith dropped out, the manager called up Celtic's record signing Steve Murray, only to be told shortly afterwards that the player did not want to join the squad, reasoning that he had played a lot of football recently and preferred to stay at home with his wife and young family. It was Jock Stein who broke the news to the beleaguered Ormond: 'He wouldn't be budged and even if his decision is the wrong one, at least it's honest.' Murray would never play for his country again. The man who benefitted was a young Graeme Souness, then at Middlesbrough. The nineteen-year-old midfielder was brought along for the experience and would, later in the year, win the first of his fifty-four international caps.

On the eve of the match it was announced that some 24,000 Scots had bought tickets for the World Cup finals. Considerably fewer were in Frankfurt for a friendly that had turned into something of a nightmare for Willie Ormond: 'Some of these players didn't even know each other when they met at the weekend. It's my job to try to establish some understanding between them and find the right blend. There are good players here – but no one knows if they will make a good side.'

When he finally pieced together his line-up Ormond handed international baptisms to Dundee keeper Thomson Allan, Hibernian left-back Erich Schaedler and Kenny Burns of Birmingham City, and there was a recall for Martin Buchan. On the plus side, he could still call on half a dozen of his trusty regulars, with Davie Hay again captaining the team in place of Bremner.

In the end, it might have been worse. West Germany scored two quick-fire goals before half-time and threatened to run riot, but Scotland hung in, got one back through Kenny Dalglish and came close to snatching a late equaliser. Given the trials and tribulations Ormond had had to deal with in the build-up to the match, a 2–1 defeat was viewed as 'no disgrace'.

The national team was kept out of the public spotlight for the next couple of weeks, the headlines reserved for one of the most shameful displays ever witnessed on a football pitch in this country. Celtic had drawn 0–0 at home to Atlético Madrid in the first leg of their European Cup semi-final, a match that saw three Atlético players sent off and seven yellow-carded, and which ended with some of the visitors brawling with police and stewards as they left the field. The brutality meted out during the game left even the most hardened of observers sickened to the core, and the Scottish Football Association took up the case on Celtic's behalf, urging UEFA to kick Atlético out of the competition. Their pleas, perhaps unsurprisingly, fell on deaf ears, the only immediate punishment being the suspension of six of the culprits from the return leg in the Vicente Calderón a fortnight later. Celtic were beaten 2–0 and denied a third final in seven years. The Spaniards were later fined 100,000 Swiss francs (around £12,000).

On April 30th – more than six weeks before their first World Cup appointment – Willie Ormond showed his hand when he named two squads, what were seen as 'probables' and 'possibles' by those reporting the story. A total of forty players were listed: twenty-two for the Home Internationals, with a further eighteen on standby. The main group read: Harvey (Leeds United), Allan (Dundee), Stewart (Kilmarnock), Jardine (Rangers), McGrain (Celtic), Schaedler (Hibernian), Donachie (Manchester City), Holton (Manchester United), Buchan (Manchester United), Blackley (Hibernian), McQueen (Leeds United), Bremner (Leeds United), Hay (Celtic), Smith (Newcastle United), Hutchison (Coventry City), Morgan (Manchester United), Dalglish (Celtic), Law (Manchester City), Ford (Hearts), Jordan (Leeds United), Lorimer (Leeds United), Johnstone (Celtic).

While the group of players expected to keep themselves fit and be ready at any moment for a call-up consisted of: Brown (Sheffield United), Burns (Birmingham City), Connelly (Celtic), Copland (Dundee United), Cormack (Liverpool), Duncan (Dundee), Gemmill

(Derby County), Hermiston (Aberdeen), Johnstone (Rangers), Lennox (Celtic), Macari (Manchester United), Munro (Wolves), Parlane (Rangers), Robinson (Dundee), Scott (Dundee), Souness (Middlesbrough), Stanton (Hibernian), Stein (Coventry City).

It was a real mixture of players who had already proved their worth at international level but had perhaps peaked, and others who had never been tested there. Some, including Archie Gemmill and Graeme Souness, would go on to enjoy stellar Scotland careers, while for others, such as Jackie Copland and Jim Hermiston, who were at the time considered surprise choices, it would be the closest they would ever get to earning an international cap.

The biggest surprise was that seven of the team which had kicked off the qualifying campaign with a 4–1 win in Denmark just eighteen months earlier were no longer considered worthy of inclusion even in such an extensive pool of players. Bobby Clark, John Brownlie, Alex Forsyth, Eddie Colquhoun, Jimmy Bone, George Graham and Joe Harper had all been dumped on the international sidelines. Of that group, four would never again feature for Scotland. Brownlie gained one further solitary cap in a European Championship qualifier against Romania, and Forsyth played four more times for his country, while Harper was recalled for the European Championship win in Denmark in 1975, in which he scored the only goal, and was later given a brief cameo role against Iran during the disastrous finals of 1978. He at least eventually got a taste of what the World Cup was all about, but as far as '74 was concerned, the dreams of those players had been extinguished.

In the end, only one of the standby squad got called up to the twenty-two who would represent the country at our first World Cup finals appearance in sixteen years. That announcement would be made three weeks later.

Those initially chosen were, as was the tradition, assembled at Largs and prepared for the first of five warm-up matches, the opening Home International encounter with Northern Ireland at Hampden. With all three games at home, the Scots were rated by the bookies as 4–7 favourites to win the domestic tournament, and at 16–1 to lift the World Cup, the same odds as Argentina, and behind only West Germany (5–2), Italy (4–1), Brazil (5–1) and Holland (11–1).

Much was being read into club-mates Buchan and Holton being paired in a practice game, and Ormond was pleased to report that injury doubts over Hay and Smith had eased, although the latter was in the doghouse for turning up twenty-four hours late after having remained in Newcastle for treatment without first advising the SFA. The only absentee was flu victim Danny McGrain, leaving the manager in the rare position of having all but a fully fit squad to choose from.

When he named his side, there were no surprises. Willie Donachie replaced the stricken McGrain in a line-up that read: Harvey, Jardine, Donachie, Bremner, Holton, Buchan, Morgan, Hay, Law, Dalglish and Hutchison.

The only quibble seemed to be about the forward line. Neither Dalglish – just two international goals to his name – nor Law – who hadn't scored for his country in two years – had shown their best form for Scotland under Ormond, and there was a growing lobby for Donald Ford to be given his chance after a season in which he had scored twenty-nine goals for Hearts. However, the striker failed even to win a place among the substitutes.

Before they left their hotel in Troon, Northern Ireland manager Terry Neill had told his players, 'Go out and enjoy yourselves.' Feeling no pressure, those players apparently spent the coach journey to Glasgow singing songs to relax themselves further. They then went and beat Scotland at Hampden for the third time in four visits. Tommy Cassidy scored the only goal after emerging from challenges by Hay and Bremner and then galloping forty yards to get on the end of the return pass before sliding the ball beyond David Harvey.

The Scots put in a limp performance and were deservedly beaten. They managed just one shot on target all game, a Dalglish effort easily held by Pat Jennings in the second half. Joe Jordan, a second-half replacement for Law, had one header that looped off the top of the Irish crossbar, but that was all the threat the home side could muster. Willie Morgan was deemed 'ineffectual', Denis Law 'looked all of 34 years old', Billy Bremner 'seemed tired after a long, hard season with Leeds United' and Davie Hay was 'strangely invisible' according to Ian Archer's match report in the *Glasgow Herald*.

Around 53,000 supporters had turned up to watch and Ormond was apologetic afterwards: 'The fans were marvellous, patient and tolerant. They were let down badly. Our attitude was all wrong. The team were attempting exhibition stuff, there was not enough fight in midfield, and there are problems up front. If we play like that against Zaire we will be struggling.'

That last sentence was remarkable given the manager's withering assessment of the Africans two months earlier, and indicated that he was perhaps beginning to feel the pressure of the job. Despite having qualified for the finals, Ormond's record as Scotland manager was a poor one. Having been in charge for eleven matches, he had led his side to victory in just two of them: a 2–0 success against Wales in Wrexham in May 1973 and the all-important decider against Czechoslovakia four months later. His reign had begun with the 5–0 humbling at the hands of England and there were successive defeats against Northern Ireland, England again, Switzerland and Brazil before the glorious night against the Czechs. The return, admittedly meaningless, was lost in Bratislava, and there was a draw and a defeat in the double-header against West Germany, before the side's latest Hampden capitulation. His figures – two wins in eleven – were exactly the same as Bobby Brown had achieved before his sacking three years earlier, and his chosen strike force had drawn another blank in front of goal, the sixth time in those eleven games his team had failed to score.

To suggest his position was under threat would be to over-exaggerate the situation, but there must have been some rumblings within the corridors of power at the SFA's Park Gardens headquarters.

Ormond planned to take his squad to the BBC studios and force them to watch a recording of the Northern Ireland match, hoping perhaps to embarrass his players into fulfilling their undoubted potential.

Meanwhile, England – under the temporary guidance of Joe Mercer following the abrupt sacking of Sir Alf Ramsey – had strolled to a 2–0 victory over the Welsh in Cardiff.

Wales were the next visitors to Hampden and Ormond spent the days in between locked in private discussions with his players. It was reported that home truths had been aired and attitudes questioned, the nature of the responsibilities all must shoulder well and truly spelled out. In a break with his normal practice, the manager chose not to make public his team selection twenty-four hours in advance of the match; he needed all the time he could get in coming to what were clearly difficult decisions. He did, however, make it clear what he now demanded: 'I want more professionalism. These are players from big clubs, from Manchester United, from Celtic, from Leeds United. They know what is expected of them – and must now start to show it to me.'

The Scotland team that took to the field showed three changes from that which had slumped to defeat the previous weekend. Willie Donachie's ankle injury, which threatened his place at the finals, kept him sidelined, while Morgan and Law were dropped. Davie Hay filled in at left-back with Jimmy Johnstone, Donald Ford and Joe Jordan all recalled. The home support had largely kept the faith, 41,969 of them turning up on a Tuesday night, and they were rewarded with a much-improved showing by their favourites.

There was an early blow, Tommy Hutchison suffering a shin injury that saw him having to be replaced within the opening five minutes by Jimmy Smith, but the Scots took that in their stride. Indeed, Smith was to the fore in the home attacks, teeing up Sandy Jardine for a shot that was saved, then crossing for Billy Bremner to head just wide. Within minutes Scotland came even closer to breaking the deadlock when Hay found Ford and the Hearts striker's header rebounded off a post. Wales were only delaying the inevitable, and the opening goal came midway through the first half. Yorath fouled Bremner in the centre circle. Martin Buchan drilled the resultant free kick into the Welsh penalty area and found the head of Jordan. The Leeds man diverted the ball towards his strike partner Ford, who in turn set up Kenny Dalglish, and his header glanced beyond the despairing fingertips of the keeper Gary Sprake.

Scotland then benefitted from the award of a dubious penalty, Irish referee Malcolm Wright harshly adjudging that Mahoney and Page had between them illegally halted the progress of Davie Hay. The protests raged on, but Sandy Jardine remained calm, before drilling the ball low into the corner of the net.

Wales threatened on occasion after the break, Harvey being called upon to make a couple of stops, but Scotland finished on a high with an eight-man move that ended in a shot by Donald Ford that required Sprake to make the save of the night, tipping the striker's fiercely struck effort over the crossbar.

It was a performance and result that left Willie Ormond purring with delight, the only negative being the injury to Hutchison ahead of the final game of the Home Internationals against England at Hampden: 'He is very doubtful and I have to bear in mind not only the English match but also the World Cup. Martin Buchan also had a groin injury and wanted to come off at half-time, but I persuaded him to stay on as long as possible [he was eventually replaced by McGrain ten minutes from the end]. Generally, I feel a lot happier, there was more work rate from the team in this match. Jardine had another tremendous game and Johnstone, who looked nervous to me at the start, settled down to play well. It was my intention to play Lorimer in the second half but the injury situation did not allow it.'

The following night England made it two wins out of two with a narrow 1–0 defeat of Northern Ireland, a result that ensured that a Scotland victory over the old enemy would see them share the British title.

Zaire, meanwhile, had embarked on their European tour as they stepped up preparations for the finals, losing 2–1 to the Swiss Second Division side FA Aarau.

It was confirmed the next day that Tommy Hutchison would be fit to travel to West Germany but that he had no chance of facing England, and the Coventry winger was in an unforgiving frame of mind: 'It was a terrible tackle. John Roberts went over the ball, I have no doubt about that, and I certainly will not forget it.'

Deprived of Hutchison, Ormond also had doubts over Buchan and Danny McGrain, the Celtic full-back having lost half a stone in weight following a bout of flu. The manager was wrapping his squad in cotton wool, well aware that more important matches lay ahead, and they spent the Wednesday relaxing by playing golf, tennis and squash. There was further light relief when the whole squad was issued with their official 'Man at C&A' suits, complete with improbably large lapels and oversized Scotland badge, to be worn during the trip to Germany. There was, however, a steely determination shared by all the players, which was voiced by their top performer over the two matches, Sandy Jardine: 'After the fright we got against the Irish last week we really buckled down to it against Wales. The victory was just the boost we needed. We can go on from there and I feel we can really raise our game against England. They will raise their game too, they always do, but I don't think they will improve more than we will.'

The renewed optimism among the squad was shared by Scotland supporters all over the country, and British Rail responded to the demand by announcing that special trains 'from Aberdeen in the north to Annan in the south' would be put on, with six 'specials' leaving Edinburgh throughout Saturday morning.

Just as everything seemed finally to be going to plan for Willie Ormond, news broke of a late-night, or indeed early morning, drama that would thereafter be known as the 'Largs Fishing Boat Incident'.

It emerged that a group of players, still pumped full of adrenalin and unable to sleep following the win over the Welsh, had decided to take up an offer from a friendly local hotelier. They spent the night quenching their thirst and as dawn broke were making their way back to base via the beach. On seeing two rowing boats sitting on the shore, Jimmy Johnstone decided to board one. Sandy Jardine playfully nudged the boat out into the water, but the tide quickly grabbed it and within seconds the Celtic winger was heading helplessly out to sea, minus oars. Erich Schaedler and Davie Hay jumped into the other vessel and began rowing to Jinky's aid, but their boat sprang a leak and the pair had to bid a hasty retreat. By then Johnstone was standing unsteadily in the boat singing at the top of his voice. It was after 6 a.m. and the players had no option but to call the emergency services, who eventually plucked Jimmy to safety. When he was finally returned to the Scotland hotel, Johnstone was nonplussed about the whole affair, commenting in typical fashion, 'I don't know what all the fuss is about. I just wanted to go fishing.'

Four decades later, a beaming smile still stretches across Davie Hay's face as he recalls those farcical moments on the beach at Largs: 'We had a few bevvies, we can't deny it. Jimmy's out there, so I get into a dinghy with Erich Schaedler, God rest him, and we decide we're going to rescue him – don't know what I was thinking about! We were using blocks of wood to try to steer it. By this time the whole squad's on the promenade at Largs killing themselves laughing. Wee Willie [Ormond] was there – I don't think he was laughing – and Erich turned to me and said, "It's OK for you, you'll be playing – I've nae chance of getting a game now!" We got towed back, we weren't too far out . . . Wee Jimmy was heading to America right enough! When we eventually got back to the Queen's Hotel, the old lady who ran it, Mrs Ganley, was waiting for us. By then Jimmy was freezing, he only had a T-shirt on, and the snotters were running from his nose. She said to him, "Oh Jimmy, you've been a bad boy." His response was unrepeatable! That night – we knew we shouldn't have done it – but in a strange way it bonded us a wee bit. The press got a hold of it, of course, and they were having a go, rightly so, saying it was no preparation for the game, the World Cup, but you dig in against it, and of course we went and beat England, comfortably. Wee Jimmy couldn't resist it after the match, there he was giving the fingers to the press box. It wasn't right, but you look back and you think maybe a wee fishing expedition was the perfect build-up after all!'

As Joe Jordan looks back, he recalls the sense that something was in the air that night, something he had no intention of getting involved in: 'Me and Peter Lorimer locked the door that night and put a chair behind it because we thought there might be a wee bit of a commotion. We slept through it, but in the morning when we went down and looked into the car park there was every emergency service you could possibly think of: the ambulance, the fire brigade, the lifeboats, the police, and they were all there for Jimmy, who didn't really think he'd done anything wrong. He'd got lost at sea in a rowing boat without any oars and he didn't think it was his fault!'

Danny McGrain was another who gave the night out a miss. A non-drinker, he was tired, and decided just to go back to his room. Unlike Jordan and Lorimer, though, he soon became aware of what was unfolding: 'I heard wee Jimmy singing out in the boat, and I heard people shouting on him, so I got dressed and down out onto the promenade. The first person I saw was the reporter John MacKenzie from the *Daily Express*. He lived there and he's got the big scoop, he's writing it all down, but there's so much happening it's difficult to keep across it all. Davie and Erich are in one boat, it's got a hole and they're sinking, trying to keep afloat using two planks of wood. We're all shouting at wee Jimmy not to jump in. He couldn't swim and he was so drunk we were worried he might decide just to get in the water. Then the tide changed. One minute he was there, the next he was a hundred yards away!'

John Blackley remembers Erich Schaedler running back to the hotel in which the players were drinking, to initially raise the alarm. But none of them was treating the situation too seriously: 'We just walked along, we took our time, there was certainly no rush . . . and then we could see this boat in the distance and there was Jimmy singing "Michael, Row the Boat Ashore" . . . Nae oars . . . ! Oh, it was so funny . . . Honestly, it was hilarious.'

Johnstone was obviously working his way through his repertoire, as Martin Buchan recalls him belting out the Lulu hit 'The Man Who Sold the World': 'I'd gone for a game of putting with Donald Ford on the green outside the hotel when Jimmy's voyage began. There was a bit of a commotion across the road, so over we went and there he was standing in the boat singing at the top of his voice . . . The rest is history. He could have lost his life!'

Locally based *Express* reporter MacKenzie had the story across the front page of the newspaper under the headline 'WORLD CUP SCOTS SEA DRAMA' and he revealed it was national team trainer Hugh Allan who had eventually realised the seriousness of the situation, dialling 999 at 6.15 a.m. He also had quotes from the coastguard, who said he had 'called out a local boatman to save time and he reported back at 6.30 a.m. to say that the drifting boats were safely ashore. The weather was pretty wild. The wind was between force seven and eight – that's 35–40 miles per hour.'

The players were, eventually, all packed off to bed and told to report at 10 a.m., when the manager would have his say. One by one, and suffering varying states of hangover, the squad assembled downstairs just a few hours later. Even then, and with an apparent dressing-down in the offing, Blackley says it was impossible to take the situation too seriously: 'Who's sitting in the seat right by the door? Jimmy! Every time the door would open he would look up and see who was coming in. We're all there and it's only a matter of time before in comes the manager and the first person he sees is Jimmy. They catch each other's eye, there's a moment, and then Jimmy goes, "That's some fucking look you're giving me, sir." The place erupted with laughter . . . and that was it; that was the meeting. It was so funny, and Jimmy being the main character . . . Jimmy Johnstone was just fantastic. Not only did he have this fantastic ability, he was just a great character. Jimmy was lovely . . . a lovely, lovely man.'

The other newspapers were all over the story, and as is so often the case in early reporting of incidents, accounts varied. One suggested Johnstone and Denis Law had been marooned; another had the quartet of Bremner, Holton, Schaedler and Ford rowing to the rescue before being thwarted. All were condemnatory, although not in the way such an incident would be treated by the media these days. The fact that Willie Ormond had, publicly at least, refused to rebuke his players was highlighted, particularly as the incident came within days of the manager calling for 'more professionalism' from his group. Further troubles lay ahead but, unaware of that, and declining to comment on the Largs incident, Ormond was instead focusing on a first victory over the English since the glorious Jim Baxter-inspired triumph of 1967: 'We have greater experience at national level. England have several new faces and they are going through a transitional period, while we are improving steadily. The signs were there [against Wales] that we are heading towards something like true form. If the improvement continues on Saturday, we will beat England. I saw them against Ireland on television on Wednesday night and was not greatly impressed.'

These were excellent quotes for the pressmen, the kind few managers offer up in the modern game, but Ormond was not finished there: 'I don't rate the present England side as highly as the one that beat us at Wembley last year, and everyone knows how unlucky we were then. If we can repeat that form on Saturday, that will be enough. I am confident of that . . . Then we can go to West Germany and fear no one.'

So confident was the Scotland boss that he reverted to his tradition of naming his side the afternoon before the game, and it was a line-up that puzzled some observers, Ian Archer again bemoaning the absence of Donald Ford, the Hearts striker who had enjoyed little game time under Ormond's command. The team read: Harvey, Jardine, McGrain, Bremner, Holton, Buchan, Lorimer, Johnstone, Jordan, Dalglish and Hay.

The one name that stood out was, of course, Jimmy Johnstone, selected rather than punished for his sea-faring antics. And Erich Schaedler's premonition was proved correct: Davie Hay was to play, while the Hibernian defender would watch the game from the South Stand.

There were kind words in the morning's papers from the caretaker England manager Joe Mercer, who hoped to put the Scots to the sword 'before I put on the tartan and root for a Scottish victory in the World Cup in West Germany. I will be in Munich cheering for Scotland and, you know, I fancy them to do really well.'

As the rain tumbled from leaden skies and the mass of fans gathered outside Hampden Park, the Scots were forced into a late team change. Buchan's troublesome groin was still causing the player problems, so Ormond instead drafted in John Blackley, the Hibernian defender, winning just his second international cap.

'About eleven o'clock in the morning I was just sitting on the stairs at the Queen's Hotel and Willie Ormond came up to me and said, "You're playing today, Martin can't make it." Then I had to phone home and tell my wife Margaret and my mother, who loved the football, to make their travel plans to get to Hampden. My father was too nervous, he watched the game in his local, the Quoit bar in Redding, and he stayed there all day. They kept buying him drinks; he had a great time.'

For Blackley, the chance to take on the 'auld enemy' was, quite literally, a dream come true: 'When I was young, the England–Scotland game was so big for me, for years my brothers used to go down to Wembley and bring back the programmes. If somebody had asked me, "What game would you like to play in?" that's the game I would have chosen. It was just a great day.'

A huge crowd of 93,274 packed onto the slopes of the national stadium and they were to be rewarded with a memorable performance by the home side.

The *Glasgow Herald* reported a Scotland side 'intoxicated by the emotion that surrounded them, high on energy and endeavour, inventive on the ball, and diligent away from it'. Goalkeeper Harvey was rarely, if at all, troubled; the full-backs Jardine and McGrain exemplary; Holton 'as solid as a side of beef'; and Blackley 'the grandest hero, rolling the ball round his instep, commanding others'. Hay, in midfield, was exceptional; Bremner 'the supreme captain'; Dalglish 'persuasive with the kind of pass no one else can envisage'. And the eulogies continued . . . Lorimer 'occasionally brought the English defence to a state of panic', while Jordan was praised for his selfless hard work: 'He chased, he harried and he headed for 90 minutes and so, at last, Scotland's striking problem seems solved.' Special praise was reserved for Jimmy Johnstone who, in the space of ninety scintillating minutes, went from bad guy to all-round good guy, Ian Archer writing, 'Then there was Johnstone, whom I select above all others, for he brought large posteriors off their seats every time the ball came within his orbit. He checked, turned, cavorted, and struck balls the like of which brought back shades of little wingers long dead but not forgotten.'

Lazarus, it seems, had nothing on Jinky!

The Scots had gone at their visitors right from the off with a tenacious all-action brand of football which had the English immediately on the back foot. Roared on by a vocal, and probably less than sober, support Ormond's men went for the jugular, and struck early.

First, Bremner won the ball in midfield and fed Jardine. The right-back's cross was met on the volley by Joe Jordan, the ball flying just over the bar. It set the tone for a frantic first half. Seconds later, Frank Worthington struggled to control a throw-in from Keith Weller and Davie Hay snapped in with a strong challenge. Bremner was first on to the loose ball and rolled it forward into the box. Shilton got there just ahead of Lorimer but failed to hold on to it, and as the ball rebounded off the keeper, Joe Jordan strolled on to it and shot left-footed. Mike Pejic made a despairing dive, and made contact, but could only divert the ball into the opposite corner of the gaping net: 1–0 Scotland! The opener was initially credited as an own goal, but later officially given to Jordan, one of eleven he scored for his country: 'For me it was a great goal, because I scored against England . . . It was a great goal for the supporters, because it was against the English . . . The execution of it was fine, I never rattled it in from thirty yards, but it was a good goal, and I'll settle for that. It was nice to win the game . . . We were going to the World Cup, England weren't, and it was a big game for them, they'd had their noses pushed out of place a wee bit and they'd come up wanting to take a little bit of the glory off us. It was a huge game for both countries and it was nice to get off to Germany having beaten them.'

Worthington had a chance to make amends, but lobbed over when in the clear at the edge of the box. It was to be a brief respite for the visiting defence. Back came Scotland, Hay surging from the halfway line before checking on to his right foot and firing a blistering shot goalwards. Shilton clawed it behind for a corner.

On the half-hour mark, the Scots deservedly doubled their advantage. Following a short throw-in on the right, Johnstone and Lorimer exchanged passes before the Leeds man's attempted cross struck an English arm. While he appealed for a free kick, the ball broke to Kenny Dalglish, who prodded it across goal. As Shilton dived to cover it, Colin Todd stuck out a foot and the ball diverted beyond his keeper. It was 2–0 Scotland: this one a definite own goal.

The second half continued in a similar vein. Jordan drove in a left-footed volley, which Shilton acrobatically kept out from just inside his post. There were a couple of scares for the Scots, Worthington and Peters each heading wide, but Shilton was soon performing further heroics, throwing himself across his six-yard box to deny first Dalglish, then Johnstone. One further chance arose when Lorimer's free kick bounced back off the England goalkeeper, but Jordan was unable to get a toe on the ball to divert it goalwards.

The final whistle sparked scenes of high emotion on the terraces, the vast bowl of the stadium a sea of St Andrew's Crosses and Lions Rampant being waved above heads. England had the decency to make a quick exit as the Scotland players celebrated with their tartan-clad followers, Hampden an altogether different place from what it had been just seven days previously following the defeat against Northern Ireland.

Study the footage of the euphoria and raucous partying in the aftermath of the game and one fleeting moment stands out above all others. In a scene that lasts no more than four seconds, a beaming Willie Ormond is seen striding across the pitch towards a distant camera. A topless Jimmy Johnstone runs into shot approaching his boss and the pair embrace. Ormond then points high up into the South Stand, where the press were housed, and says something to his mercurial winger. Johnstone turns, mouths an obscenity, and twice flicks the Vs in the direction of the reporters. 'Get it right up ye': the unmistakable message from player and, it seems, manager.

The signal to the men of the press was noted by Archer, but instantly forgiven: 'It seemed fair in the light of the match, for the doubting ones were proved wrong and that early morning escapade had done no damage to legs and lungs.'

John MacKenzie was similarly understanding in the *Daily Express*: 'Not for a second do I grudge Jimmy Johnstone his joyful Harvey Smith gesture to the press box after the game . . . Having proved that he could still turn it on, he was entitled to his show of elation.'

For Joe Jordan, it had been a dream come true to pull on the dark blue of Scotland alongside his boyhood hero in a game against the 'auld enemy': 'Jimmy was a world-class player. He was an idol to me, I used to go and watch him in that great Celtic team. Jimmy could do things that other players couldn't even contemplate trying . . . He was courageous as well . . . He would take the ball all day. People would kick him, he never flinched. He would take people on, beat them, then beat them again . . . and I got to play with him. It does take a bit of sinking in . . . It was a privilege to play with

93

him. He had an edge to him, he was always on the line and must have given big Jock Stein a few sleepless nights, but he spoke for Scottish football, he entertained, he produced magic, but there was also an end product: his teams won trophies. He was a star player. And that game against England . . . Willie forgave him, he played, we won 2–0 and Jimmy was fantastic.'

Davie Hay's face lights up as years later he recalls his team-mate's contribution that wet afternoon in 1974: 'He was phenomenal against England. I remember he swapped jerseys at the end, he was wearing Peter Shilton's shirt, and it was down to his knees during the lap of honour . . .' Hay pauses, smiles, and adds, 'He was just brilliant that day.'

Johnstone faced his nemeses the following day, but no mention was made of his salute to his inquisitors twenty-four hours earlier. Instead, they wanted his thoughts on what had undoubtedly been his best performance in a Scotland shirt, one that had guaranteed his seat on the aeroplane to West Germany. Johnstone told reporters: 'I was elated, as were the rest of the boys. How could we fail with that wonderful crowd of supporters behind us? They were magnificent, and I am only too happy that I helped in some way to make it a great day for them. Before we went out we were determined to put on a show for the fans, and for Willie Ormond. The boss has stood by us all during the past couple of weeks, and I suppose our performance against England was our way of saying thanks to him. He really deserves it.'

Johnstone then turned his attention to an even bigger occasion, now less than four weeks away: 'We proved on Saturday that we are the best side in Britain and are worthy of our place in the World Cup finals. Take it from me, we will do well in Germany.'

At that moment, basking in the glow of his superb individual performance and the demolition of the English, and with the finals just around the corner, there was no reason to suspect that Jimmy Johnstone's sometimes tempestuous love affair with the national team was in its dying stages. But it was.

94

He would be substituted in each of the remaining warm-up matches, would get just three minutes in a friendly against East Germany in the October of 1974, and would win the last of his pitifully small total of twenty-three caps in a European Championship qualifying defeat at home to Spain the following month.

He would not kick a single ball during the World Cup finals.

5

MUNICH, MUNICH HERE WE COME

On Monday, May 20th 1974, Willie Ormond strode into the basement room of the SFA building in Glasgow's leafy Park Gardens in which news conferences were at that time held. He walked in on a state of disarray, as that was the very room in which five large hampers were being packed in readiness for the trip to West Germany. Dirty shirts and socks were strewn around waiting to be sent to the laundry; muddy tracksuits and bandages lay piled in another corner. There were footballs, inflators and shin guards. Hardly the ideal setting for such an important announcement, but Ormond would not need much time; he had no real surprises to spring on assembled reporters.

Of the provisional squad he had announced three weeks earlier, only one man would not be going to the World Cup finals: the Newcastle United winger Jimmy Smith. His place would instead go to the Liverpool midfielder Peter Cormack, a player who had not featured for his country since the defeat in Amsterdam in December 1971 during the early days of Tommy Docherty's reign.

Smith, it has to be assumed, was paying the penalty for his failure to inform the manager of his delayed arrival ahead of the British tournament: he had arrived almost two days late, but no explanation was offered. Of the group announced, all had seen action over the previous week, apart from goalkeepers Thomson Allan and Jim

Stewart, and Gordon McQueen and Erich Schaedler. Willie Donachie's return to training following his injury against Northern Ireland ensured his selection, while George Connelly was ruled out, having failed to prove his fitness, his broken ankle deemed not to have repaired sufficiently. McQueen and Stewart were the only uncapped players in the squad. Those on the standby list were urged not to engage fully in 'holiday mode' in case any mishaps befell the chosen twenty-two; Ormond had until June 5th before officially handing his list into FIFA.

The television companies were, meanwhile, drawing up their own lists as they geared up for what would be the first World Cup finals to be shown extensively at a time suitable to most viewers. The 1970 tournament from Mexico had been broadcast live, but local kick-off times and less than reliable satellite links had proved major hurdles for both the BBC and ITV. Those finals were the first at which 'The Panel' had been introduced, as both companies gathered current and former professionals in their London studios to comment on games. The BBC had Frank Bough and David Vine heading up their programmes, with Ian St John, Bob Wilson, Don Revie and the ever-controversial Brian Clough wheeled in as talking heads. David Coleman was in Mexico to host and commentate. ITV went for a similar format, with Jimmy Hill and Brian Moore fronting their programmes, aided by Pat Crerand, Derek Dougan, Bob McNab and Malcolm Allison. Floral shirts, big collars and cravats were much to the fore, and the panellists were also seen smoking cigars on screen. ITV's coverage was certainly the livelier, with the guests getting regularly into heated debate and ferocious arguments. It struck a chord with the British public, the independent station attracting higher audiences than the BBC, a rare feat at that time.

A similar format was used in 1974. By then Jimmy Hill had been transferred to the Beeb, and he and Bough hosted from a studio in West Germany. Jock Stein, Bobby Charlton, Bob Wilson, Joe Mercer, Lawrie McMenemy and Frank McLintock were among their guests, with Coleman, Barry Davies and the emerging John Motson commentating on the matches. ITV dropped McNab but added Clough, Bobby Moncur, Ron Greenwood, Sir Alf Ramsey and Jack Charlton to their panel and introduced a phone-in section. In a thinly veiled swipe at their rival's approach, the BBC's Head of Sport, Sam Leitch, announced, 'We are going for style, experience and knowledge. We don't want gimmicks. We don't want fancy ties.'

Viewers of either channel north of the border had their own commentators for the Scotland games, legendary broadcasters Archie MacPherson and Arthur Montford describing the action.

Opportunities to do live matches were still relatively limited for either station in the 1970s. One such chance had been the opening qualifier in Copenhagen, while the home encounter with the Danes was seen only in highlights form. Scottish TV and Grampian secured the rights to transmit both the Czechoslovakia games live.

All thirty-eight matches at the 1974 World Cup finals would be broadcast live, a rare treat for stay-at-home fans that offered them not only the chance to see Scotland but also, for many, a first opportunity to watch closely some of the star players in the global game.

Before the event kicked off the Scots still had two warm-up matches to prepare for – neither of which would be shown live on television – and in typical fashion there was a shock around the corner for Willie Ormond as he assembled his troops in Glasgow ahead of their departure for Belgium and Norway. Only twenty-one players reported for duty; the missing one, Martin Buchan, was still in Palma, where he was enjoying a week-long holiday with his club, Manchester United. As the party headed for Largs to begin training for their continental sojourn, Buchan was making his apologies over the telephone, explaining that a telegram had been sent to the Scottish FA and that he would be with the squad the following day. Ernie Walker, then assistant secretary of the SFA, confirmed the communication had been received, but Ormond was furious: 'I am most displeased. I have all the players here except Buchan. He knew when we were gathering and he should have been there. It is enough to say that his Manchester United team-mates, Jim Holton and Willie Morgan, stayed at home to train and they are here. It is the duty of each player to be present at the correct gathering time in Glasgow. Take it from me, Buchan will not play against Belgium on Saturday.'

The twenty-five-year-old did arrive the following day and had face-to-face talks with his angry manager. Ormond declined to comment further: 'There will be no statement.' And the player, presumably under instruction, had little to say either. 'I am here for as long as Mr Ormond wants me' was all he had to offer.

Rumours circulating at the time suggested various reasons for his late arrival. It was indicated that Buchan had not known when the squad was due to gather, that he was delayed because of discussions over a new contract with his club and that he was still recovering from the groin injury that had forced him to miss the England match. Whatever the reason, the SFA decided to accept his private explanation, and Buchan's place in the World Cup party was safeguarded.

Four decades later, while being interviewed for this book, Martin is more forthcoming and says it was all a misunderstanding, something that was blown out of all proportion: 'I was injured, and with the lads going off to Majorca for a week at the end of the season, I thought it best to go with them and get treatment from the physio, Laurie Brown. He was good, I trusted him, and I wasn't due to report for Scotland anyway. I asked Tommy Docherty, he said that would be fine, and that he would square it with Willie Ormond. But he didn't, he forgot, and that's where it all kicked off, where the confusion arose. There was nothing more sinister than that.'

Quite why the SFA chose not to make that explanation known to all remains a mystery, but as the controversy rumbled on Buchan soon tired of being painted as the bad guy: 'I apologised to Willie and explained that I'd thought The Doc had sorted it out in advance. I said to him, "I've just driven up from Manchester, if you don't want me here and there's going to be all this nonsense I can just put my case in the back of the car and drive up to Aberdeen for the summer instead." He obviously didn't want that, but I wasn't going to be messed about because of something that wasn't my doing.'

Ormond had other, more important, matters to consider and put his men through a tough training session. Bremner and Jardine took part despite suffering from sore throats, and John Blackley was packed off to bed as a result of a similar complaint, but that apart there were no further worries for the manager – at least for the meantime.

As Yugoslavia were being beaten 3–2 by Hungary in the latest of their warm-up games, Ormond continued to train his players hard, determined to ensure there could be no question marks over their physical fitness for the challenges that lay ahead. With Blackley rising from his sickbed there was a full complement of players on show, leading a smiling Ormond to declare, 'We have absolutely no worries.'

The party would leave for Belgium the following day, Friday, May 31st, move on to Norway on the Sunday, then head for West Germany. By then there would be little over a week before the competitive action got underway, and Ormond admitted he was starting to sense a change of mood in the camp: 'I am beginning to feel the tension and it is spreading through the party. The pressure is building up, and that is the way it should be.'

He went on to describe how he felt there was nevertheless a good atmosphere, a bond between the players, who all got on well with each other. He talked of his determination to win both matches in the coming days, how that would be a tremendous morale booster, and he reaffirmed his strong belief that Scotland had what was required to make headlines for all the right reasons at the finals: 'We have so many players who could win a game on their own, brilliant individualists. We certainly don't fear anyone in the World Cup. I prefer to let the rest of the teams worry about us.'

Of those teams, he picked Italy and the hosts as likely winners, but he was not ruling out bringing the new trophy with him when the squad finally returned to these shores: 'After we beat Zaire, we have to face Brazil, then Yugoslavia. These will be two very hard games. If we can qualify from that section, I firmly believe we can go on and win the tournament.'

Four years later, Ally MacLeod's managerial career would crash and burn after making similar predictions ahead of the debacle in Argentina. MacLeod was a showman, given to razzamatazz, and certainly shouted louder than the understated Ormond; perhaps that was why the two were treated in such different ways after their World Cup exits. Or perhaps it was simply that Ormond's squad flew home with their heads held high, while MacLeod's men slunk home in near-disgrace. Willie Ormond clearly had total confidence in his team and was not afraid to say so publicly; what he now had to hope was that they would go out and justify his bold statement.

Sadly for the manager, the players' focus was being distracted by other concerns, and on the eve of their departure the squad met up with their business manager Bob Bain for 'a stormy four-hour confrontation' at the team hotel. Bain had breezed into Largs, full of bluster as always, but when Billy Bremner spotted him, the skipper, who had been playing putting on the front lawn, threw his club to the ground and rushed to his room, demanding the forty-two-year-old follow him. They were joined by other members of the players' committee: Denis Law, Davie Hay, Jimmy Johnstone and Willie Morgan.

Bain had previously claimed the Scots squad members would all make more money than the English had from the 1970 World Cup finals, but when asked how much they had made, he had admitted he did not know.

He had suggested that each member of the group could expect to collect around £5,000 from contracts already signed, and pledged there were more in the pipeline. 'I am sure at the end of the day everyone will be quite happy' was his latest promise, but many now feared that sum could be considerably less, which was why Bremner had demanded a showdown. In his time in the job Bain had produced sponsored cars, a record deal and contracts for themed bags and posters. He was quoted as saying things were going 'relatively well', but captain Billy Bremner held an altogether different view, telling reporters: 'I am not happy at all about the situation. I had expected offers from soft drinks manufacturers and others. These don't seem to have materialised. A lot of harsh words were spoken at the meeting.'

Willie Ormond, clearly troubled by the effect the saga might be having on player morale, was scathing in his assessment of the businessman: 'He's all promises, but he has nothing concrete to offer. He's no further on than he was last November.'

Four decades on, Davie Hay would describe Bob Bain as 'a loveable rogue'. In 1974, the *Evening Times* labelled Bain 'a fast-talking, cigar-smoking agent', dubbed by some squad members the 'Tartan Pimpernel'.

Willie Ormond, while sympathetic, had to settle his players down, to calm minds, to ensure such distractions would be fleeting, as he led his men up the steps of the aeroplane sitting on the tarmac of Glasgow airport. First stop Ghent, and thereafter a journey that the whole nation hoped and prayed would not end until July 7th, the date of the World Cup final.

Throughout the second half of the domestic football season, and at all subsequent Scotland matches, a familiar chorus among fans had been the simple, hopeful chant of 'Munich, Munich, here we come!' It had been repeated over and over, it had become the mantra of Scottish supporters, but the truth was that the Scots would only play in the Bavarian capital if they were to reach either the final or the third/fourth play-off tie. Our group matches would be staged in Dortmund and Frankfurt, while none of the second-stage group games were scheduled for Munich. Either the Tartan Army was ignorant of that fact or its members had the utmost conviction the team was going all the way.

On arrival in Belgium, Ormond was quick to reveal his starting line-up. It was an easy selection: he simply trotted out the names of the eleven players who had kicked off the win over England. He expected to win both warm-up matches, and wanted above all else good performances, but also indicated that nothing that might happen during the next couple of matches would alter his thinking for the World Cup. He made it clear he had already decided upon his team to face Zaire.

Behind the scenes, however, there were still murmurings of discontent, players openly complaining about business contracts – or the lack of them – and the role played by the man who had been tasked with negotiating on their behalf. Bob Bain was still in the firing line, but it was Ormond who was suffering collateral damage, and he was clearly getting frustrated with reporters keen to quiz him on that subject rather than the forthcoming game: 'Look, there's no chance of this matter affecting the players' performance on the pitch. This is the best set of lads I have ever worked with and the morale could not be higher. The business side is one thing, the football another. There's no relationship between them.'

Billy Bremner agreed with his boss: 'I don't want to say another word about Bob Bain. We are just looking forward to playing some football now.'

That may well have been true, but having made the short journey to Bruges for the match, the Scots then disappointed, failing entirely to replicate the form shown against the English a fortnight earlier. The Belgians admittedly offered stiff opposition, as they had romped through their qualification group unbeaten and without conceding a goal, their undoing coming in two 0–0 draws with Holland, who progressed thanks to a vastly superior scoring rate against the cannon fodder of Norway and Iceland. Nevertheless, the Scottish display was a sobering reminder that nothing could be taken for granted, the paucity of their performance shocking even the Belgium coach Raymond Goethals, who, when facing the media, covered his eyes with his hands and said, 'This is how Scotland played. Like blind men.'

In measured tones the Belgian elaborated: 'I would have expected, at this stage, Scotland to have had more of a pattern of play, a method. But out there they looked like strangers to each other. They do not look where they are going and I'm sorry about this, but I think Brazil and Yugoslavia will qualify in your World Cup section.'

Willie Ormond had been forced into one late change to the team. Jim Holton injured his right knee in training, allowing Gordon McQueen his international debut in central defence, but that alteration had little if any bearing on the outcome.

The home side moved ahead midway through the opening forty-five minutes, Van Moer setting up Roger Henrotay to slip the ball beyond Harvey. Scotland responded soon after when McQueen's long free kick was spilled by Christian Piot, allowing Jimmy Johnstone to side-foot the equaliser. The visitors' only other serious attempt on goal was a well-struck Lorimer effort that failed to find the net, and the Belgians clinched victory with a late penalty. Dalglish was adjudged to have pushed Van Himst in the box and Lambert easily converted the spot kick.

It was a decision that left Ormond raging, and in the immediate aftermath perhaps blinded him to the inadequacies of his team's showing: 'The penalty decision that cost us the match was nonsense. The referee was a homer and the linesmen were terrible.'

Such a scathing assessment in the current climate would lead to the perpetrator being handed a sizeable fine or lengthy touchline ban. In those simpler times, Ormond's accusations were ignored by the authorities.

And so the party moved on to Oslo, where fears were growing about Jim Holton's readiness for the finals. The Manchester United defender attended a specialist and was given an injection in his knee. He was to take part in a practice match in a bid to prove his fitness, and remained confident he would make it: 'It's improving all the time. I'm sure it will be all right.' Meanwhile, his manager lodged his squad list with FIFA, or at least twenty-one names. The other space was left blank, with Wolves' defender Francis Munro favourite to replace Holton if required.

They had arrived in the Norwegian city to find it shrouded in grey clouds, with rain hammering down in torrents, and sat morosely on the long coach ride from the airport. Oslo boasted many fine, luxurious hotels, but the Scotland HQ had been set up at a somewhat less salubrious establishment: a busy students' hostel. It came as a shock to the players, who were hoping for some rest and relaxation ahead of the rigours of the World Cup finals, one unnamed member of the party telling journalists, 'I don't believe it. I thought Ghent was bad enough, noisy and inadequate, but this is ridiculous. There's nowhere to relax, nothing to look at, and by Friday I'll be stark, raving mad.'

John Blackley was perhaps a little less demanding than his anonymous colleague. He recalls their base as somewhat spartan but perfectly adequate: 'It was like a college, with football pitches around it . . . It wasn't the best, but at the end of the day it didn't faze me. I was on that flight, I was going to the World Cup, that was the main thing for me, but obviously others, who had been playing in Europe with the likes of Leeds United, and living in the best hotels, they knew what to expect and what they got wasn't good enough for them. They were probably right, but I didn't mind.'

Their accommodation was in a high-rise campus block, one part of which was open to summer tourists. There was nowhere to snatch a few private moments, nowhere to unwind. In the *Glasgow Herald*, Ian Archer warned the players would have 'no release from the unending boredom which afflicts footballers – and which has frequently been ruinous to the Scottish cause. The omens for a Norwegian week are bad.' His worst fears were soon to be borne out.

In addition, the bad feeling over commercial issues was rumbling on. There had been a disagreement with the press after the newspapers had refused to pay £5,000 for an official squad photograph. With West Germany just around the corner, this was not a happy group.

By the following day they were front-page news again. Billy

Bremner and Jimmy Johnstone had been drinking in the campus bar, which was packed with students, when an 'incident' occurred. Davie Hay recalls the lead-up as if it were yesterday: 'We were on the plane from Brussels to Oslo and they were plying us with champagne. We get there to find we're staying at a university. There were wee single beds and the rooms were spartan. Inevitably a party gets going – believe it or not, I actually went for a lie-down – and wee Jimmy and Billy are worse the wear for drink, they didn't turn up for the team dinner, and ended up having words with Willie. Actually, they were ready to go home: they pulled their waistcoats and jackets on, packed their bags, they were for the off, but they got talked out of it. The whole story didn't come out, but it hits the press and we're branded a mad squad again. To be fair we didn't do ourselves any favours, we probably put ourselves under more pressure, but it led to an "us against the world" type mentality.'

The *Evening Times* headline blared: 'BREMNER, JINKY IN OSLO HOTEL SCENE' and the Norwegian newspapers were equally captivated by the story, going with 'THE FIRST WORLD CUP SENSATION' and 'IT'S A SCANDAL'.

It does, however, seem as if the situation was rather hyped-up. No tables were overturned, no punches were thrown; the players were apparently noisy and over-exuberant rather than aggressive. But it was the last thing Willie Ormond and the Scottish FA needed.

The SFA convened a meeting in the immediate aftermath. It lasted two hours and ended after midnight. There was a clear groundswell of opinion that the duo should be sent packing. No comment was made that night, the players were left to sweat it out, but the next morning SFA secretary Willie Allan read from a prepared statement: 'On Sunday evening the manager drew the attention of the members of the International and selection committee to an extremely serious breach of discipline on the part of two of the players. The president, chairman of the committee, and the secretary later interviewed the players, who offered profuse apologies and gave an assurance that there would not be a recurrence. In view of this assurance, members of the committee, who had been of the mind to send the players home, decided, with some hesitation, that they be allowed to stay. They were severely reprimanded.'

It later emerged that Willie Ormond had pleaded their case, requesting clemency. Peter Lorimer believes there was a dual motive for the manager: first, it would have been hugely damaging for morale, and second, Ormond himself had got involved in the aftermath, as Lorimer explained while being interviewed for this book: 'We'd had a few drinks on the plane – with permission – but the session continued and the SFA had a chip at Willie to go and sort it out. Billy and me were in the same complex bit, and I'd locked myself in my room and was pretending I wasn't there because I'd had enough. But they were carrying on ... I could hear them because they were just through the door and didn't know I were there because the door was locked. They thought I'd gone some- where else. Willie came up and said, "Right, lads, it's got to stop, the SFA aren't very happy," and the lads said, "Come on, Willie, we're not doing any harm, get yourself sat down and get a drink." And then, of course, he did sit down and had a drink and within an hour, he's giving it, "Ah, tell them to go fuck themselves ..." He's just as bad as the rest of them ... So it was quite funny, you can imagine, listening to it all going on. He's come up to give them a bollocking, then he's right in the middle of it.'

Like Davie Hay, Lorimer believes the two players were set on leaving the squad, on giving up on their World Cup dream, so angered were they by the SFA reaction to what they believed was no more than a 'loosening-up' exercise: 'The SFA took it a bit further ... and Billy and Jimmy, they were going to go home ... I was rooming with Billy and I was trying to talk him out of it, but he was adamant: "Bollocks to them, I'm off." That would have been it ... It was quite worrying.'

The following morning saw the *Daily Express* – at the time, the most-read paper in Scotland – taking a hard line on its back page.

'NOW WE NEED NEW SKIPPER: Bremner, Johnstone should have been sent home' was the heading, under which John MacKenzie, tagged the 'Voice of Football' by his employers, pulled no punches: 'Billy Bremner cannot be allowed to continue as captain of the Scotland team that heads into the World Cup in ten days' time . . . If Ormond allows him to continue he is failing in his duty as team manager.'

It was a view that would see MacKenzie banned from travelling with the official SFA party, accused of 'muck-raking' and 'causing distress to players and families at home'. One such family member, Agnes Johnstone, Jimmy's wife, had her say on the front page of the newspaper, telling young reporter Gerald McNee (who, better known as Gerry, would later inherit the 'Voice of Football' tag during a lengthy media career) of the pain and embarrassment her husband was causing her: 'I wish he would realise he is nearly thirty and give up the night life.'

Publicly, the manager felt 'bitterly disappointed' and let down, but knew expulsion would end the international careers of the pair and believed that to be too harsh a punishment. Quite apart from his own role in the partying, there must also have been a more pragmatic side to his argument; Ormond knew he needed them, Bremner in particular, if the Scots were to be successful in West Germany.

As it turned out, Johnstone would spend the tournament watching from the sidelines, and his old friend Davie Hay has long since wondered whether he did so as punishment for his Oslo escapade: 'The tragedy of that was that wee Jimmy never got picked, even coming off the bench. Whether there had been a directive, or whether wee Willie himself decided because he felt so let down, I don't know. What I admired about Jimmy, and I roomed with him for five weeks, was that he never complained about not playing. A player of his ability never got to play and yet there was no sulking, no remonstration. He was probably the most skilful player in that squad, but he just accepted it.'

Meanwhile, our World Cup opponents, apparently free from such diversions, were continuing their build-up to the finals. Brazil, based in Switzerland, beat FC Basel 5–2, while Zaire won by an identical scoreline against German amateurs VfB Oldenburg, their first victory in six warm-up games.

There was better news for Ormond as Jim Holton was passed fit, so the manager was finally able to register his full squad with FIFA, and the newspapers reported that all the players were safely tucked up in bed by eleven o'clock that night, the heads of Bremner and Johnstone the first to hit the pillows.

Ormond hoped now to fully focus on the game against Norway and attempted to lay the controversy to rest when he said, 'I want to make it plain – Bremner will still captain the side. He is a very good leader.'

The squad was put through a rigorous training session on a pitch behind their living quarters, Ormond keeping a close watch on Holton, John Blackley – whose shin had been gashed by Denis Law in an accidental challenge – and Danny McGrain, who was suffering from a slight stomach-muscle pull.

Afterwards they mingled with students, queued in the super-market to buy provisions, made friends and signed every autograph book proffered; they were perfect Scottish ambassadors.

There was another slight disturbance the next day as Willie Ormond banned the Scottish press from attending the squad's training at the Ulleval Stadium. He later said it was because he wanted to work on some new tactics, an explanation that sounded hollow given that the Norwegian manager, Englishman George Curtis, was in attendance throughout. The disgruntled reporters felt they were being punished for reporting the antics of two days earlier.

Yet another distraction was due to arrive in the shape of the team's commercial manager, Bob Bain, for further talks with Bremner and Ormond. Representatives of Tennent Caledonian Breweries were also due to fly in for a meeting with the SFA, early

109

reports suggesting the company might be prepared to offer up to £10,000 to be shared by the squad. When details emerged of the deal, however, that estimate proved to be way off the mark. Instead, each player stood to pocket a slice of an amazing £115,000 incentive-based prize fund.

Details were announced by Tennent's sales director Bill Findlay, who confirmed that £7,500 would be paid immediately for an exclusive colour team photograph to be used in the brewers' promotions. There was to be an initial sum of up to £15,000 handed over, which would be upped by a further £7,500 should the Scots qualify from the group. That additional payment would be increased to £10,000 for finishing third or fourth, £50,000 for a runners-up spot, and £100,000 for lifting the cup.

Mr Findlay met Willie Allan to put the proposal forward and was promised a response by 6 p.m. that day. As that time passed, Findlay was left sitting in his hotel room still awaiting a reply, while the SFA delegation, including its secretary, left to attend a banquet held by the Norwegian FA. It would be the following morning before agreement was eventually reached and the players whisked off to be photographed.

Given everything that was happening behind the scenes, the match against Norway was not afforded the usual build-up in the press. When the manager finally announced his team, both Billy Bremner and Jimmy Johnstone were included in a starting line-up that read: Allan, Jardine, McGrain, Bremner, Holton, Buchan, Johnstone, Hutchison, Jordan, Hay and Lorimer.

The previous night, Yugoslavia had drawn 2–2 with England, highlights of which were shown on ITV across much of Britain, but not in Scotland, and there was to be no television coverage of the Scots' final World Cup warm-up encounter, so fans back home had to rely on the words of reporters from the national newspapers. For the most part, their assessments did not make happy reading, although Ormond's side staged a late rally to at least head for West Germany with a win under their belts.

Billy Bremner was apparently unimpressive for much of the match, although it was from two of his free kicks that Scotland eventually snatched the goals to secure victory against their amateur opponents, while Jimmy Johnstone was 'out of sorts' or 'invisible' depending on which newspaper you read.

There was alarm among the assembled hacks when the teams ran out onto the pitch, Holton clearly limping before the game had even kicked off, and he hobbled throughout ninety error-strewn minutes during which he was booked after unceremoniously dumping Norwegian striker Tom Lund onto the cinder track surrounding the pitch.

The 18,432 crowd sat huddled against the elements, strong winds and driving rain aiding a positive opening spell by the home players as Thomson Allan endured a torrid start to just his second international appearance. Within the first few minutes he turned away a shot from Barkelund; next he denied Lund as his defence parted to allow the Norwegian a clear run on goal; then Helge Skuset rounded the Dundee keeper only to shoot wide of the gaping net. The inevitable was only being delayed, however, and Norway forged ahead in the seventeenth minute. Geir Karlsen, who plied his trade in the Scottish First Division with Dunfermline, punted a long clearance down-field from his own penalty area. The ball flew over Holton's head, evading Buchan, and Lund gathered it before striking a powerful left-footed shot beyond Allan's despairing reach.

Martin Buchan remembers Tom Lund well: that he was an impressive and troublesome striker to try to contain, and he also remembers some less than helpful advice dispensed by Willie Ormond before the match: 'Willie had, in all seriousness, told us to "watch out for the six-foot blond lad at free kicks". Well, when we got out onto the pitch we looked across at the Norwegians and they were all six-foot blond lads!'

The Scots finally woke up, and Karlsen twice denied Lorimer, before saving from Jordan, in the run-up to the interval. In the second period, Jardine crossed for Jordan's head, but the Leeds striker's effort rebounded from a post, with the goalkeeper rooted to the spot. Jimmy Johnstone's time was up: his frustrating evening ended after seventy minutes as he was replaced by club-mate Kenny Dalglish, and the substitute made an immediate impact, setting up Peter Lorimer to score, only for the goal to be incorrectly ruled out for offside.

That galvanised Scotland further and they equalised soon after with a goal of utter simplicity, Bremner's free kick easily headed beyond the keeper to give Joe Jordan a deserved goal. A similar move contrived the winner, Jordan this time heading across the box for Dalglish to apply the finishing touch from all of six inches out.

As the sodden players trooped from the pitch, the stadium announcer bellowed, 'We wish you well at the World Cup!' A reminder, if one were needed, that the serious business was finally about to get started; the kick-off against Zaire now just a week away.

The beaten manager, George Curtis, offered some encouragement: 'You did not reveal your form against us, but I still think you will do well, and qualify.'

The overall performance might have been less than convincing, and few of the players, Dalglish excepted, had offered anything to enhance their individual reputations, but there were at least some small positives to take from Oslo.

Above all else, it was a win, a much needed confidence-restorer after the events of the previous week. It represented Willie Ormond's first victory on continental soil as Scotland manager (his only previous away success coming in Wrexham more than a year before) and was the team's first since opening their qualifying campaign with a 4–1 stroll in Copenhagen in October 1972.

Satisfied rather than elated, the squad returned to its campus quarters, and there, in the very downstairs bar in which two of them had 'disgraced' themselves a few days earlier, drank and made friends with locals. When asked for a song, the players responded with 'Bonnie Scotland'. Applause broke out, there were friendly handshakes all round, before the Scots – all of them – retired in time to meet their 11 p.m. curfew.

Next stop, Frankfurt.

6

THE FINALS

On Friday, June 7th 1974 – just one week before their opening encounter with the 'Leopards' of Zaire – the official Scotland party touched down on West German soil. After a sixteen-year wait, they were back at the World Cup finals.

As their aeroplane taxied across the tarmac, those sitting in window seats were given an immediate indication of just how seriously the West German authorities were taking the issue of security, determined there would be no repeat of the terrorist atrocities that had scarred the Munich Olympic Games just two years earlier.

There had been no signs of any trouble as that event had moved into its second week, the organising committee having encouraged an open and friendly Games. That all changed in the early hours of Tuesday, September 5th 1972. Eight members of the 'Black September' group, a faction of the Palestine Liberation Organisation, scaled the perimeter fence. They were armed with automatic rifles, pistols and grenades. Facing little resistance, the terrorists located their targets, members of the Israeli Olympic squad, and soon had eleven of them held captive. There followed intense negotiations, the hostage-takers demanding the release of more than 200 Palestinians imprisoned in Israel, along with two infamous German terrorists, Andreas Baader and Ulrike Meinhof. By early evening the group had demanded safe transport to Cairo, and the authorities agreed, planning to ambush and kill them before they could leave the Fürstenfeldbruck air base. The plan failed after the terrorists realised they were being tricked, and in the ensuing battle the hostages were massacred and a German policeman shot dead.

The tragedy continued to cast a dark shadow over West German society, and the inquests and investigations would go on for years. The '74 World Cup finals were an obvious target for a repeat mission and no expense was spared in ensuring the visitors from around the globe, especially the high-profile sportsmen, were kept safe and secure.

As the Scotland plane drew to a halt, forty uniformed and heavily armed police officers surrounded it. Plain-clothed security men, also armed with holstered revolvers, led the players and officials into the terminal building, from where they were quickly escorted into coaches and hustled away some forty miles to their base in Erbismühle, which nestled quietly in the foothills of the Taunus mountain range.

They later discovered every room in the hotel had been checked for bombs, every visitor scrutinised. The levels of security were maintained throughout the Scots' stay, and Davie Hay admits he and his team-mates were left somewhat bemused by it all: 'Of course we knew what had happened in Munich, but I don't really think it was on any of our minds. It became apparent right away the Germans weren't going to let it happen again and we had a squad of special security people travelling with us all the time. We had our own designated bus and they were always there, at training, at the games. They'd be following us, there would be helicopters flying overhead. We'd never experienced anything like that before, but we were young, naive, and we made light of it. Maybe that was our way of brushing it to the side . . . Subconsciously, you're trying not to think about it.'

Goalkeeper Jim Stewart remembers being shocked by the level of security put in place: 'A few of us had gone for a wander around the grounds and the first thing we saw were guards walking around carrying machine guns. That really brought it home to us that it was a high-profile tournament and reminded us of the enormity of what had happened at the Munich Olympics. The German authorities were clearly determined that nothing similar was going to be allowed to happen at the World Cup.'

On arrival at the hotel, staff had insisted the party attend a champagne-cocktail reception, eager to impress upon their visitors a friendly and helpful welcome. Every measure would be taken to guarantee a relaxing stay, to ensure the Scotland squad was ready for the big kick-off.

Not everyone was happy, though, as Jim Stewart recalls: 'Martin Buchan and I were to be sharing, but when we got to the room there wasn't a shower and Martin says, "I'm not having this." Now he's captain of Manchester United, I'm just a part-time player with Kilmarnock, so I'm not wanting to rock the boat . . . He went off to the manager and told Willie he'd better get him a room with a shower. He got his way – Martin ended up getting one of the officials' rooms and I had to share with Willie Morgan and John Blackley. Three of us in one room, which was interesting . . . but, hey, I was just happy to be there.'

Occasional overcrowding apart, Davie Hay remembers Erbismühle as being a near perfect base from which the squad could prepare for the rigours ahead: 'It was pretty idyllic, it was way out in the country, and we had the hotel pretty much to ourselves. I thought on the whole it was good . . . There were some complaints from one or two of the boys who felt some of the SFA men got better rooms than some of the players, but the way it worked out wee Jimmy and me were at the better end of the hotel, so we were fine! I had no complaints about it.'

It was a settling-in process for all the players, who, according to striker Joe Jordan, were now on a very steep learning curve: 'It was all new to me, as it was to everybody in the Scotland camp, so we just took it as it came, but we were discovering new things every day. It was a great World Cup, because it was my first World Cup. It was a great experience . . . the build-up, being around all these terrific players that I had been brought up with: Law, Johnstone, Bremner. It was fantastic.'

Around that time, details were emerging of a handbook published in West Germany that offered a much less friendly approach to the Scots. The book, *The World Cup Championship '74*, made some astonishing claims and so enraged people back home that it hit the front page of the *Evening Times*, which bore the headline 'UGLY FACE OF SCOTTISH SOCCER: How Germans see life in Glasgow . . .'

The article began with the sentence 'TWO DEAD and 50 injured are the norm for local derbys between Glasgow Celtic and Glasgow Rangers'. Quoting from the publication, the paper went on to describe how it painted a grim picture of the city, of a life so wretched football and whisky provided the only relief. It further claimed: 'Scottish football is the toughest, most aggressive in the world. In Scotland they don't play, they fight mercilessly. In Scotland they don't take defeat like gentlemen – above all in Glasgow, the centre of Scottish football. It is an ugly city by the sea, where the sun won't shine, where the damp gets into everything, where men toil for wages that, after food, leave enough only for whisky and football tickets. The whisky could help one forget that one is living in a city better suited to rats than human beings, but the whisky is too dear and therefore one goes to the football.'

The book also turned its attention to the Scottish national side, referring back to the 1–1 result against West Germany the previous November. It said the Germans had been lucky to escape with a draw, 'but not for years had they been so shaken – constantly on the run from their small, tough opponents'. The authors described Billy Bremner as 'the wildest of all' and berated the team as 'instinctive, plodding tradesmen'.

Some of the claims were not particularly outlandish, indeed some pride might have been taken by the players from those references to their determination and fighting spirit, but the overall picture painted was that of a grossly over-exaggerated national stereotype, and had such a book been printed in the modern day it would have been viewed as a serious national incident, one that would have sparked outcry and debate at the highest levels of government.

Oblivious to all that, Willie Ormond was settling his players into their headquarters and had a few injury worries on his mind, with Harvey, Jardine, Holton, Blackley, Bremner and Hay all receiving treatment for what were described as 'minor knocks'. Of more concern was the damaged ankle suffered by Erich Schaedler following a rash tackle by Peter Cormack during their first training session. The Hibernian player had to be carried from the pitch, leaving Willie Donachie as the only fully fit full-back in the squad.

Despite that, Ormond remained buoyant: 'Our preparations are well in hand for the challenges ahead. The build-up over the next few days will be vital ... and, of course, we must win our first match next Friday in Dortmund against Zaire. The players will train at the World Cup stadium in Frankfurt [the games against Brazil and Yugoslavia would be staged at the Waldstadion] tomorrow morning; in fact, we have the honour of being the last team to train there before final preparations are made for the World Cup kick-off.'

The Celtic manager Jock Stein was in West Germany as part of the BBC television commentary team and had been asked by Ormond to cast his eye over Yugoslavia when they played their final warm-up game the following afternoon against a local Second Division side. Stein spoke to reporters and expressed his admiration for the Slavs, warning that the Scots faced a tough task in qualifying from the section: 'Scotland can do themselves a real favour by winning well against Zaire. However, we would be foolish going into this game with the wrong attitude and, of course, we tend to do better when we are up against it. Complacency is the last thing Scotland need at this stage.'

Yugoslavia won the match in Neu-Isenburg 9–2 as they gave a number of squad players the chance of a run-out.

'This wasn't anything like the team that will face Brazil,' Stein later commented, 'but it was a good public-relations exercise, something Scotland might have thought of, giving players who haven't played for some time a taste of the atmosphere, and getting the German crowds on our side.'

There was some criticism in the press of Ormond's decision not to attend that game, and even more when the manager revealed he would not be going to watch Brazil and Yugoslavia open Group 2 the day before his side took on Zaire. He explained that the players had requested the party move to Dortmund a day early and he was happy to go along with that. He and the group planned to watch the Frankfurt encounter on the television.

The Brazil coach, Mário Zagallo, took an entirely different view, announcing that after his team's match he would be heading straight for Dortmund with a camera crew to film the Scots in action. He felt it imperative to see for himself what Ormond's men had to offer: 'Scotland must be taken seriously in this competition. They have many fine individual players and are capable of turning any game in a matter of minutes. I believe they can give us a lot of trouble, and therefore it is in Brazil's interests to be in Dortmund on Friday.'

When the squad rolled out of Erbismühle for the Waldstadion that Sunday, they did so without Peter Lorimer, the Leeds man left behind suffering from a badly upset stomach. Goalkeeper Jim Stewart would sit out the session after being struck by the same complaint, prompting team doctor, John Fitzsimmons, to consult with his West German counterparts. He was given telephone numbers for various Frankfurt-based medical specialists, German prescription forms that he would be permitted to fill out, and an assurance that all facilities would instantly be made available in the case of further illness or injury.

Willie Ormond had requested the Scots' training be conducted behind closed doors but was in for a shock when the garishly painted Mercedes team coach pulled up at the ground, finding the terraces populated not only by media from all around the world but also by curious locals out for a Sunday stroll who had wandered in to see what all the fuss was about.

'There are more people here to watch this practice than there would be for a league match in Perth' was Ormond's dry observation, before adding, 'It seems there's no way they can be kept out and I've no idea where we can go to work quietly and experiment.'

While the manager became resigned to his very public training stint, he was less than delighted when he discovered the Yugoslav coach Miljan Miljanic was also in attendance. The pair later shook hands and exchanged pleasantries, but Ormond was furious at the intrusion. He and the players were having to come to terms with the fact that this tournament would be like nothing they had previously experienced. It would be an event during which every incident would be examined both on and off the pitch, and where transgressions, real or imagined, would be reported worldwide – and, of course, the Scots came with something of a reputation in that respect. News of the Largs and Oslo troubles had spread far and wide; perhaps foreign reporters had also availed themselves of the less than flattering book that so demonised Scotland, and our reputation as a nation of 'bevviers' went before us.

Only the Argentine squad seemed to be under more scrutiny, with reports painting them as a group of players out of control who 'have become frequent visitors around the night-spots and who actually went on strike for an hour during a training session in a dispute over commercial bonuses'.

Local reporters were clearly hoping the Scots would drop a similar story in their laps, with some 'patrolling the corridors of the team hotel in the early hours, waiting for sounds of revelry'. Thankfully, on this occasion, the players gave them nothing to write about on that score.

With the tournament on the verge of kicking off, FIFA delegates had arrived from all corners of the globe, and while for most it would mean weeks of being wined and dined and being treated like VIPs, there was some official business to take care of first. Among the decisions taken was the acceptance of a South American Confederation proposal that the 1978 World Cup finals be extended to include twenty teams (this never actually happened, as the Argentina extravaganza retained the exact format being operated in West Germany). Top of the list, however, was the election of a new president, with Sir Stanley Rous eventually voted out after thirteen years in the post. His successor would be the Brazilian João Havelange, who – having spent an estimated $400,000 during his three-year campaign – would remain in position for almost a quarter of a century. It was to be a period during which FIFA's income would increase unimaginably, but was not without controversy, Havelange having to face repeated accusations of bribery and corruption before eventually standing down in 1998.

Brazil had been allowed to permanently retain the Jules Rimet Trophy after winning the competition for a record third time in Mexico, so details were also announced of the prize on offer to the 1974 world champions. Called simply the FIFA World Cup, the new trophy had been designed by Italian sculptor Silvio Gazzaniga and crafted from eleven pounds of 18-carat gold. It was priced at around £8,000, but its value to the eventual winners would be inestimable.

World Cup organisers were, meanwhile, outlining further security plans, with the old Olympic Stadium in West Berlin high on their agenda. With Chile due to play two matches there, reports had been received of plans for large-scale protests to be held against the military junta operating in the South American country. The authorities were clearly intent on quelling any such uprising, announcing that in addition to 1,000 police officers, 1,300 security guards would also be in place, along with 100 plain-clothes men who would be mingling with fans and keeping an eye on potential troublemakers.

By the eve of the tournament the world's broadcasters were all in place, assembled together in what was the largest such gathering football had ever known. Estimates suggested 132 commentators and around 2,000 technicians from 180 television and radio stations were now based in West Germany. A further 1,000 journalists, reporters and photographers had also been accredited. Those figures would be dwarfed these days but were seen as quite startling at the time. The BBC had sent over sixty-nine members of staff and ITV forty.

The pictures would be beamed worldwide by the German broadcasters, who were relying on fifty-six 'colour' cameras to cover the nine venues. By contrast, at the 2010 World Cup final in Johannesburg there were thirty-two cameras in place to monitor that single match. The hosts could also offer sixteen outside broadcast units and ten slow-motion machines and were estimating that an unprecedented global audience of one billion viewers would tune in to watch the finals.

Still attempting to find more secluded training facilities, Willie Ormond had procured the use of a small village pitch near to the Scotland HQ, and oversaw what was described as a 'furious' session watched only by members of the Scottish media and 'a few bemused Germans'. It was a full-blooded couple of hours during which team-mates scythed into each other with no apparent fear of inflicting injuries that might end World Cup dreams. John Blackley and Jim Holton were particularly guilty, and Martin Buchan and Joe Jordan got so embroiled at one stage that captain Billy Bremner had to wade in to separate them. In any other walk of life such an incident might be seen as damaging to workplace morale, but of course football is an entirely different beast, and Ormond declared himself delighted by the passion shown by his men: 'It was just the type of incident I had been hoping to see. It shows that the needle has crept in and that they are ready to go. They are beginning to play for their places in earnest, although I was a little bit worried throughout just in case it got out of hand.'

Reserve goalkeeper Jim Stewart was on the periphery, working alongside Thomson Allan and David Harvey, who, as the senior keeper, and in the absence of a specialist coach, was in charge of working out training routines for the trio. He remembers watching on as the outfield players got stuck into some pretty ferocious sessions: 'They were pretty intense! It was very different then, of course. Willie Ormond didn't really have much back-up, just the physios Hugh Allan and Ronnie McKenzie, so the players took a lot more responsibility for what they did. They were certainly giving their all, they treated training as they would the games, because everyone was desperate to take part in the finals. They trained full-out, they played full-out . . . It was certainly different in those days.'

Fortunately, the players all emerged unscathed and were by that stage simply desperate for the action to get underway. Just hours before the opening ceremony and the first match, the Brazil–Yugoslavia encounter, Billy Bremner spoke to reporters, once again drumming out the positive message he had maintained all along: 'If I didn't think Scotland would win, you wouldn't catch me in this hotel. I'd be lying on a beach in Majorca having a good holiday. I think, I believe, we will win – and I'm not just being a rampant Scottish nationalist in saying that. I'm being a hard-headed realist who knows we have the players, the skill and the conviction.'

The captain went on to explain his reasoning: 'Take it match by match in the first section. We won't make the mistake of under-estimating Zaire because we have been caught that way before. We won't relax either because goals are important all the time [an interesting comment worth returning to given how that first game panned out]. It's only against England we like to show our superiority in terms of flashiness. Against the Africans we will play the British way, hustling and bustling. Then, against Brazil, we must change, for if you give them possession, you are beaten. So we will keep the ball, and be patient. I played for Scotland in Rio two years ago and we were destroying them. We were most unlucky to lose by a single goal and I am sure they are not the side they were. Yugoslavia will be the more difficult as they are physically harder and, unlike the Brazilians, they don't get dispirited when they go a goal behind. After the first round, who knows? But we are going to win this competition or I will want to know the reason why not. We are afraid of no one.'

As rallying cries go, it could hardly have been more inspiring, more confident, and yet there was little in Scotland's recent record to back up Bremner's confidence. Of Willie Ormond's fifteen games in charge of his country, only five had been won. Admittedly, three of those had come in the Scots' last four outings, but the most recent had been an undignified scramble against the Norwegian amateurs, secured only by two late goals.

A similar statement by the national captain in the twenty-first century would be greeted with a mixture of derision and disbelief, but in the mid-1970s it was simply reported factually, hidden away in the journalists' copy and with no great fanfare or headlines. In fact, the climate would have changed just four years later, when Ally MacLeod's assertions – no more emphatic than Bremner's – were given much more prominence across the media and in Scottish society in general.

Media coverage of the finals had been growing throughout the build-up, with more and more column inches being devoted to it. There were historical articles, interviews with former players, features on the other competing nations and the potential stars of the tournament. The *Daily Express* even costed the overall expense of the tournament to the Scottish Football Association, assessing an outlay of £971 for each of the twenty-two squad members. That sum included travel and accommodation, not only for the finals but also for the warm-up trips to Belgium and Norway. The official World Cup suit was reckoned to have cost £60, each player's tie £3 – the same price as the jersey they would wear during the matches – and shorts and pairs of socks were priced at £1.50 each. Also included was a figure for the expenses our World Cup heroes could claim from the Association: the princely sum of £5 a day.

The hard work done, and with just twenty-four hours left to fill, the Scotland party transferred to Dortmund, where they would settle down and watch on television as 'the greatest show on earth' finally kicked off.

It was a show that would, at long last, once again feature Scotland and offer one of the game's most respected figures the opportunity to belatedly sample the unique experience of a World Cup finals. Denis Law had just missed out on the '58 tournament, making his international debut in the very next game after those finals, and he then had to suffer through a series of frustrations and disappointments as campaign after campaign ended in defeat. It was, he admitted during an interview for this book, a difficult period to endure: 'You've got to think about the quality of teams in the draw in those days and the fact that only one team qualified, there were only sixteen teams in the World Cup . . . So you were playing against the cream of Europe; you never had any easy games. You had Czechoslovakia, Poland, Italy, West Germany . . . These were huge teams, I mean Czechoslovakia got to the final in '62. Whereas today you're in a group where there will be difficult games, but you look at three of the countries and expect to get a result against them. I think it was harder back in the day to qualify.'

Law missed out on three successive tournaments, but it was the middle one, 1966, which hit him the hardest. Those were the finals he really wanted to play in: 'Oh, I think if we'd qualified in '66 we could have done extremely well. It would have been like playing at home . . . A lot of the players played in England, the support we would have had from the Scottish fans would have been fantastic . . . That was the most disappointing one we didn't qualify for.'

No one reading this book will need reminding of how that World Cup turned out, and on the day of the final itself, Denis did everything he could to avoid the game. He went golfing.

'I was playing against a friend who was not a good golfer, but he beat me that day because I couldn't concentrate. As we came round to the eighteenth green just in front of the clubhouse, all the guys came to meet me and they were giving me plenty of stick as they celebrated. It was a sad day . . . a sad day.'

125

7

ZAIRE 0–2 SCOTLAND

Westfalenstadion, Dortmund, Friday, June 14th 1974

Having relocated some 130 miles north, Willie Ormond and his players settled down to watch on television as their two main rivals prepared to slug it out in the tournament's first match. Before the action got underway, they were 'treated' to the opening ceremony, a somewhat listless affair – certainly in comparison to more recent extravaganzas – the main feature of which was sixteen giant footballs that opened up like eggs to release singers and dancers representing each of the competing nations. There was also an appearance by Pelé, carrying the old Jules Rimet Trophy, and West German legend Uwe Seeler, holding aloft the new FIFA trophy.

When the game at last kicked off it proved to be a disappointing affair, as opening encounters so often are, and the 0–0 draw probably suited both sides. The 62,000 inside the Waldstadion and the millions watching across the globe saw no evidence of the Brazilian magic that had so thrillingly captivated the world four years earlier. Rivelino and Jairzinho, so mesmerising in Mexico, were pale imitations on a sodden pitch, and the Yugoslavs, after overcoming a nervy start, went on to dominate the match, with Petkovic and Acimovic coming closest to breaking the deadlock in a fixture of few clear-cut chances.

There was certainly nothing in the play of either side to frighten the watching Scots; what may have concerned them was the fact that both had picked up a point from their head-to-head and were now up and running in the group.

As Ormond digested what he had seen, he was giving final thoughts to his line-up and released it to reporters on the eve of the encounter with Zaire. There were no real surprises in his selection, which looked like this: Harvey; Jardine, Holton, Blackley, McGrain; Dalglish, Bremner, Hay; Lorimer, Jordan and Law.

It was a side that lacked width – one report dubbing it the Scottish version of Sir Alf Ramsey's 'Wingless Wonders' – but was overloaded with attacking talent, the manager's clear intent to go for the goals everyone believed would probably be vital in deciding their fate.

Among the forwards, one name stood out. Having made his international debut on October 18th 1958, and having scored in a 3–0 win over Wales at Cardiff's Ninian Park, Denis Law would at last feature in the finals on the day he won his fifty-fifth Scotland cap. While there was undoubtedly something of the fairy tale about Ormond's decision, the choice of Law was also a pragmatic one, the manager making it clear that he could not allow emotions to dictate in such important circumstances. Scotland needed a handsome victory and Ormond knew only too well that despite his advancing years Denis Law could help them do just that: 'Of course I think we will win, but there's no chance of us underestimating Zaire. That can't happen now we have seen just how big this World Cup stage is – and how important a part we could play upon it. We go for goals, as many as possible, for that is the only way we will make Brazil and Yugoslavia respect us.'

For Denis Law, a fervent patriot, it was to be a richly deserved chance to finally play on the biggest stage of them all, something he had missed out on by just a few months sixteen years earlier. Now in his early seventies, the legend's eyes sparkle as he looks back: 'I was too young in '58 . . . it would have been nice to have been part of that, but it just came a little too early.'

Within four months he did get the call for that game in Cardiff, but admits he did not find it easy making the transition to international football: 'Not really, no. You could imagine, it was a huge step. I was not playing in the First Division down in England, I was in the Second Division at that time and I was playing alongside players who were household names – Bobby Collins, Tommy Docherty, Dave MacKay – they were all superstars in those days . . . For me, it was an unexpected pleasure to be selected. In fact, I was told I was selected by the guy who sold the papers, the *Huddersfield Examiner*, in the square in the town centre. I was walking through that day and he said, "Denis, you've been picked to play for your country," and he showed me the paper. Unbelievable! The manager didn't tell me, the SFA didn't tell me; it was the guy in the square with the old bunnet on.'

Law would go on to become perhaps the most celebrated Scottish footballer of all time, but back then, just eighteen years old, he says he found it a struggle to begin with: 'I was helped a lot by the experienced players in the Scottish team . . . Remember I was also playing against guys who were household names . . . Even Wales had superstars – John Charles, Cliff Jones of Spurs, Ivor Allchurch . . . It was a huge step up, it wasn't easy for me.'

By 1974, Law had emulated all the greats, had won trophies and was respected worldwide for his immense talent, and had been part of one of the most revered Manchester United sides in history. He was now capping all that with an appearance in the World Cup finals but now admits it had been an anxious wait to discover if he would be chosen; he had taken nothing for granted: 'No, no. Never. You were just happy to see your name if you were selected. It was a relief to hear I was in. I was a big friend of Dave MacKay's, and you look back at Dave, he never got to play in a World Cup; in fact, if you look at the number of caps he won [MacKay played just twenty-two times for Scotland] he should have had many more. The competition for places in those days was so tough . . . so I never took it for granted.'

Although they were at opposite ends of their respective careers,

Law and John Blackley had one thing in common: they were about to get their first taste of the finals. While the legendary striker was winning his fifty-fifth cap, the Hibernian defender was about to make just his fourth appearance for his country: 'I got lucky on two fronts. One, if George Connelly had continued to play [the Celtic defender had suffered injury problems and had missed matches because of a contractual dispute] I wouldn't have been there. Two, Martin Buchan pulling up injured on the morning of the English game; I don't know if I'd have made the tournament if I hadn't played well against England. One of the nicest things was the squad numbers. When they came out, I got number six, and that really surprised me . . . and now, every time I see Martin, I point to myself and say "number six" and we have a laugh.'

Buchan smiles as he recalls that: 'I was number fourteen, wasn't I? I didn't know if I was going to be playing, you don't know until the team is read out. I was disappointed because everyone wants to play in a World Cup . . . but I was pleased for John, I like John, I liked him as a player and he's a good guy, I didn't bear any malice towards him.'

And so the big day dawned.

Scotland's last appearance at a finals had been on June 15th 1958, a 2–1 defeat to France. Sixteen years later they were to return to the top table, and although there were some nerves among the players, there was also a strong belief that this was their time. As the squad bundled onto their coach, the second game of the tournament was being played out at the Olympiastadion in West Berlin, with the hosts coming out on top against Chile thanks to a solitary long-range strike from Paul Breitner. The Chilean national anthem was booed by a large group of protestors, still trying to enlighten the world about the atrocities carried out by the military junta, and in a sign of the stringent security enforced by the authorities, the fans were immediately surrounded by 2,000 riot police, who remained in place throughout the match.

The Scots had their own security in the form of officers who never left the party, an armed-guard escort and helicopters flying overhead. Their trip to the stadium would be an untroubled one, but Martin Buchan says it left everyone in no doubt as to how seriously their hosts were taking their safety: 'We were surrounded by guards with guns and we were given the drill, told that if anything happened while we were on the bus that we had to get down onto the floor. There was the helicopter flying alongside the bus . . . Quite an experience looking out the window and seeing it there, the lad sitting in the open side door with his feet dangling out and the machine gun in his lap. They were certainly taking it seriously.'

Buchan had been given another example of just how thorough the security forces were being just a few days earlier: 'There was a little hill just outside the hotel, we'd just finished training, it was a nice sunny day and I thought I'd just go over and sit there and read my book. I'd got to know a couple of the security guards pretty well and one of them came across and said, "I don't think it's a good idea to be up here." It never occurred to me, but they were obviously worried about the threat from snipers.'

Willie Ormond had scouted the opposition and had a clear picture in his mind of what he felt was required on the day, but decades later Danny McGrain recalls it had still felt as if the players were taking a step into the unknown: 'We never really knew anything about Zaire, nothing. We feared they might hurt us, but we didn't know their good players, their bad players . . . We just went out there and got on with it.'

The official team photo taken just before kick-off shows a grim-faced and resolute group of young men giving the clear sense that they just wanted to finish all the preliminaries and get down to business. Of the eleven, only Peter Lorimer's face shows even the hint of a smile, while the others are looking away in various directions. John Blackley, on the extreme right of the shot, seems ready to walk off, while at the other end of the back row, Jim Holton's outstretched arms appear almost to be holding David

Harvey and Joe Jordan in place. The six players in the front row are crouched in a variety of different poses, giving the picture an unstructured look and emphasising the fact it was a snatched shot before they hurriedly broke away to get the action underway.

Blackley recalls the tension as they posed for that photograph and admits it had been just as bad in the changing room a few minutes earlier: 'I remember the nerves. I don't think I've ever been in a dressing room with so many nerves. I'm talking leaders . . . I'm talking Billy Bremner, Denis Law, looking you straight in the eye and not having a word to say to you. It was unbelievable . . . We were just sitting there, looking at each other.'

McGrain is another for whom the pressure that day was palpable: 'Myself, Kenny, Joe Jordan, Sandy, it was our first World Cup, so we're looking for some reassurance, some calming words, not from Willie Ormond, but from the senior players . . . Us forgetting, it was also their first World Cup, probably their last as well, while we're going to go on forever . . . But Denis and Billy were as nervous as we all were. Nobody knew quite how to behave, nobody knew what to say.'

Law remembers that dressing room well, and the feelings he was experiencing at the time: 'Absolutely, it was very tense, although to be fair I was nervous before every game. It didn't matter if it was for Manchester United or Scotland, every game, but more so for Scotland. It was worse that night. You're playing in the World Cup, it's a dream we all had and some of us would have hoped to have done it years before, but we never had the opportunity. Here it was, you had been selected, and all you wanted was to get out onto that park and get the game underway. Although, I have to say, I can't remember anything about the game at all. Not a thing. So, yeah, I was nervous, it was a new experience completely.'

It is interesting that Lorimer is the only one of the group in that picture not apparently suffering from nerves. He says that should not come as a surprise; unlike Denis Law, he was never affected in that way before a game, not even one of this magnitude: 'I never

131

personally had nerves before any football match I ever played in. My idea of a game was to go out, enjoy yourself, give everything you've got . . . I'm not one of those who would get over-excited if we won, or go in the sulks for three days if we lost. For me, the moment the referee blew the final whistle, the result was the result, and I moved on and got on with my life. It was what I did best, just get me out there and let me show people what I can do, that was my attitude. Didn't make any difference to me that it was the World Cup finals, it could have been a First Division match or a cup tie against a team from the Fourth Division, I treated them all the same. I went out there and did my best, I had good games and I had bad games, but I never allowed nerves to get in the way of my performance.'

There were some nerves evident very early on as the Scots looked to get a foothold in the match, and they almost had the perfect settler as early as the second minute as Peter Lorimer pumped the first of many high balls into the African penalty area. The bewildered Zaire defenders failed to react to the Leeds man's corner and a leaping Joe Jordan headed narrowly wide at the back post. Jim Holton presented the next opportunity, failing to convert his header, before Denis Law had his first sight of goal. Lorimer got the break of the ball midway inside the opposition half and it fell perfectly for Kenny Dalglish, whose pass set Law racing towards the eighteen-yard box. With three Zairian defenders in his wake, the veteran striker, perhaps fleetingly aware of the potentially historic moment, scuffed his shot, and goalkeeper Kazadi flopped onto the ball before Jordan could profit from his team-mate's weak effort.

The Africans then manufactured their first opening of the encounter and should have taken the lead. Their captain, Mantantu, delightfully controlled a high diagonal cross twenty yards from goal and in the same movement flicked the ball into the Scotland area directly in the path of Kakoko Etepé. As Holton moved to close him down, the striker first took a touch, then had a complete fresh-air swing before recovering his composure and racing goalwards.

Harvey careered from his line, but from a narrow angle Etepé fired the ball under him only to find the side netting.

Danny McGrain remembers the side getting a real wake-up call as Zaire threatened to take a shock lead: 'They had two breakaways and Dave Harvey had to be alert. I think that helped to focus our minds.'

Scotland were indeed clearly stung by that scare and raced back up-field. Kenny Dalglish gathered the ball inside the right touchline, moved it onto his left foot, and swung an inviting cross into the penalty area. Jordan leapt highest and nodded it back into the path of Davie Hay. The midfielder cushioned the ball on his thighs, steadied, and unleashed a powerful left-footed volley that rebounded back out off the inside of Kazadi's right-hand post, with the keeper, despite a spectacular dive, well beaten.

Before frustration could set in and erode Scottish confidence, the goal finally came in the twenty-sixth minute. McGrain, marauding down the left, checked and rolled the ball back towards Hay. He looked up and measured a diagonal cross deep into the Zaire box, where Jordan once again out-jumped a clutch of markers. His headed pass fell perfectly for Peter Lorimer, whose stunning volley was in the net before Kazadi could even think about moving. As the ball rebounded out, Denis Law lashed it gleefully back into the goal and Lorimer applauded his own effort before celebrating with his jubilant team-mates.

'At that particular time, I was probably at my peak. I was really playing well both for Leeds and for Scotland and I was full of confidence . . . as for that powerful shot I had, it was totally natural.'

Lorimer was renowned as having perhaps the hardest shot in football in the 1970s, surpassing speeds of 90 mph during tests that were carried out: 'I don't know where it came from, it was just a natural thing. I suppose it was simply down to timing, or bone structure . . . But it was certainly a weapon for me, and I was scoring a lot of goals back then.'

With the pressure off, Scotland could now surely be expected to

133

systematically destroy their unfancied opponents and rack up an impressive goals advantage? That appeared to be the plan, and the lead was nearly doubled almost immediately when McGrain's angled cross found the head of the unmarked Law just six yards out. The striker, renowned as one of the greatest-ever headers of a ball, failed to convert, though, looping his effort well over the bar.

When the second did arrive, it was in bizarre circumstances.

Billy Bremner had been fouled some twenty-five yards from goal and took the resultant free kick himself. As he slanted the ball into the box, the Zaire defenders, strung out untidily across the edge of the box, stood motionless as Joe Jordan raced beyond them and headed goalwards from eight yards out. Given his splendid isolation it was a pretty weak header, but the goalkeeper seemed stunned by the unfolding scenario, and although the ball was directly at him, Kazadi somehow allowed it to slip between his thigh and right hand and over the line.

The only other opportunity in the first half fell to Zaire, and once again it was in the clear-cut category. John Blackley was caught out as a through ball skidded off the surface, allowing Etepé free possession. He surged forward and slid an inch-perfect pass along the edge of the box. With Holton having been dragged wide as a result of his fellow central defender's error, there was no one to prevent Kidumu Mantantu from running on to the ball and bearing down on goal. His first touch was just a little heavy and that allowed David Harvey the split second he needed to race forward and throw himself bravely at his opponent's feet, smothering the ball and safely grabbing it.

At the interval 2–0 seemed a reasonable enough return, particularly given two major scares in their own penalty box, and Willie Ormond later admitted he was satisfied and confident his men would go on to increase their winning margin.

When the sides re-emerged for the second half they were almost immediately halted again as a section of the floodlighting failed. The delay was a short one, some four or five minutes, before

German referee Gerhard Schulenburg decided to press ahead with the offending lights on half-power. Archive television footage certainly shows a remarkable difference in the brightness between the halves, but it was clearly still playable as Scotland set about building on their advantage.

They nearly did so when poor defending by Zaire allowed Dalglish and Law to race clear. It was the latter who took the ball into the area, but with the keeper racing from goal, Law declined to shoot, and as he tried to feed his younger colleague, Kazadi leapt on the ball to thwart them.

The Africans were not about to lie down and showed considerable spirit as they forced the Scots onto the back foot. Mayanga gathered the ball forty yards out, turned in-field, and raced goalwards before thumping in a low long-range shot with his left foot, for which Harvey had to dive smartly to his left to scramble beyond the post.

Back came Scotland. Holton headed straight at the keeper; Hay whipped in a left-footed cross from which Lorimer brought a superb diving save out of Kazadi, although he was then ruled offside; and minutes later Jordan missed a sitter. Lorimer drove round the outside of the Zaire defence and crossed from the right, the keeper scrambled the ball out and the striker poked it wide from just seven yards out.

The next Scottish attack came down the left, with Kenny Dalglish the supplier. His cross was headed out by Buanga Tshimen and dropped invitingly on the edge of the box. Lorimer thrashed in a stunning volley, only for the keeper to get the slightest of touches onto the crossbar.

In the dying stages, McGrain linked up with Tommy Hutchison – a seventy-sixth minute replacement for Dalglish – and the winger chipped the ball up to Denis Law. He took advantage of a fortunate bounce, turned, and sent a shot towards the keeper's left post, only to see Kazadi leap through the air and claw it behind for a corner. In the act of shooting, Law had tumbled to the ground and sat on the turf for a few seconds after seeing his effort saved. As he bowed his head in disappointment, the message was clear: the 'Lawman' seemed to know he was now destined never to score a goal at the World Cup finals.

Zaire then spurned another gilt-edged chance when, after a flowing move, Ndaye Mulamba found himself in space just eight yards out. His weak shot screwed across the six-yard box and wide of the far post. Ndaye – top scorer with nine goals as his country had won the Africa Cup of Nations earlier in the year – then attempted to make amends from a free kick, his effort tipped over the bar by Harvey, although given it had been taken from inside the eighteen-yard box, and had obviously been indirect, the Scottish keeper's save should not have been required.

That was to be the last serious action of the match, the final whistle sounding soon afterwards, and the players trooped off, the jeers of a number of less than impressed 'neutral' German supporters in the 27,000 crowd ringing in their ears.

After lingering on the somewhat muted on-field celebrations, the cameras cut to the technical areas just in time to see a grim-faced Willie Ormond making his way from the dugout and up the tunnel. Even at that moment, seconds after Scotland's first-ever victory at a World Cup finals, the manager clearly feared the two-goal winning margin was not going to be enough.

He later declared himself pleased with the performance, the positive result being the main priority, and he maintained it was the sort of platform from which Scotland could still mount a successful challenge to qualify for the latter stages.

Billy Bremner admitted that despite the Africans having been watched in advance, and written off, the Scots had been caught out by their unfancied opponents: 'Zaire surprised us. They played better than we ever believed possible. But the manager told us the way to beat them, with those high balls. Maybe in the second half we could have done more, but it was a dreadfully sticky night, players were gasping for air every time they made a long run. And

Tommy Docherty was in charge when Scotland kicked off their World Cup qualifying campaign with a 4–1 victory in Copenhagen in October 1972.

Kenny Dalglish opened the scoring as the Scots followed up with a 2–0 win over Denmark at Hampden.

Willie Ormond took over the national team when Docherty quit to become Manchester United manager.

Ormond's first game in charge was a 5–0 thrashing at the hands of England in February 1973. Peter Lorimer's own goal in the 5th minute set the scene for a night of humiliation.

Joe Jordan is congratulated by Tommy Hutchison and Billy Bremner after scoring the winning goal in the deciding qualifier against Czechoslovakia … sparking scenes of celebration inside Hampden Park.

The Scotland party was kitted out by C&A for the trip to the finals.

The 'Largs Fishing Boat Incident' was headline news after Jimmy Johnstone had to be rescued from the Firth of Clyde in the early hours of the morning.

Ormond kept faith in the winger and Johnstone was man of the match as the Scots beat England 2–0 at Hampden three days later.

The World Cup squad hit the charts with the single 'Easy Easy' and released the album *Scotland Scotland*.

The Hotel Erbismühle, Scotland's base during the finals.

The accommodation was fairly basic, with two or, in some cases, three players sharing a room.

June 14th 1974. A nervous-looking Scotland side line up for the team photograph ahead of their return to the World Cup finals for the first time in sixteen years.

The legendary Denis Law made his one and only finals appearance in that opening match against Zaire.

Joe Jordan headed the second goal in the 2–0 win over the Africans.

One of the most iconic images in the history of Scottish football as
Billy Bremner comes agonisingly close to scoring against Brazil, a
goal that would have seen the Scots qualify from their group.

June 22nd 1974. Scotland line up ahead of the decisive encounter with Yugoslavia.

Joe Jordan nets the late equaliser in the 1–1 draw at the Waldstadion, Frankfurt.

A crestfallen Billy Bremner leaves the pitch after Scotland's elimination had been confirmed.

Daily Record

SCOTLAND'S BIGGEST DAILY SALE

4p   Tuesday, June 25, ★   No. 24,518

FAN-TASTIC!

That's what our World Cup team think of the fans—and the welcome home

Picture by WILLIAM THORNTON

THERE'S only one word for it. Fan-tastic! Scotland's
World Cup squad couldn't believe their eyes—or ears—
at the deafening welcome by 10,000 fans at Glasgow Airport yesterday.

Waving back to the singing, roaring crowd are soccer
heroes Hay, left, Hutchison, Schaedler, Bremner, Blackley,
McGrain, McQueen, Johnstone and Jordan.

It seemed as if the Scots had won the World Cup. And,
as far as the fans were concerned, they had.
FABULOUS FANS—Centre Pages.

WILSON DROPS A BOMBSHELL
—Back Page

HOME RULE ROW GROWS
—Page Two

Despite being knocked out at the group stage, the squad returned home as heroes.

at the end, with the crowd behind Zaire as they came at us, I had to do something to calm it all down. That explains the possession stuff. It wasn't done to show off.'

Bremner was referring to the closing stages of the match, a period during which he sat deep and orchestrated a series of sideways passes, the Scots retaining the ball rather than attempting to further hurt the Africans, the exact opposite of the plans he had outlined to reporters the day before. His thinking was perhaps understandable, particularly if the players were physically drained, but it was a tactic that would over the years be criticised and seen as a major reason why the adventure ultimately ended in tears.

Reflecting four decades later, Danny McGrain certainly doesn't remember getting any instructions to that effect. As far as he was concerned, the team had but one thought in mind – to score more goals: 'There were no orders that we should just keep the ball, play about them, that we were happy with two-nothing. We wanted to go on and score three, four, five. We should have done that. I overlapped, Sandy overlapped, big Joe tried to score, Peter Lorimer tried to score, but for some reason it just didn't happen. The problem was that it was the first game, we had nothing to gauge it against, and of course history shows that it might have been very different.'

There was also, Davie Hay argues, self-inflicted additional pressure because of the well-publicised disciplinary problems in Largs and Norway before the finals: 'I think for the first time it really struck us: given everything that has happened, we can't afford to lose this game. The first game in the World Cup is always important, but because of the adverse publicity we put ourselves under unnecessary pressure. It was extremely warm that night, it was very humid, and later in the match, when we had it under control, I think we did take the foot off the gas, knowing there were big games coming up, but not of course, at that point, knowing the consequences. It was 2–0, we'd won the game; there was no doubt we could have got more if we'd really pushed it.'

Joe Jordan had scored, the first of four goals he would net at that level, becoming, along the way, the only Scot ever to score in three World Cup finals. It is a record that right now seems unlikely ever to be beaten, let alone matched, and it was a proud moment for the Leeds striker, the realisation of a boyhood dream.

And yet he still looks back on that match with feelings of frustration and regret: 'We maybe were a little naive. We held a two-nothing lead and we were comfortable. In hindsight, we could have got more goals, and I think if the game had been the last of the three and we knew what we needed to get to win the game, to get out of the group, we would have gone on and scored more.'

Looking back, Denis Law agrees with his strike partner, but is at pains to point out the pressure all the players felt to achieve their first priority – taking maximum points from the match: 'We had to win the game. You have to understand that; we knew with it being the first one, we simply had to win the game. We didn't want to get beat, we didn't want to go into games with Brazil and Yugoslavia having dropped points. I just remember coming off the park and being delighted we had won. They were the weakest team in the group, but we were just pleased we'd got the points. Maybe if we'd had a bit more experience of being at the World Cup we'd have gone on and tried to get more goals.'

As the Scots were beating Zaire to complete the opening round of Group 2 fixtures, the other match in Group 1 saw East Germany beat Australia 2–0 in a bad-tempered encounter in Hamburg to leapfrog their rivals from the West and top the section.

The following day's *Evening Times* reported, 'Travel agents throughout Scotland were inundated with phone calls today as football fans made last-minute arrangements to get to the World Cup.' The 'eleventh-hour rush' was attributed to the Scots winning their opening game and to a desire to see the side take on the defending champions in a match that could determine their fate in the group. The paper quoted Mr Brian Doran, boss of Blue Sky Holidays: 'If Scotland win this one they can't fail to qualify, and the fans don't want to miss it. I hardly had time to sit down at my desk this morning before the phone started ringing, and this is only the start.'

The planned exodus made headlines on the front and back pages. Also contained was this extraordinary advertisement, one that was offering potential travellers all the time they could possibly need to decide whether or not they might take the plunge.

VAUXHALL WORLD CUP SPECIAL

DAY TRIP BY JET TO

SCOTLAND v BRAZIL

in FRANKFURT, June 18th,
including best reserve seat ticket

Only £65

Depart 9am Glasgow Airport. Bookings accepted up to 1 hour before departure. Pay at Vauxhall check-in desk at airport on the day. Or phone 061-236-0268

ONLY A LIMITED NUMBER OF
TRIPS AVAILABLE

**PLEASE REMEMBER TO BRING
YOUR PASSPORT**

As the squad headed back to their 'home' in Erbismühle, Ormond was already casting his mind ahead to that game against Brazil. Uppermost in his mind were three injury concerns that might have a big bearing on his plans. Jim Holton had hurt his back, captain Billy Bremner was nursing a knee problem, and Danny McGrain had suffered a bad gash on his left leg.

139

Given he had already decided to make what he felt were necessary changes from the win over Zaire, it would be an anxious couple of days for the Scotland manager, who was keen to avoid having to make too many enforced alterations. Ormond liked stability and knew he needed his key men on the park if he was to get the result he required to help deliver to the nation the success he had promised.

8

SCOTLAND 0–0 BRAZIL

Waldstadion, Frankfurt, Tuesday, June 18th 1974

Over the weekend, the two other sections in the competition got underway. Holland took an immediate hold on Group 3, with an impressive 2–0 beating of Uruguay, while Sweden and Bulgaria finished in a goalless stalemate. Italy were given a shock in Group 4, falling behind to Haiti, but recovered to save face with a 3–1 victory, while Poland gave notice that they, having knocked out England during qualification, were going to make an impact in the finals, kicking off with a 3–2 win over Argentina.

Monday, June 17th was a rest day, at least in terms of the competitive action, but the Scotland squad were hard at work in preparation for their showdown with Mário Zagallo's side.

There had been time to relax and recuperate following the return to their headquarters in the Taunus foothills, but now Ormond and his squad were getting back to business. As the players trooped out onto the training pitch, the manager, apparently quite relaxed, paused to share his thoughts with the travelling press pack: 'The pressure is now on Brazil. They are the ones with all to lose, we are the side with all to gain.'

Even a cursory glance through the newspaper reports from that day makes it clear to the reader there had been a decided shift in mood, with journalists buying into Ormond's optimistic take on events. Zaire, long written off as no-hopers, are described by Ian

Archer in the *Glasgow Herald* as 'undervalued Africans' offering a 'challenge larger and more insistent than any thought imaginable'. Archer goes on to point out that while the Scots scored just two goals, 'only Poland and Italy in the first series of matches have gathered more. They have become the fancied ones to beat Brazil. That is no mean performance in the first four days of play.'

Ormond's assertion that all the pressure was on Brazil might have been slightly overstated, but Zagallo was very much in the spotlight, with reports suggesting the government back home might fall should the football team fail in its stated objective to retain the World Cup. The coach, trying to concentrate of footballing rather than political matters, was focused only on the upcoming match: 'We hope that Scotland play football and do not make war. As far as the Scots are concerned I have been impressed – and I say it quite frankly – by their captain Billy Bremner. He is capable of playing a decisive role in the match.'

Zagallo revealed to reporters that he would be likely to field the same eleven players as had started against Yugoslavia, a match in which the Brazilians had faded spectacularly in the closing stages after the heavens had opened and the Frankfurt pitch had become a sodden mess. When asked if he would therefore be praying for rain the following night, Ormond replied, 'I'll just be praying, full stop.'

If he had indeed been seeking help from above, his pleas had been answered with the news that his injured trio had all recovered over the weekend. In fact, his entire squad of twenty-two was fit and available, a clean bill of health that allowed the manager the luxury of choosing what he deemed to be his best side.

After training, it was the turn of Bremner to be interviewed, and the Scotland skipper admitted the pressures of the World Cup finals had, despite his vast experience and success-laden career, struck him to the core and left him a nervous wreck: 'When we went to loosen up an hour before the match, I just could not run. I had to sit on the bench, hunched up, a bundle of nerves. It was all so emotional, especially later at the national anthem. The only other time I felt that way was in my first cup final for Leeds in 1965 when I was only 22. But Friday was worse. Ridiculous, isn't it, but that's how we felt about our country, and the World Cup.'

Willie Ormond was in a reflective mood as he sat down to lunch, admitting that he had not pushed his men too hard during their light workout. The hard work, he felt, had already been done; now it was just a case of keeping the players ticking over: 'Possibly last week I worked them too hard and that would explain why we fell away during the second half against Zaire. We played five full practice matches in the days beforehand because the players wanted them. I could not stop it – but all that is over now.'

Ormond decided against revealing his team in advance, preferring to wait until he was officially required to do so, but his counterpart Mário Zagallo showed his hand later in the day, eventually making one alteration, Mirandinha replacing Valdomiro from the side that had opened with that goalless draw.

It was a much-changed Brazilian line-up from that which had been crowned world champions in such spectacular fashion four years earlier. There was no Pelé, Gérson or Tostão, and the captain, Carlos Alberto, had retired. His place as leader of the team was taken by Wilson Piazza, one of only three survivors from the 4–1 demolition of Italy in Mexico City in the summer of 1970. The other two were Rivelino, reputed to have the hardest shot in world football, and Jairzinho, who had scored in every game during those Mexico finals.

Despite the inclusion of that illustrious duo, it was a side without the sparkle and creativity Brazil had become renowned for. It was a more functional, pragmatic team, one capable of mixing it up physically when required. It was not a side of which Scotland needed to be overly wary. It was a side Scotland, on top form, could beat.

Despite his apparent confidence, Zagallo had refused to allow cameramen to film his last training session with his squad, fearing the crew, which included Jock Stein, who was there as part of the BBC commentary team, would pass on the footage to Willie

Ormond. The Scotland party instead visited the BBC's Frankfurt studio to watch a re-run of the draw with Yugoslavia.

In the present day, every cup final or similarly important match, is previewed in part by players who have been signed up by the various media organisations to give a behind-the-scenes look at preparations, to write, or more likely dictate, columns that reveal the 'secrets' their team-mates might prefer not to be made public. Details such as who was worst in training, who plays the noisiest music in the dressing room or who leaves his dirty boxer shorts lying around have become a staple of the coverage. In the mid-1970s such pieces were far from prevalent, but the *Glasgow Herald* of Tuesday, June 18th featured a lengthy, and much less frivolous, article written in the first person by the Hearts striker Donald Ford. It gives an interesting insight into life in the Scotland camp and makes it clear there was still lingering resentment among the players over some of the pre-finals coverage of the squad's supposed antics.

High spirits in the Scottish camp, but Frankfurt is no frolic
By DONALD FORD
of Scotland's World Cup squad

IT WOULD be reasonable to assume that the multitudes of husbands, wives, and children who invade the Hotel Erbismühle, 30 miles from Frankfurt, each Sunday afternoon are coming to enjoy the crazy golf, table tennis, swimming pool, or indoor bowling. Either that, or to sit on the terrace with a glass of beer and gaze at the magnificence of the tree-lined slopes of the Taunus Mountains.

The fact of the matter is that they are not. They have, instead, arrived by car, motor bike, push-bike, and on foot in their hundreds to admire 22 handsome rugged Scotsmen.

Disappointed at the non-appearance of kilts or haggis,

they wend their way home at teatime, but not without arming themselves with umpteen autographs, written on books, on postcards, on footballs, or on anything that is available for signature.

To be stared at by pleasant German people is infinitely more desirable than staring at a sub-machinegun held by Arab terrorists (the threat of which has meant enormous security arrangements being mounted by the German government) and so I suppose we should be thankful for small mercies.

At least these Sunday visitors mean new faces and fresh interest to a team who have spent so much time in one another's company – from a showery and blustery Largs, via a new and very poorly staffed 'top class' hotel in Belgium, a glorified youth hostel in Norway, and finally to Germany.

One would gather from some reports that nothing but nasty incidents happened in the Scottish squad's build-up to the competition.

The events of the last fortnight are now history but it is safe to say that every player was deeply hurt at the thought of fervent Scottish football supporters at home being led to believe that the whole event was similar to a visit to a Playboy Club.

What should be emphasised is the effort expended on the training field – including some voluntary sessions by some of the players – or about the magnificent team spirit of Denis Law, Jimmy Johnstone, and Billy Bremner – the finest captain Scotland has ever possessed – carried on by the less experienced members of the squad, and then eventually enveloping everyone so that never a day goes by without half-a-dozen interludes that would do credit to a Morecambe and Wise show.

Even this statement might lead some to think that the

145

whole business is being treated as a joke but nothing could be further from the truth. When football is involved the job is done thoroughly and to the best of each player's ability.

The fitness of the whole squad is unquestionable – and the mental attitude which is so important is kept at a peak because the spirit is tremendous.

Ford goes on to write at some length about the importance of Denis Law in particular, how his room had become the 'common room' and how the veteran's force of character spilled into everything, touched everyone. He writes that being with Law is 'exciting, interesting, amazing and exhausting all at the same time. The simple fact is that he loves life and the way he is living it. Intentionally or not, he passes it on to all who pack his room to chat, play cards, talk about football or drink tea.'

The column continues:

> And so, despite the attempts by many to write off our attempt to win the World Cup as an incident-strewn frolic, we find ourselves awaiting the challenge of the world champions, who are below us in the section and were by no means clever in their match against Yugoslavia.
>
> They will lose matches in this World Cup, of that there is no doubt, and the first of these could well be very near.
>
> Should Scotland lose, there is no doubt that all the knives will be drawn again. But, win or lose, no one will be entitled to point a finger at any player in this team and resume hysterical criticisms, because none will be deserved.
>
> There are no doubters in this camp; only lads determined to win a football match and stuff a lot of words down some throats. Far too much rubbish has already been aired, and no opportunity will be afforded for any more.

The players are aware of the stakes and will react accordingly.

To all loyal Scottish football followers, we send our good wishes and thanks, as well as a promise that we have given and will give of our best at all times.

It is a forthright and well-written piece, carefully constructed by an experienced and intelligent man – Ford was twenty-nine at the time of the finals and had played well over 200 games for Hearts – and makes it clear that mistrust of the media is not a modern phenomenon: it was alive and kicking four decades ago.

The most surprising aspect of the article was the lack of prominence given to it by the newspaper, situated as it was on page fourteen alongside the leader column and above the readers' letters.

As Donald Ford and his team-mates woke and slowly gathered their senses that morning in Erbismühle, the realisation began to sink in that within a few hours a number of them would be involved in what might just be the biggest match of their careers to date. Although the manager would not be revealing his squad of sixteen until much nearer kick-off – 'I have still got a couple of things to iron out before committing myself to a team . . .' – most of them would have been well aware of their likely fate; there were only a few places up for grabs. Jimmy Johnstone and Peter Cormack were being tipped to be called up, with Kenny Dalglish's place apparently under threat. Everyone assumed that Denis Law's outing against Zaire would prove to be his only one of the tournament.

As those players peered from their bedroom windows there would have been delight that the weather had apparently turned in their favour. After two days of brilliant sunshine and humid conditions – which it was assumed would have suited the Brazilians perfectly – there had been heavy rain overnight and the forecast was for a cloudy, colder day with occasional showers.

Some 900 miles away, Glasgow airport was, according to the

Evening Times, 'bulging at the seams as hundreds of tartan fans set off on a World Cup pilgrimage'. The supporters were bundled on to a series of chartered planes, and 'as soon as one party was on its way, another horde arrived' reported the paper. It also gave details of a special VIP departure at 10.30 a.m., a plane that carried Glasgow's Lord Provost, Sir William Gray, and 'most of Scotland's football managers and a number of directors'. Among that group was a certain Ally MacLeod, then boss of Ayr United, but who would of course have his own World Cup 'adventure' just four years later. His parting shot was a typically patriotic one: 'I think that all of us who know the game feel that logically Brazil will win. But every damn one of us is hoping that we're wrong and praying that once more we can turn it on when it matters and hammer the Brazilians.'

The advance party had already set up camp in West Germany, thousands of them streaming into Frankfurt ahead of the match, which was expected to attract a sell-out crowd of just under 65,000. Supporters had already arrived by car, bus and even caravanette, according to journalist Jim Blair, who was mingling with them on the streets of the city. He wrote of 'singing Scots fans waving St Andrew's flags and Lions Rampant, decked in tartan from head to toe, who brought the Frankfurt streets to life from early morning as the astonished Germans made their way to work'. The story had been headlined 'FRANKFURT HAS BEEN HI-JOCKED'.

Such was the hysteria ahead of the game that that day's *Evening Times* was awash with World Cup-themed stories. Quite apart from the page-one report on the fan exodus and the match previews further back, there were some bizarre articles.

Page five offered tips on international sign language that travelling fans might use to make themselves understood by Germans or Brazilians with whom they wished to communicate. Although given that 'FOREFINGER DRAWN SLOWLY ACROSS THROAT', 'CLENCHED FIST' and 'V-SIGN' were among those listed, it hardly seemed to be the most helpful advice to tourists.

Page nine led with the headline 'IT'S A WORLD CUP CLASH: Beauty v the box' before detailing how organisers of the Miss Maryhill contest planned to forge ahead with their beauty show, albeit with a television set at the side of the stage to allow the audience to keep across the Scotland game. The event organiser, Mr David Forrester, admitted unsurprisingly to the paper, 'We've still got quite a few tickets left for tonight.'

On page eleven could be found the story of two Glaswegians, Ronnie Keenan and Eddie McDowall, who were pictured standing alongside a German autobahn attempting to hitch-hike their way to Frankfurt, having successfully negotiated Holland and Belgium in that way.

A few pages on and the traditional 'vox pop' could be found. *Times* reporters had been out on the streets, their clear remit to find women who did not want to watch the big match. 'WIVES IN TV SOCCER TIZZY' summed up their findings. Mrs Pauline Evans from Crofthill Road told the paper, 'Football? It drives me round the bend. Our television set will be on BBC2 for the film, whatever it is.' Meanwhile, Mrs Helga Thompson from Carmunnock had been warned by her husband before he left for work 'not, under any circumstances, to be in the house at kick-off time, or at best, not in the same room as the TV'.

In its football coverage, the paper also had an interview with the legendary Pelé, who was returning from a public appearance in Spain to watch the game. He was anticipating his fellow countrymen would be given a demanding ninety minutes: 'Some people are saying that now we have drawn with Yugoslavia the rest of the group will be easy. But we all know only too well that Scotland have never been easy to us. I recall passionate battles with the Scots and I am expecting a close affair.'

Group 1 also resumed that day, and in the afternoon kick-off the hosts romped to a comfortable 3–0 win over Australia, with Overath, Cullmann and Gerd Müller all on target. East Germany would later draw 1–1 with Chile, a result that ensured the West Germans would qualify; all that had to be decided was which country would top the section.

The other match in Group 2 was at the Parkstadion in Gelsenkirchen, where Yugoslavia were next to take on Zaire. They would do so with Dusan Bajevic restored to the side, having completed his two-game ban for being sent off in his country's qualifier against Greece, and the Velez Mostar striker – who would go on to score twenty-nine goals in thirty-seven career appearances for the national team – would have a major part to play that night. Coach Miljan Miljanic, erring on the side of caution after Scotland's experience against the Africans, followed Willie Ormond's lead and refused to name the remainder of his selection until duty-bound to do so.

Last-minute preparations were being carried out in the Scots camp, with trainers Ronnie McKenzie and Hugh Allan leaving nothing to chance. The pair were responsible for the vast quantities of kit required for match days and training, as well as administering medications and providing rubdowns for aching limbs. Sports science was in its infancy forty years ago and the pair had a much more basic approach to maintaining fitness, but, well aware that the team had faded in the heat during the final part of the opening match, slow-release soda pills were dispensed to the players to guard against dehydration.

By then the squad had boarded their coach and travelled the thirty miles into downtown Frankfurt, their progress – despite the ever-present security convoy guiding them through the traffic and a helicopter again hovering overhead throughout – slowed by excited fans as they closed in on the Waldstadion for what would be just a fourth meeting with the mighty Brazil.

The Scots had failed to win any of the previous three. Stevie Chalmers had given Scotland a first-minute lead at Hampden in June 1966, only for the visitors to hit back to snatch a 1–1 draw. Brazil had then secured 1–0 wins at the Maracanã and in Glasgow in the summers of 1972 and '73.

As the players picked their spots in the changing room and settled down, Ormond addressed them. He had announced his squad of sixteen and had told them the eleven who would start the match; now was the time for a few last words of encouragement.

One hour before kick-off, that news filtered out to everyone else with the official confirmation of the line-ups. Mário Zagallo had, as promised, gone for a 4–3–3 formation that read: Leão; Luis Pereira, Nelinho, Marinho, Francisco Marinho; Piazza, Rivelino, Mirandinha; Jairzinho, Leivinha, Paulo César.

While Ormond had eventually decided on the following team: Harvey; Jardine, Holton, Buchan, McGrain; Morgan, Bremner, Hay, Lorimer; Dalglish, Jordan.

The manager, who later confessed he had needed a dram of whisky to settle his pre-match nerves, had settled for two changes from the victory over Zaire. The more experienced Martin Buchan replaced John Blackley in central defence, while Willie Morgan was the man to benefit from the expected absence of Denis Law.

Law's World Cup, at least in a playing sense, was over. Blackley had the consolation of a place on the substitute's bench, alongside Thomson Allan, Peter Cormack, Tommy Hutchison and Jimmy Johnstone, but that was of little comfort to the Hibernian defender. He knew only too well that managers rarely make defensive changes during the course of a match; he was relying on Buchan or Holton picking up an injury, and he felt that unlikely. As far as Blackley was concerned, he, like his great boyhood hero Denis Law, had kicked his last ball in the 1974 World Cup finals: 'It was the saddest moment in my football career, being dropped for the Brazil game. I felt I'd done all right against Zaire, I'd made one bad error, but I'd done fine. I remember we were in a room in the hotel the day before and the manager read out the team. I was distraught. I'd always wanted to play against England, and I got that chance . . . The other team I really wanted to play against was Brazil, and here was an opportunity . . . It might have been my one and only opportunity . . . and it was taken away from me. I was in tears. I went to my bed and one or two of the lads came in and tried to cheer me up, but there was no cheering me up. It became a different World Cup for me then ... I sat there, pretty much relaxed, obviously involved in the games, but relaxed. I knew I was never going to get on. I mean, I'm not complaining ... Me, a boy from the villages, playing against Zaire in the World Cup ... fantastic ... but it could have been better ...'

John Blackley clearly felt then, and still feels to this day, that the decision was the wrong one, that it was unfair to drop him. And he harbours the suspicion that some pressure was applied on the manager: 'I heard there was a delegation went up to Willie Ormond after the first game and said, "If we're not playing we might as well go home." ... I don't know if that's true ... Anyway, I didn't play. That was the outcome.'

Peter Lorimer had also heard the stories at the time: 'There was a bit of a rumour that they'd had a go at Willie and then they were in the team. He was under pressure from the SFA and I don't think in those days it was totally down to Willie Ormond to pick the team as such, I think they would have a meeting where they would have their say ... so it could well have happened. I don't think they [the players] would have been able to do it with Tommy Docherty, but I think they would have been able to do it with Willie Ormond. I do clearly remember Jinky talking about Willie Morgan and saying, "How's he got in and I haven't?" He said he wouldn't mind being kept out of the team by me, but he couldn't understand how Morgan kept him out. Jimmy was a fantastic player and I remember him going off on one, insinuating he felt there had been a bit of skulduggery going on, but obviously you don't know yourself, do you? And to be quite honest, when you know you're playing you're not all that bothered, you're just delighted you're in yourself.'

Was Ormond the type of manager who might have bowed to that kind of pressure? Blackley resists giving a definitive answer: 'I don't think he'd have wanted to see anybody going home from the camp at that particular time and I just felt that would have brought extra pressure on everybody . . . but . . . I'd heard this, it's never been verified, so . . .'

Did he ever ask Martin Buchan about it?

'I've bumped into him a few times . . . but, no.'

Martin looked taken aback when that suggestion was put to him four decades later. Did he deliver such an ultimatum to the boss?

'No . . . no . . . I wouldn't have dared. I think I got the vote because I was quicker than John. End of story. He was a good reader of the game, but I had a bit more pace and I was a good man-marker. That was the thing at the time, you put somebody on the opposition's playmaker, and I was good at that and I think he wanted me to do a job on Jairzinho.'

Buchan says he felt a sense of great pride when he was given the news he would be playing: 'When you start kicking a ball around the streets of Aberdeen, you dream of playing for Scotland, and the pinnacle is playing for Scotland at the World Cup. It was a very proud moment standing out there lined up on the pitch in Frankfurt before the game.'

If there had been nerves ahead of the Zaire game, Danny McGrain was experiencing a somewhat more intense sensation before kick-off against Brazil, and the man who had scored in every match in Mexico was also uppermost on his mind: 'I was shiting myself! Jairzinho was the outside-right, he'd had a great World Cup in 1970, and I'd just moved to left-back and I'm thinking this guy is going to give me a hard time. I've no evidence of it at all . . . but I think he'd enjoyed his four years as a World Cup winner, and he'd slowed down a little bit thankfully.'

As it was, Buchan shackled the Brazilian legend 'so heavily as to render him invisible' according to one match report, so McGrain had to deal with him only fleetingly.

The whole match can be viewed online; the version I tracked down is accompanied by typically frantic South American commentary. Two things immediately strike the viewer: the relatively pedestrian pace of play and the simplicity of the television coverage.

Anyone born in the past couple of decades will be amazed by how few cameras are utilised and by the lack of replays from all sorts of different angles, although this one at least had cameramen stationed behind the goals to give a slightly different perspective.

The first couple of minutes saw Scotland trying to press forward with little success, and the first chance fell to the Brazilians when Davie Hay fouled Paulo César twenty-five yards out. With a myriad of options to take the free kick, it was Nelinho who stepped up and curled his effort just wide of David Harvey's right post.

The Scots then won a free kick themselves, which Lorimer fired in from all of forty yards. He found the target, but Leão saved easily.

As the pace of the match began to pick up, it became more physical, and Scotland tried to utilise the high ball on occasion without seriously threatening. Brazil showed better technique and forced some last-gasp defending from Ormond's side, with Harvey called into serious action for the first time in the twelfth minute. Dalglish, back helping his rearguard, nicked the ball away on the edge of his own penalty area, but only as far as the onrushing Wilson Piazza. The Brazil captain sent a wickedly curving shot goalwards, forcing Harvey to leap to his left and claw the ball round the post. From the resultant corner, Leivinha crashed in a volley just under the bar, the keeper reacting quickly to touch it over.

The Scots were finding it next to impossible to get out of their own half, possession regularly being given away too quickly, as the yellow shirts flooded towards David Harvey. Sandy Jardine hooked one dangerous cross to safety just two yards from his own goal line, while Jim Holton was regularly being pressed into winning headers.

Bit by bit Scotland edged back into the match, confidence growing as a result of having prevented Brazil from scoring what had, on occasion, looked like an inevitable early goal. In the nineteenth minute Willie Morgan got on the end of a Jordan header, but nodded wide of the post. The Manchester United winger then wriggled clear on the left and found Jordan with his cross, but Leão was smartly off his line to grab the ball before Dalglish could make contact.

Brazil were still dangerous and Paulo César found space in the box, only to shoot straight at Harvey from an angle.

Joe Jordan then required treatment from Ronnie McKenzie for a facial knock – the incident missed by the few cameras covering the game – and during the break for treatment there was a rare cutaway to the bench, where Willie Ormond sat impassively, his face betraying none of the tension he must have been feeling at that stage.

After an impressive performance against Zaire, Davie Hay was continuing his fine World Cup in the second match, attempting to assist in Scotland's rare attacks, but more often dropping back to close down space and utilise his defensive talents. Time after time Brazilian attacks ended with the Celtic midfielder intercepting or crunching into a tackle.

The Scots claimed for a penalty in the twenty-ninth minute after Joe Jordan had headed down a driven cross from Peter Lorimer. Dalglish pounced, turned and shot towards goal, and as Marinho threw himself in to block, the ball seemed to strike his outstretched arm. Jordan was insistent, but Dutch referee Arie van Gemert dismissed his claims. Television did not bother even to show a replay.

Lorimer and Morgan were seeing more of the ball, Jardine was pushing forward, and Bremner was snapping into challenges, but still Brazil came forward and Leivinha was next to threaten, his header easily gathered by Harvey.

Mário Zagallo's hope that Scotland 'do not make war' was beginning to seem somewhat ironic given the physical approach of his team, and first Bremner, then Morgan, Lorimer and Dalglish were the victims of crude Brazilian fouls as frustration began to set in for the defending champions.

At the other end of the pitch, Martin Buchan was justifying his selection with a commanding and assured performance, sliding in on a number of occasions to blunt Brazil attacks. It was a performance he reflects upon with pride: 'I was very fortunate. I played thirty-four times for Scotland and three of them were against Brazil. I kind of knew what I was up against because I'd played them when The Doc took us over there in '72, so I wasn't as nervous as I might have been if it had been my first time against the famous Brazilians. It also helped that I'd played in Frankfurt previously in the friendly with Germany, so that helped to put me at ease as well. It wasn't as daunting as it might otherwise have been. They didn't have too many chances, but I don't think you can ever feel comfortable against Brazil because they're always capable of moments of individual brilliance. You can never take it for granted you're heading for a clean sheet.'

Despite that caution, the first half ended with Scotland looking more and more in control, and while Harvey had been the busier keeper – Leão had yet to make a significant save – it would be Willie Ormond who would return to the dressing room the happier manager.

The second period began in a similar fashion with the champions offering little threat, the Scots enjoying more possession and probing forward more often. In one of those attacks Bremner surged over halfway and fed Davie Hay. The midfielder looked up, carried the ball some fifteen yards, then unleashed a long-range effort that Leão tipped over the bar. Lorimer swung across the resultant corner and Joe Jordan crashed through Francisco Marinho to power in a header that the keeper saved at his left post.

Bremner was revelling in the challenge and broke free again and again to set up crossing chances for Willie Morgan and Peter Lorimer, none of which could be converted.

In the fifty-ninth minute David Harvey was called into action for the first time since the interval, easily clutching a Leivinha header after a free kick had been conceded by Sandy Jardine. Again the camera cut to Ormond; again he looked relaxed and at ease, chatting with Hugh Allan on the Scottish bench.

He had reason to be, as his side was taking a firm grip on the match with first Hay and then Lorimer forcing Leão to pull off smart saves. The Leeds man then hammered in a thirty-five-yard free kick and got the ball swerving, but the Brazil number one was again up to the task and palmed the shot over for a corner.

That effort was about to lead to one of the most iconic moments in the annals of Scottish football.

Lorimer drove the ball in from the right and the Brazilians made a mess of clearing it, succeeding only in conceding another corner. The winger this time hung a high ball across goal, and Joe Jordan, timing his run from the edge of the box to perfection, rose to meet it seven yards out. Leão pounced forward and unconvincingly pushed the ball out. Billy Bremner, rushing in to try to profit from any slip, had no time to react, and the ball rebounded from his shin and trundled agonisingly wide of the post, missing the upright by inches.

The sight of a distraught Bremner, face buried in his hands, is one that has burned itself indelibly in the history of our national game.

In the STV commentary, a devastated Arthur Montford is clearly stunned as he wails 'an unbelievable miss by Billy Bremner . . . inches away from the sensation of the season'.

Forty years later, Peter Lorimer still winces as he relives the moment when his close friend might have won the game for Scotland: 'That was sickening. Ninety-nine times out of a hundred he'd have stuck that away. I know it just bounced off him, but Billy had very sharp reactions; being little, he had quick feet. Normally, he'd have scored that . . . but you only get one chance and that one just didn't go in for us. I never did speak to him about that afterwards, there was no point.'

Bremner's partner in that impressive Scottish midfield was Davie Hay. Like Lorimer, he can see that opportunity playing out in his mind as if it were yesterday: 'It was like pinball, it came off him rather than him directing it. He was just a yard out, the assumption is he has to score . . . I couldn't believe it when I realised the ball had rolled wide. There's a photo of the incident and if you look at it I'm about two yards away from him . . . I still can't believe it wasn't a goal.'

John Blackley did not have quite such a close-up view of the incident; he watched it unfold from the bench back at the halfway line: 'The excitement of that, because you knew if that goes in we're beating Brazil, we're going through. I knew it was close; just how close I didn't know until I saw it later on the telly. Billy was just ahead of it, he had no time to adjust . . . So, so close . . .'

Undeterred, the Scots pressed forward, forcing a succession of corners, continuing to dominate the match, with Bremner, seemingly determined to make amends, becoming more and more influential, Davie Hay surging from midfield, and Lorimer and Morgan teasing the Brazil defence.

It was not until the seventy-third minute that Zagallo's team next threatened, a delightful flick freeing substitute Carpegiani to make an angled run into the box, but Harvey raced from his line to smother the ball as the Brazilian attempted to poke it under him.

As players tired, so the contest became more physical, and there were a series of late challenges by both teams. Hay was being singled out, and Sandy Jardine was chopped to the ground by a retreating Rivelino as he overlapped down the wing. The Brazil number ten had been booked in the first half for an assault on Bremner and seemed certain to be sent off, but referee van Gemert took no action other than to award the Scots a free kick. He did brandish the yellow card at Francisco Marinho for his extended protestations. It is astonishing to reflect that those were the only cautions handed out in the entire ninety minutes – had the match been refereed under today's laws and regulations, neither side would have finished with a full complement and the card count would have been in double figures.

There followed a near carbon copy of the Bremner 'miss' as Lorimer pinged the dead ball goalwards, Jordan again won the header and Leão again spilled it, but this time the ball rebounded beyond the sliding Scotland captain.

Joe Jordan was then lucky to escape a red card. After late challenges on both himself and Billy Bremner, the Leeds striker seemed to stamp on and then kick Nelinho as he lay on the ground. The Dutch official awarded Scotland a free kick and urged them to take it quickly, the Brazilian left lying in a heap on the turf as the Scots mounted an attack from deep in their own half. Kenny Dalglish carried the ball far into the Brazil half before he was crudely hacked to the ground by Luís Pereira. Hay eventually sent an angled shot just over the bar, and in the next attack the Brazilian full-back scythed down Jordan as he attempted to wriggle clear down the touchline.

In a rare counter by the defending champions, Rivelino was blocked by Bremner and reacted angrily, clearly punching the Scots captain on the chin in retaliation. The referee, no more than three yards away, again ignored the incident and seconds later the pair were shaking hands, a clear mark of respect between two great warriors.

The free kick, from thirty yards out, was deflected well wide, and the resultant corner cleared. Seconds later, the final whistle blew. It was a second successive 0–0 draw for the South Americans, who still trailed Scotland in the group, but they would be the happier of the teams with the outcome.

That was a point not lost on Joe Jordan, who to this day reflects on a superb Scottish performance, but one tinged with frustration; it was, he believes, a lost chance: 'They were the world champions at the time and it was the sort of game all us players wanted to play in against the big names, guys who had made their reputations in Mexico . . . and all I can say is, we were the better team, we were the better team that day, and despite the result, that was pleasing to players like Billy Bremner who had taken on the World Cup winners and proved, on that occasion, that they were as good as them.'

For Jordan and the rest of the Scots who trooped off that pitch, there was clearly a sense of what might have been, of an opportunity missed. The victory they came agonisingly close to achieving would have secured their place in the next stage with a game in hand. Having to settle for a draw meant that game, against Yugoslavia, would now be the decisive one, and it promised to be a tough examination. As the players gathered back in the dressing room, word came through from Gelsenkirchen of the score in the other match being played that evening.

It had ended Yugoslavia 9–0 Zaire.

The victory equalled the World Cup finals record, previously achieved in 1954 by Hungary against South Korea, and was set up early in the game as the returning Bajevic notched the first goal in the eighth minute. He would go on to complete his hat-trick late in the match, by which time Zaire had been overwhelmed. At the interval it was 6–0, the only comfort for the Africans that the final result might have been even more damaging. Even the Yugoslav manager felt for his opposition, saying afterwards, 'I hoped that Zaire would score once or twice. I am very sorry there were so many goals because our opponents were very likeable.' The Africans' cause was not helped by the sending-off, midway through the first half, of talisman Ndaye Mulamba for a dispute with the referee, by which time goalkeeper Kazadi had already been replaced by substitute Ndimbi Tubilandu, a move which did nothing to stem the flow.

If that scoreline had dented Scottish confidence in any way, it was not apparent in the immediate aftermath of the match when Billy Bremner spoke to reporters: 'After they missed a couple of chances early on I felt it could be our night. It's something you sense as a player . . . and in the second half I was convinced we would win. It will be very, very difficult now for us against Yugoslavia, but I am confident we can do it. We will never be beaten until the last whistle.'

Willie Ormond picked up on the same theme: 'We've made it a bit difficult for ourselves to qualify by having to beat Yugoslavia

[but] if the boys turn on the same type of football and get the breaks we will win the game.'

It had been a rough ninety minutes, with a string of illegal challenges by players from both sides, but Bremner claimed Brazil had to shoulder the blame for that: 'We did not think they would be so physical. They didn't give us a chance to play.'

That was something of an over-exaggeration, as the Scots had performed well and caused the champions plenty of problems. Mário Zagallo, in his post-match briefing, tried to deflect attention from his side's poor showing by blaming the Scots for the 'rough stuff'. It was a claim that infuriated his opposite number, Ormond hitting back angrily: 'I suggest Zagallo comes down to my dressing room and looks at the shins of my players. I have the opinion that the Brazilians tried to play European-style football, but they should leave that to those who know about it. They have lost their key players like Pelé and they do not have the individual ability now, and that is the reason why they play so tough.'

Pelé had himself been in attendance, and was later introduced to British prime minister Harold Wilson in the VIP room at the stadium. The PM's thoughts on the match are not recorded, but the football great was happy to talk: 'Scotland certainly belonged to Bremner. I was greatly impressed by the way he improvised his game and by his stamina and will. It wasn't really a match, it was a fight at times. I have never seen Rivelino so involved physically and while this was all going on in midfield Brazil lacked the penetration they needed to have won. Now they are going to be hanging on for goal difference calculations . . . I don't like the look of it.'

Even as the Brazilian superstar was speaking, the thousands of Scots who had made the day trip to Frankfurt were piling into planes and heading for home. On arrival at Glasgow airport they were met by a lone piper alongside the tarmac, who apparently did little to raise spirits. The fans had been heartened by the team's performance, but now feared the worst. Among those interviewed by waiting reporters was ten-year-old John Cullis from Largs, who offered the following insightful analysis: 'We were great at times, but we failed to take our chances. This was my first trip abroad with Scotland and I'll never forget it.'

The stay-at-home supporters had also been fixated on the occasion, with overnight figures suggesting a staggering 22 million viewers across the UK had tuned into the match. The BBC had claimed 16.5 million of them, the others watching on the various ITV regional opt-outs.

The combative nature of the game had left Willie Ormond with an extensive casualty list. Bremner and Danny McGrain were badly bruised on both shins, Joe Jordan had suffered light concussion – hardly surprising given the number of aerial challenges he had contested – and the rest of the players had incurred 'bruises and knocks'. Some patching up would be required, but they were all expected to be fit for the weekend.

Upon returning to Erbismühle, the players had settled down for a quiet drink, the general feeling, according to the manager, one of deflation, but as the night wore on, and as more alcohol was consumed, spirits were raised and a certain pride had kicked in. The mood was helped, no doubt, by the appearance of comedian Billy Connolly, who had been invited back to entertain the squad, and when he was joined on the small stage by Jimmy Johnstone, the party moved into full flow. The night ended with Johnstone, always an enthusiastic performer, singing 'Amazing Grace'.

Glasses were drained, the players retired to their rooms and the lights were switched off.

In less than four days' time those players would be required to drag themselves once again to the heights, to meet one of the greatest challenges of their careers. It could be a match that would see them attain legendary status, one that would never be forgotten.

An expectant nation would be right behind them, demanding one final push. Each one of those players was determined not to let anyone down.

9

SCOTLAND 1–1 YUGOSLAVIA

Waldstadion, Frankfurt, Saturday, June 22nd 1974

The first step in the build-up to the decider was to allow the players to relax and recover, both physically and mentally, and so Wednesday, June 19th was to be a quiet one for the Scotland party. The sun beat down on the hotel, the security guards were in short-sleeved shirts rather than their combat gear, and Ormond and his men were able to digest the overwhelming praise heaped on the Scots for their performance the previous night.

After being booed from the pitch following their beating of Zaire, neutral West German fans and reporters had now, it seemed, taken the Scottish players to their hearts, with Billy Bremner their clear favourite for his outstanding showing against the defending champions.

The manager was rightly proud of his players' efforts, but as he sat with journalists on the sun-soaked terrace of the hotel, Willie Ormond also turned his attention to the forthcoming encounter, now just seventy-two hours away: 'I don't fear them. Certainly with 250,000 Yugoslavians living around here, they will have the support, but there are only eleven players on the field. With the same kind of performance as we gave against Brazil and a break or two we can beat them.'

It was a reinforcement of the message he had been keen to get across in the bowels of the Waldstadion just after the game, and

163

Ormond was determined to stay upbeat and optimistic: 'Sure, they are a helluva side – but weren't we against Brazil? Every time you ask this team to get their teeth into something they bite and they bite. I'll be asking once again – and they'll do it for me. These players are great people.'

He then went on to admit that he had allowed his team to dictate, at least in part, the tactics that they felt would work against Brazil: 'They told me how they wanted to play the game, with Morgan and Lorimer wide, Dalglish up among the attack. In my heart I knew it wasn't on but I said OK, we'll give it twenty minutes the way you want it, you are the ones that count. It didn't work, I knew it wouldn't, but you have to respect and listen to the opinions of players. The style was changed, with Lorimer going inside and Dalglish coming back, but I didn't have to say a word, the captain and the others worked it out for themselves. I'm proud of them for that and didn't they play well afterwards?'

It was an interesting glimpse into Willie Ormond's managerial style. He was seen from the outside as a quiet, unassuming man, but those who knew him and worked with him talk of a genuine football man, one who understood the game and was prepared to treat his players as adults. That approach undoubtedly backfired on him on occasion, as events in Largs and Norway proved, but by the time of the World Cup finals Ormond clearly had the respect of his players, and he obviously trusted them to go out and do what was required.

With no training scheduled that day, Ormond chose just to relax at the hotel while the squad wandered down into town on a shopping expedition. The following day it would all be stepped up again.

If there was confidence in the Scotland camp, it was positively flowing from the Brazilian base as they surveyed the task facing them. Coach Zagallo knew exactly what was required and exuded positivity: 'All we have to do is beat Zaire by three goals to make sure. If we can't do that, then we really shouldn't be here.' His defender Luis Pereira was even more forthright in his assessment: 'We will qualify because Yugoslavia and Scotland will draw, while we will beat Zaire 10–0.'

They might not have had the opportunity, as that day reports emerged in a West German newspaper that the Zaire players had wanted to quit the competition and return home in the wake of their humbling by Yugoslavia. In fact, it later emerged there had been similar talks even before their second match. It took eight hours of bargaining by their coach Blagoje Vidinic to persuade his squad to fulfil the fixture. The Zairian FA released a short statement, which read: 'We will play against Brazil hoping to come out of that game with not too bad a defeat.'

Had the Africans chosen not to turn up, Brazil, according to competition rules at the time, would have been awarded a 2–0 victory. That would have meant a scoring draw between Yugoslavia and Scotland, and would have seen the Scots progress.

That evening, both Group 3 matches ended in draws, Uruguay scoring late to snatch a 1–1 against Bulgaria, while Sweden thwarted the Dutch with a backs-to-the-wall performance in which keeper Ronnie Hellstroem did most to keep the scoreline blank. The results meant all four teams retained hopes of qualifying.

In Group 4, Italy and Argentina also fought out a draw, 1–1, while the impressive Poles clinched qualification as they romped to a second successive victory, swamping Haiti 7–0. The Haitians' cause had not been helped by the expulsion from the tournament of one of their players, Ernst Jean-Joseph, who had failed a drug-test after their opener with the Italians. He later admitted having taken an illegal stimulant and was sent home in disgrace. Four years later it was the Scots who were embroiled in a similar controversy, but that is a tale for another book.

Another controversy – one that regularly came to the fore in the 1970s – was rumbling away and getting prominent coverage in the media: that of which music the Scots players should line up to before their games.

According to reports, 'God Save the Queen' had been 'jeered, howled and whistled throughout' by the travelling fans prior to the matches with Zaire and Brazil, prompting the Scottish National Party to contact the SFA. A telegram was sent to the Scottish camp suggesting 'Scotland the Brave' be played instead and it was a move the manager was happy to lend his weight to. 'I don't see any reason why we shouldn't have a Scottish anthem for a Scottish occasion. Why antagonise our supporters before the game begins?' was Willie Ormond's reasoning.

It would have come as no surprise to anyone that the pleas fell on deaf ears; Scottish FA secretary Willie Allan's response was unequivocal: 'There is no question of us playing anything other than the national anthem.'

On the eve of their crucial decider, the Scotland players rose, had breakfast and were back on the training pitch. Or, at least, twenty-one of them were. Willie Morgan had suffered what was thought to have been a badly bruised toe in the Brazil encounter and sat out most of the session, his chances of being fit for the remaining group match rated at no better than fifty–fifty. He was later taken down into Frankfurt by team doctor John Fitzsimmons, where an orthopaedic surgeon examined and X-rayed his foot.

'If the match had to be played tomorrow then I certainly could not pick Morgan for the team,' revealed Willie Ormond. 'As it is, he remains extremely doubtful.'

That news would have been of significant interest to Yugoslavia. Coach Miljan Miljanic had been astonished to discover Morgan had been given the nod ahead of Jimmy Johnstone for the previous game. The *Evening Times* reporter Jim Blair had spoken to an unnamed Yugoslav 'spy' who had drawn up a detailed dossier on all the Scots players for Miljanic. The mystery man told Blair the Slavs could not believe 'Jinky' had thus far remained an unused substitute: 'People in my country still talk of Johnstone because of his fantastic performance against Red Star Belgrade several years ago at Parkhead when Celtic won 5–1. Why did Mr Ormond play

Willie Morgan? Surely Johnstone would have been better in that role. Still, he is now a fresh player and I suppose he could play against us. Scotland will be doing us a favour if he is not in the team.'

The injured trio of Bremner, McGrain and Jordan all fully took part in the training; all were declared fit for Yugoslavia.

That news cheered Willie Ormond, who was himself undertaking a bit of espionage, reacquainting himself with the towering Dusan Bajevic, the striker who had bagged a hat-trick against Zaire after completing his FIFA suspension. The feeling was that Miljanic would name an unchanged line-up on Saturday, and Ormond wanted to ensure he had all the information he required to prepare his players for the challenge ahead.

The Slavs boasted a team of talented, technically proficient players, at the hub of which was midfield playmaker Branko Oblak, the man who pulled the strings and made the side tick. The likelihood was that Billy Bremner would be detailed to try to prevent that from happening.

Ormond, though, refused to get too hooked up on the opposition; he felt his men had what it took to dictate the flow of the game and how it might pan out. 'I don't fear Yugoslavia at all,' he proclaimed at his latest news conference, before adding, 'In fact, no one in the camp fears them. We are not going into this game with any inferiority complex. We know they are a good team, we know we must win, and we know we have the ability to do just that.'

Centre-half Jim Holton also spoke to reporters, and he was just as 'on-message' as his team-mates and manager: 'I don't think they are going to come at us in the way they attacked Brazil in their opening match. That will suit us. In fact, it's what we want. We're at our best going forward. All the boys are confident we can win. All we need is a lucky break, because we're playing tremendous stuff at the moment.'

The Celtic manager Jock Stein, in West Germany fulfilling media duties, was an occasional visitor to the Scotland camp. Before the competition had even kicked off he had tipped Yugoslavia as potential champions and felt they might just put an end to Scottish dreams: 'We had a real chance of qualifying against Brazil, and although we were unlucky it was our best chance of reaching the last eight. Yugoslavia present a different problem – and of course a draw is of no use at this stage.'

On the eve of the all-important match, the Scotland party suddenly had more pressing matters on their minds. Just twenty-four hours before the meeting with Yugoslavia, a death threat was issued, purportedly by the IRA, in which it claimed two of the Scots players were to be killed. The letter was received by police in Munich and passed on to the German security headquarters in Wiesbaden. The threat was immediately relayed to the SFA and the number of security forces at Erbismühle doubled. Thirty armed police stood guard and stopped visitors from getting anywhere near the wing of the hotel populated by the squad. Troops were sent into the surrounding tree-lined hills to search for snipers.

Willie Ormond told the players of the threat – aimed at 'two unnamed Protestants' according to newspapers reports at the time – and ordered them to remain in their rooms and not to go wandering around the terrace or gardens. Helicopters were put on standby and fire appliances rushed to the hotel, while the team coach was checked for bombs and all cars in the nearby area were searched.

It was announced that roads would be sealed off and extra escorts arranged for the following day to ensure the safety of the party as the bus made the thirty-mile journey back along to Frankfurt.

The manager was understandably nervous and edgy: 'We are taking the threat seriously. This is the worst kind of thing that could have happened on the eve of such an important match and there is no doubt that it will affect some of the players.'

The 'targets' were later revealed to have been Sandy Jardine and Jimmy Johnstone.

In typical fashion, the rest of the players took a gallows humour approach to the emergency and there was plenty winding up going on. In the 2006 BBC Scotland documentary *That Was The Team That Was: Scotland 1974*, winger Tommy Hutchison summed up the mood of the camp at the time: 'Everywhere we went, even the hotel, we had to have police with us, and they all had guns. Wee Jimmy was frightened to death, which gave the rest of us a laugh. He kept saying there could be snipers. He used to walk out the hotel with his Celtic bag up at his face. He'd say, "Look, I play for Celtic," as if that was going to save him.'

While Johnstone was not getting much sympathy from his team-mates, neither, according to Danny McGrain, was the other 'target', Sandy Jardine: 'We all made fun of it. Sandy would sit down on the bus and nobody would sit beside him because there were snipers about. I remember Erich Schaedler pestering one of the security guards to show him how to neutralise someone, like Spock from *Star Trek*. Erich was a strong, fit guy and he'd be trying it out on the rest of us . . . He was always busy, could never sit still . . . His way of relaxing was to try and paralyse you!'

Jim Stewart also recalls the rest of the players using humour to try to defuse what was, potentially, a very traumatic situation: 'You know what footballers are like, there was a bit of levity. It's all about trying to turn disadvantage into advantage. It wouldn't have done anyone any good for us to be worrying too much about it. The guards, the police officers, generally kept a low profile and I certainly never felt at any time we were under any immediate threat.'

A spokesman for the German security services was taking the matter a little more seriously, telling the *Glasgow Herald*, 'The threat was contained in a letter which was posted abroad. We do not intend saying where exactly it came from. I understand it was posted in England.'

More details emerged. The *Daily Express* revealed the letter had indeed been sent from England, it was handwritten, and contained the chilling message: 'We have sent two killers to eliminate two Scottish Protestant bastards.'

It was then reported that both wings of the IRA in Dublin had denied any involvement, and restrictions on the players were relaxed somewhat. Four of them – Bremner, Hay, Harvey and Jordan – were permitted to carry out a live television interview on the hotel lawn, while armed guards and around fifty bemused tourists watched on.

As darkness fell, security was tightened up again and police took up positions around the hotel, on the lookout for anything or anyone suspicious.

In the midst of the furore, Willie Ormond had also announced his team.

Incredibly, and against all the odds, Willie Morgan had been able to train in the afternoon and declared himself fully fit. Ormond had no hesitation in naming the same starting line-up and five substitutes as had faced Brazil.

The news would come as a pleasant surprise to Yugoslavia coach Miljanic – no Jimmy Johnstone – but as a crushing blow to a number of the Scotland squad. Ormond's decision meant that of the twenty-two who had travelled to the finals, only thirteen got the chance to start a match. The one other player who saw any action at all was Tommy Hutchison, who had replaced Kenny Dalglish against Zaire, and would do so again in the final match.

Eight of the pool never saw even a single minute of action: goalkeepers Thomson Allan and Jim Stewart, Peter Cormack, Willie Donachie, Donald Ford, Gordon McQueen, Erich Schaedler and Johnstone. Four of them – Stewart, Donachie, McQueen and Schaedler – did not even enjoy the consolation of a place among the substitutes; they watched all three matches from the stands.

There is no room for sympathy or sentiment in a football manager's job. Ormond thanked each and every individual for their contribution, made it clear they all had a part to play, and then simply chose the men he felt best suited to achieving their collective aim. Before he retired that night, looking strained and exhausted, his nerves shattered by having had to deal not only with the demands of the World Cup, but also a potential terrorist attack on his squad, Willie Ormond had allowed himself a glimpse into the future.

A victory the following afternoon in Frankfurt would see Scotland top their qualifying section to secure a place in the second group stage. The likelihood was they would then face Sweden, Poland and East Germany. None of those countries would represent an insurmountable hurdle. Win that mini-tournament, and a place in the final beckoned, and that remained Ormond's ultimate objective: 'I always said qualifying was the hardest task. We need one break. That's all.'

As it panned out, Group 1 was turned on its head when the team from the East shocked the hosts with a 1–0 success, Jürgen Sparwasser running on to a long through ball, skipping beyond two defenders and firing his shot over a despairing Sepp Maier into the roof of the net.

The victory, watched by a crowd of 60,350 at Hamburg's Volksparkstadion, was proclaimed as a great political success by leaders on the other side of the Berlin Wall, and the result clearly shook the West, but there is no question Helmut Schoen's side benefitted most from it. By finishing in first place, East Germany landed in a second-phase pool with Brazil, Holland and Argentina. Their neighbours, by contrast, were rewarded with a much easier route.

The dead rubber in Group 1 saw Chile and Australia battle out a goalless draw.

Group 2 would be decided in Frankfurt – where the Scots would take on Yugoslavia – and Gelsenkirchen, where Brazil were expected to run riot against the hapless Zairians.

The Yugoslavs were clear favourites and coach Miljanic, as antici-pated, named an unchanged team from that which had destroyed the Africans. He had only done so, however, after a four-hour-long meeting with his advisers – the national team was run then by a five-man coaching commission, of which Miljanic was the senior appointee – and there had, according to reports, been significant debate about how best to meet the challenge the Scots posed, before the head coach eventually won the day.

His team read: Maric; Buljan, Katalinski, Bogicevic, Hadziabdic; Acimovic, Oblak, Surjak; Petkovic, Bajevic and Dzajic.

It was a talented side and the Scots were well aware how difficult a hurdle faced them. Looking back, Martin Buchan admits it was always going to take something special to beat them: 'They had good players . . . Their ball-control . . . They were like the Brazilians of Europe . . . Their technical skills were far ahead of the Scots. A good side.'

Despite the scare of the death threat the previous day, there were no problems for the Scottish party as it made its heavily protected way to the stadium. Joe Jordan was stunned to see just how much the ring of steel around the Scots squad had been tightened: 'There was a lot of security . . . I remember that last game, we had a helicopter escort giving us security cover, there were soldiers, we had paratroopers. I was just trying to concentrate on the game, we had to win the game, had to beat Yugoslavia . . . It was just a sign of the times, there were a lot of terrorists around, they had to take precautions. It was exciting, a little bit crazy really.'

Inside were around 15,000 Scots fans mingling with double that number of Yugoslavs. The match had also attracted plenty of locals and supporters from other countries; the eventual estimated attendance varies between 56,000 and 60,000 depending on which report you read.

The match once again attracted a huge television audience, with the streets of many towns and cities across Scotland deserted by the 4 p.m. kick-off time. Both the BBC and STV showed the game live north of the border, with Archie MacPherson and Arthur Montford describing the action for those back home.

Yugoslavia had won the toss to wear their 'home' kit, so when

172

Billy Bremner led his men out to a cacophony of noise around the Waldstadion he did so in an eye-catching, and very simple, all-white strip. The only adornments were the dark blue numbers on the shorts and the backs of the shirts, a tiny Umbro motif and an oversized Scotland badge on the players' chests.

Both sides lined up for the national anthems – the jeering of Scots fans during 'God Save the Queen' had sparked a bit of controversy throughout the tournament and had led to calls for a more appropriate song to be adopted, although it would be almost two decades before 'Flower of Scotland' was introduced – before peeling off to their respective halves in the late afternoon sunshine.

Willie Ormond, in short sleeves and wearing sunglasses, took his seat on the bench. The task was now largely out of his hands; it was up to the men he had entrusted to deliver the hopes and dreams of a nation.

If those players had been surprised by the physical challenge offered by Brazil, they fully expected one from Yugoslavia, and it very quickly became apparent this was not going to be a contest for the faint-hearted.

Early on, Lorimer was scythed to the ground and required treatment before recovering. Billy Bremner had clearly been targeted and was the victim of a series of bone-jarring tackles, with Bogicevic the enforcer-in-chief.

By then, Brazil had already taken an expected lead against Zaire, Jairzinho at last finding a semblance of the form that had made him one of the stars of Mexico 1970, as he fired an angled volley low across the Africans' penalty area and into the bottom corner of the net.

In the main, Jim Holton's prediction that Yugoslavia would be happy to sit back and defend was being borne out, but they were dangerous on the counter-attack and twice had chances to open the scoring. First, Surjak crossed from the left and Petkovic volleyed high over at the back post, then captain Dzajic found himself free on the angle, but his chipped effort drifted beyond the crossbar.

The clearest opportunities in the first period, however, fell to Scotland. Midway through the half, Willie Morgan, skipping along the right touchline, passed in-field to Lorimer. The Leeds man lined up one of his powerful long-range efforts, but scuffed the shot, and Katalinski stuck out a foot in an attempt to clear the ball. He succeeded only in teeing it up for Jordan, who quickly pounced, but as he stabbed the ball goalwards from seven yards, goalkeeper Maric raced from his line to block it.

Morgan then swung a cross in from the right aimed at the Scotland striker who was clearly held back by Buljan in the box. It was an obvious penalty, but Mexican referee Alfonso González Archundía chose to ignore it.

In the next Scotland attack Davie Hay played a dangerous chipped pass through the middle of the penalty area. Bogicevic decided inexplicably to duck away from it, and as Maric flung himself desperately to his right, the ball bounced agonisingly wide of the post.

In the final minutes before the whistle blew for the break, Morgan jinked in-field, but shot over the bar from twenty yards.

There was little Willie Ormond could say to his players back down in the dressing room, other than to ask them to repeat their performance in the second half. They had dominated a side that had received rave reviews in their previous matches; the only thing missing was that potentially all-important goal.

The encouraging news from the Parkstadion was that Brazil had failed to capitalise on their early opener and had reached the interval leading Zaire just 1–0. As things stood, Scotland were in a position to qualify, but there was still a firm belief that the champions would get the total they needed in the remaining forty-five minutes. That would mean Ormond's men had to win their game.

With that in mind, from the restart the Scots once again took the initiative and created chance after chance.

Lorimer's free kick found Danny McGrain, improbably, in acres of space deep inside the Yugoslavia box. Had he been more accustomed to being in such a position the full-back might have chested the ball down and shot for goal; instead, he headed back across the six-yard line and Maric grabbed it before Jordan could make contact.

Billy Bremner then dropped another free kick invitingly into the box, but Jordan failed to direct his header on target. Bremner, once again a dominant figure, next found the overlapping Sandy Jardine, and the full-back, more comfortable in the opposition penalty area than his team-mate on the left of the Scots defence, fired in a powerful angled drive, which Maric held by his post.

The Scotland captain intercepted a desperate Yugoslav clearance and orchestrated another attack, passing to Peter Lorimer, who teed the ball up with his left foot before unleashing a right-footed piledriver, which the keeper clutched gratefully.

Around that time Brazil finally breached the Zaire rearguard for a second time as Rivelino ripped a twenty-yard shot high into the top corner of the net. Mário Zagallo's team still had twenty-four minutes to get the third goal they so desperately required.

The Scottish players were unaware of that, and still pushed forward, with Lorimer coming even closer to opening the scoring soon after. From two yards inside his opponents' half Jardine lifted a free kick high into the penalty area. Joe Jordan climbed above Katalinski and headed the ball diagonally across the box, where a stretching Bogicevic jumped but missed it. The ball bounced further wide off Lorimer's chest, but the Scot was quick to react, and with Maric advancing he hooked it back over the goalkeeper. Almost in slow motion the ball arced towards goal, and seemed about to drop inside the post, but Katalinski had been alert enough to cover and was able to hitch-kick it behind for a corner.

By then Hutchison had replaced Kenny Dalglish, but the Coventry winger had been given little opportunity to shine. Rather, it was the Leeds trio of Bremner, Lorimer and Jordan that was involved in every Scotland move.

And then, suddenly, with just nine minutes left on the clock, Yugoslavia scored.

Substitute Stanislav Karasi had replaced danger-man Bajevic – who the Scots had neutralised throughout – just ten minutes earlier. He collected the ball on the edge of the centre circle and strode forward, dummied to shoot, and then skipped beyond the retreating Scottish midfielders. Twenty-five yards out, he clipped the ball wide to Dragan Dzajic, then peeled off into the box. Danny McGrain had been drawn in-field and had to quickly double back to try to avert the danger. He did enough to halt his opponent, but the Yugoslav captain bought himself a yard and rolled the ball back away from goal on to his left foot. It is a moment that still rankles McGrain all these years later: 'I don't know if it was the heat, but I lost concentration then, I forgot they had switched the wingers so I thought he was all right-foot, and I showed him back on to his left, his good foot. He must have thought, "Oh Merry Christmas," and he dinked it to the far post. That goal was my fault.'

At that point Martin Buchan was seven yards out in line with the near post; Jim Holton was a couple of yards further forward, nearer the penalty spot; and Sandy Jardine was off to his right in line with the back post. As Dzajic crossed towards goal he had only two targets, but crucially there were gaps for both to run into. He chose Karasi. The ball floated over Buchan and Holton; Jardine reacted, but a fraction too late, and as he dived forward the Yugoslav got there just ahead of him to bullet a header across the helpless Harvey and into the far corner of the net.

It was the first time the Scottish defence had been breached during the tournament, but that single goal looked like being enough to crush their World Cup dream.

Scattered across the pitch, the players looked devastated. Shoulders slumped. Heads bowed. But they somehow dragged themselves back up the park in search of an equaliser that might yet lead to unlikely salvation. It came in the eighty-eighth minute.

Bremner and Morgan exchanged passes and the Manchester

United winger drove forward. Jordan dropped deep and his first-time pass found Peter Lorimer. Avoiding the temptation to let fly, the Scotland number eleven switched play down the left, where Hutchison controlled the ball, swept beyond Buljan and made for the byeline. He looked up and crossed low. Lorimer and Surjak arrived simultaneously. The Scot got a touch but could only slice the ball towards the far post, where Jordan first controlled it, then lashed a left-footed shot under the despairing Katalinski and into Maric's net.

The Scottish fans erupted with hope on the terraces as down below the striker was mobbed briefly by his team-mates, before the group raced back towards halfway, Lorimer pointedly placing the ball on the centre spot. Scotland were far more eager to get the game resumed than Yugoslavia were.

Joe Jordan had again scored at the World Cup finals, but there was to be no dramatic winner for the men in white: 'They were a really, really good team and it was a tough fixture. Again, I thought we were the better team on the day . . . but, we never got the goal or the points that were necessary to go through.'

In the last move of the game, Hay lifted the ball to Bremner, who headed on to Jardine. The full-back's pass found Morgan free on the right wing, but as soon as he took a touch, and shaped to cross, the referee raised his whistle to his lips and signalled the end of the encounter.

Fireworks were let off around the stadium and there was a mini-pitch invasion by some Yugoslavian fans. All that was left for the Scots players to do was to shake hands with their opponents and find out the final score from Gelsenkirchen.

When the news arrived, it was devastating.

That Brazil had achieved the 3–0 win they needed came as no surprise; it was the manner of the third goal that left the Scottish squad anguished. With little over ten minutes remaining, Zaire had held firm and the Brazilians were feeling the pressure. As frustration mounted, they had probed again, the ball played wide to Valdomiro.

The substitute took a poor first touch and was forced even wider. He was a few feet outside the penalty area, level with the six-yard box, when he nudged a speculative cross towards the near post. There was no great power in the delivery and Kazadi was well positioned to gather it, but the goalkeeper somehow allowed the ball to slither through his hands, under his body and into the net.

There was one comical moment during that second half in the Parkstadion, an incident even the distraught Scottish players would later find amusing. It was a little cameo that has gone down in football folklore. The Zaire defence was strung out across its eighteen-yard box ready to defend a Brazil free kick. As three of his opponents discussed who might strike it, and before the referee had blown his whistle, the African right-back Mwepu Ilunga raced from the wall and booted the ball fifty yards up-field. As the bemused Brazilians fell about laughing, the stern-faced Romanian referee flashed a yellow card in the face of Ilunga, who himself seemed stunned by what he had just done.

It was light relief, but in truth it did nothing to lessen the desperate hurt felt by everyone in the Scottish camp. There was, however, more to the incident than seemed immediately apparent, as will be discussed in chapter 11.

The players returned to the dressing room, those who had watched from the stands made their way forlornly downstairs, and the backroom team began gathering the kit and other paraphernalia ahead of the return trip to Erbismühle.

The feeling was one of sickening, crushing despair.

Despite that, Willie Ormond, a gentleman to the last, had gone to the Yugoslavia dressing room to congratulate his opponents, a gesture later highlighted by his opposite number Miljanic: 'Nothing finer will happen in the tournament. You are the greatest sportsmen in the world – and good, good players.'

10

END OF A DREAM

As the players finally dragged themselves out of the stadium ready to board the coach back up to their hotel, they were met by thousands of Scotland supporters who had flocked from their vantage points to pay tribute to their heroes. As they surrounded the exit, those fans sang in praise of the team.

Ian Archer reports in the *Glasgow Herald* of hearing them chant, 'We're on our way to Argentina, we shall not be moved!' If only those misguided souls had known what lay ahead at the next finals, they might not have been quite so quick to make such a pledge.

Unable to see into the future, they poured into the streets of Frankfurt to indulge in those two traditional pursuits of the Scottish football supporter: drowning their sorrows and dreaming of what might have been. It would be a noisy and drunken but trouble-free night in that sprawling city in the heart of Germany, after which the British Consul General, John Fearnley, said, 'The behaviour of the Scottish supporters was first class.' Police spokesman Horst Wogel joined in the praise, thanking the travelling Tartan Army for livening up his town: 'Your Scotsmen were no trouble at all.'

The bus finally pulled away from the Waldstadion carrying a group of exhausted young men, the manager and his coaching staff, and various others. It was a quiet journey up into the Taunus mountains.

A party had been arranged at the hotel, planned to take place irrespective of the outcome, and unsurprisingly it began in a quiet, morose way as players sat around lost in their own personal thoughts. Slowly, very slowly, as the alcohol began to lubricate the winding-down process, a few of them shared their thoughts.

The manager went first, his mood yet to lighten, telling Archer, 'I've died a thousand deaths on this trip but when we got back to the hotel I went into his room [he points at Adolf, the chief security guard, now dancing a Highland fling dressed in bonnet and scarf] and I looked at all the revolvers. I could have shot myself.'

The next song played out from the speakers around the room: Frank Sinatra signing 'My Way'. As Sandy Jardine – one of the top performers throughout the finals – heard the great crooner belt out, 'The record shows, I took the blows . . .' he turned to the journalist and said, wryly, 'That's our story, our history. Isn't it?'

He then went on to explain just how demanding the match against Yugoslavia had been: 'It was like running through a furnace out there. They said it was 82 degrees. I had ice cubes in my hands and I was stuffing them down my throat, but they melted. I couldn't catch my breath. See when that goal of theirs went in, I was done, I couldn't care less. That's dreadful, isn't it? I've never felt so bad in my life.'

Davie Hay had been an outstanding presence in the Scottish midfield in all the games. He too was shaken by the realisation that it was now all over, frustrated by just how close the Scots had come: 'One break in the three matches would have made all the difference. I'm convinced had we beaten Yugoslavia we were capable of winning the World Cup. The fact that we played so well and didn't lose a match proves a point – and it's a bit hard to accept defeat when you don't lose.'

Peter Lorimer also paused to reveal he had just called home and been overwhelmed by the release of emotion all the players were now experiencing: 'I've just rung my wife, she's English. I thought she would be happy to see me coming home. But she was bubbling, and so was I.'

Ian Archer had also shed tears, he admits as much in his dispatch for the paper, and his assessment of the adventure was a generally positive one. He writes of the SFA having to learn lessons, understandable after sixteen years' absence from the top table of world football, and urges that further back-up, both administrative and in a coaching sense, would be required for future campaigns.

He notes that the finals had not been a lucrative venture for the players, each having received just £300 in match fees – although the few commercial tie-ups that had been struck did eventually bring in a little more money – but quotes one of the squad as dismissing the payments as irrelevant: 'Whoever thought of money? We would come again for nothing.'

Archer's article concludes thus: 'As hard-working Germany relaxes on a warm Sunday, dirty Scottish socks are thrown into cases, boots and strips packed safely into hampers, and the carnival is over. The World Cup of other countries awaits this sad correspondent, and for the later stages he has little enthusiasm. Yes, I cried for my beloved country.'

The German newspapers were that Sunday morning unanimous in their backing of and sympathy for Ormond's team, with the *Berliner Abdenpost* bemoaning 'THE GREAT BAD LUCK OF THE SCOTS', *Die Welt* claiming 'IT WAS A PITY BRAZIL QUALIFIED' and *Bild* summing the situation up perfectly with 'THE BRAVE BUT LUCKLESS SCOTS'.

As those Scots players bundled together their possessions, packed away gifts for loved ones back home and spent time bidding farewell to their generous hosts, footballers of other nations were taking their chance to make history.

The four remaining group matches were played simultaneously. Holland and Sweden secured their qualification with comfortable wins over Bulgaria and Uruguay respectively, while Argentina – after taking just a single point from their first two matches – and

Group 4 winners Poland enjoyed wins over Haiti and Italy to ensure their progress.

Only seven teams emerged from that opening phase with unbeaten records. Most impressive were the Poles, with three wins out of three. The Dutch, the Swedes and the East Germans had also yet to taste defeat. The three other unbeaten sides came from Group 2: Yugoslavia, Brazil and, of course, Scotland, the only one of those countries not to make it through to the last eight.

One by one, the undefeated records tumbled. Yugoslavia's was first to go, in a 2–0 loss to West Germany. Miljanic's side would go on to lose all three second-phase matches. Poland handed Sweden a first defeat, and later that day East Germany went down 1–0 to Brazil.

As the competition progressed, Holland destroyed a brutal Brazilian team 2–0 in the deciding group match, Luis Pereira at last collecting an overdue red card as the Dutch booked their place in the final. The Waldstadion in Frankfurt staged another decisive encounter that same night, Wednesday, July 3rd, when Gerd Müller snatched a late winner to finally end the Polish challenge.

Holland were the one side left in the tournament yet to suffer a loss, but it came four days later in Munich's Olympiastadion. Johan Neeskens gave them an early lead from a penalty, but Paul Breitner later levelled, again from the spot, and just before half-time Müller wriggled clear to turn and hook what turned out to be the winner past Jongbloed in the Dutch goal.

And so it was Franz Beckenbauer who became the first man to hold aloft the new FIFA trophy as West Germany celebrated being named 1974 World Cup champions.

Had Scotland managed to rattle in a few more goals against Zaire; had Billy Bremner managed to scuff the ball into the Brazil net from a few yards out; had one more of the many chances created against Yugoslavia been taken . . . Might it have been Bremner holding aloft the golden prize? It might indeed, according to Peter Lorimer: 'I honestly believe that team had a serious chance of winning the competition, but we played those group games the wrong way round. To have Zaire first was the worst thing that could have happened. That was their one big game, they were up for it, they ran and chased and looked like they couldn't do any more after that one. Plus, we didn't have a target. We could have won by more goals, there's no question about it. If we had really gone about them we could have got four, maybe five, but we had a big game coming up midweek and we just wanted to see it through, not pick up any injuries. We were confident we wouldn't lose, we thought one of them would beat the other, we didn't think everybody would go and draw with each other in every bloody game. It was disappointing. Not only did we think we had a chance, in general we were seen as a danger to the big teams over there, especially after the way we played against Brazil. We outplayed them, we outplayed Yugoslavia, but they put the shutters up . . . We should have beaten them both.'

Willie Ormond had always asserted his team would improve as the competition progressed; he saw qualifying from the initial group as the hard part. Matches against the hosts, Sweden and Poland would have been tough but would not have scared that Scotland team.

By the time the final had been won and lost, those Scottish players had been home for almost a fortnight and many had scattered to various parts of the world to enjoy family holidays, to relax and wind down. And yet every one of them must have allowed themselves to have a 'what if . . .' moment that Sunday afternoon at the start of July.

Two weeks earlier they had left Erbismühle one last time to take their final journey in the coach that had transported them daily throughout their German adventure. That trip ended at Frankfurt airport, and after being eased through security and bundled aboard their plane, the players wondered what awaited them back home.

The welcome they received blew them away.

Even before their British Airways Trident touched down at

Abbotsinch – as Glasgow airport was then known – at 12.55 p.m. on Monday, June 24th, the squad members in window seats could clearly see a mass of fans assembled around the terminal building. They were crammed on to balconies, standing on roofs and hanging out of windows.

As the plane taxied to a halt, the cheering got louder, and when Billy Bremner, wearing a tartan scarf, led his men down the steps, the fans erupted as if a goal had just been scored. Their message to the players was clear: they were returning home as heroes.

It came as a relief to a few of them who had feared they had let the country down by failing to make progress. They had been aware that the newspaper coverage had been generally quite supportive, there had been the odd phone call back home during which reassurance had been sought, but in the days long before wall-to-wall sports news on satellite television channels beamed all across the world, and social media sites, there had been no real way for the players to gauge the mood of the nation.

In that one moment they knew.

Airport officials said the scenes were unprecedented, the crowds much larger even than those that had in the past assembled to greet pop stars arriving there. They put the numbers at around 10,000.

As they strolled across the tarmac, the players stopped to wave towards the supporters, many of whom had gathered hours earlier. Willie Ormond was blown away by the reception. As his men soaked up the acclaim, he slipped out of the rear door of the aircraft. A slight figure, looking tired and drained, the manager carried his coat in one hand, an airline bag in the other. He paused to survey the scene, later telling reporters, 'We expected a welcome, but nothing like this. It is fantastic! This is an emotional moment for myself and the players. I think we showed we are one of the best teams in the world. There must be a lot of sides glad we are out of the competition.'

As he soaked up the adulation of the tartan-clad hordes, the manager turned his attention to the future: 'We do not worry about

184

anyone now. We have taken a bit of stick from the English press – but England are kindergarten now.'

Captain Billy Bremner was also taken aback by the turnout, the patriotic Scot close to tears as he admitted, 'It is really fabulous this welcome. It is fantastic. You'd think we had won the cup. We went out there with the object of getting through to the final and I firmly believe we could have done it.'

It had been a long hard shift for the squad. They had first been brought together – most of them, at least – on May 7th ahead of the Home International Championships. There had been a brief interlude before the trips to Belgium and Norway, and then on to West Germany, but they had in effect been together, away from their families and loved ones, for the past forty-nine days. For a number of them that had been difficult, others had revelled in the adventure, but while they would all have loved to have still been part of the World Cup, there was also a sense of relief that the pressure was now off and life, for a time at least, could revert to some kind of normality.

Four players – Willie Morgan, Denis Law, Martin Buchan and David Harvey – missed the tumultuous occasion, as they had earlier flown to Manchester, where their reception had been somewhat more muted. Law recalls an exclusive welcoming party: 'My wife and five kids were there!'

As Law's team-mates in Glasgow boarded the single-deck bus that would take them into the city centre, around 100 police officers had to hold back fans, forming a cordon to prevent them from swamping the squad. The players quickly opened the roof windows. Some stood on seats and looked out, others climbed out onto the roof as the vehicle inched away from the terminal.

The *Scottish Daily Express* gave over its front page to the scenes at the airport, a large photograph of the coach, surrounded by excited supporters, topped by the heading 'YOU'LL NEVER WALK ALONE – And this is 10,000 fans saying it to Scotland'.

Glasgow's Lord Provost, Sir William Gray, had been among those

185

to meet the returning heroes, and he was quick to pledge that a civic reception would be organised in their honour. He also sent a personal letter to each of the squad congratulating them on a 'magnificent effort'.

Meanwhile, the coach was making slow progress en route to the North British Hotel on George Square, from where the squad would finally disperse.

The scenes at the airport and along the M8 have stuck in the minds of those players. Goalkeeper Jim Stewart says the reaction was phenomenal, much more frenzied than the squad had imagined it might be: 'I've got scrapbooks up in the attic, my wife kept them, and when we were moving one time we came across them. My boys hadn't seen anything like it. Some of the photographs were amazing. I'll never forget those scenes all the way in to the hotel where our families had gathered to meet us. It wasn't an open-topped bus, but the skylights were getting opened and there were guys on the roof. The supporters were hanging over the fences and railings just to get a vantage point to see the team. It was absolutely fantastic.'

'It was a riotous welcome,' recalls Danny McGrain, 'but we didn't want that, we didn't feel as if we deserved it. OK, we came back undefeated . . . but in a sense, we were defeated, because we didn't get through.'

The outpouring of emotion has lived long in the memory of John Blackley, who still marvels at the reaction of the Scotland supporters: 'I don't think any of us thought we were going to get a welcome like that. It was mind-blowing and it just showed how much the country was behind us . . . George Square was packed. It was incredible. None of us could believe what was happening and it made you wonder what it would have been like if we'd made the second group stage.'

John still had one further act to undertake before he could finally return to his family home just outside Falkirk. His journey was via what was, at the time, one of the roughest and most notorious areas of nearby Stirling.

'I gave Billy Bremner a run home to Raploch . . .' He bursts out laughing, 'Imagine that, me dropping Scotland's World Cup captain off at his parents' house in the Raploch. I'd never been there, but I knew about it, and it was wild . . . There you go, it was just a surreal time for me.'

After all the welcomes from the fans, and the long goodbyes as the travelling party finally dispersed from the city centre, Willie Ormond returned home to Musselburgh. His plans for the next few days were, he revealed, to read and relax: 'I'll be taking it easy for a day or two, but I'll be back in Glasgow on Thursday and hoping to meet up with SFA officials. There's a lot to be done yet. We have to start planning for the next stage, which is the European Nations Cup.'

When he got back to his house in the East Lothian town, neighbours were there to greet him, all keen to congratulate and shake the hand of the man who had so very nearly led his country to the heights of international football.

Only one person was missing: his wife Margaret. She had gone to Munich with a group of friends and would not be returning until the end of the week.

As Mrs Ormond continued to party with the tens of thousands of others who were soaking up the World Cup atmosphere, her husband no doubt poured himself a glass, sank down into his favourite armchair and dreamed of what might have been.

11

CONSPIRACY?

One of the main topics swirling around Willie Ormond's mind might have been Yugoslavia's record-equalling 9–0 thrashing of Zaire, a result that had clearly tipped the group in their favour and left Scotland in a do-or-die position.

The Scots would have rendered that scoreline far less important had they beaten Brazil in their second group match, played out at the same time as the Slavs were destroying the hapless Africans. But the 0–0 draw in Frankfurt had left Ormond's team with a huge challenge ahead of them, while at the same time handing the Brazilians the undoubted advantage of knowing exactly what they had to do in their final encounter, against Zaire.

As has been outlined in this book, Scotland were held 1–1 by Yugoslavia while Brazil, aided by a lucky final goal, secured the exact winning margin they required to progress. It is a scenario that has been debated over the years, with occasional rumours and suggestions of potential foul play emerging.

The Hibernian central defender John Blackley played in the opening match and was substitute for the other two. He, for one, has his suspicions: 'I still think there was a conspiracy in the camp. Not in our camp . . . in Zaire's camp and in Yugoslavia's camp. I still think there was a conspiracy.'

Blackley is a solid football man. Now in his mid-sixties, he has amassed almost five decades of experience in the game, first as player, then as coach and manager. He is not a man given to flights of fancy, nor one for making controversial statements just to stir things up.

Forty years after those '74 finals, he still shakes his head as he recalls how that section unfolded: 'Zaire . . . they were never a nine-nothing team. Never. I'll give Yugoslavia their due, they were probably the best side in the group, technically really good players . . . but they were never nine-nothing . . . And who's at the top of Zaire? A Yugoslav [Blagoje Vidinic] . . . he's the coach . . . and for me, I always believed that nine-nothing was a ploy. Honestly, I just felt they took . . . Zaire, Yugoslavia . . . they took the table away from us. We couldn't do anything about it . . . other than go and beat Brazil, which we should have, we should have beat Brazil.'

Blackley admits it was not something he ever discussed with the Scotland management, or the other members of the squad. It is his own personal belief, but it is one that still lingers: 'I just always felt that, and I still do to this day. No way was Zaire nine-nothing . . . no way! We could have played two games against them and we'd never have scored nine goals. Never. Zaire weren't that bad. I don't think any of us could believe Zaire had been beaten nine-nothing. Honestly . . . no way.'

It was a remarkable scoreline, one that had only once before been achieved at the World Cup finals, by the brilliant Hungarian side of Puskás, Kocsis and Hidegkuti in 1954. The only time it has since been emulated was also by Hungary, with a 10–1 demolition of El Salvador in 1982.

The victory by Yugoslavia in '74 stands out a mile.

Scotland scored two, Brazil three, and in neither match did the Zaire goalkeeper have to perform heroics to keep the score down. Kazadi certainly made saves in both games, there were defensive blocks and clearances and the Africans were spared by the woodwork on occasion, but neither encounter would be considered out of the ordinary.

As Blackley accepts, Yugoslavia were the best team in the group. But were they seven goals better than Scotland? Six goals better than Brazil? The scorelines in the other matches – all drawn – seem to suggest not.

There is footage of the Yugoslavia–Zaire game available online, and it is worth studying. The overall impression of the Africans is that they were naive – something they displayed in their two other games – and lacked defensive discipline, again a failing much in evidence against both the Scots and the Brazilians. What they did not lack was enthusiasm and effort, and they actually created more scoring opportunities in that middle encounter than they did in either of the other two.

As for the goals they lost, some might have been prevented, but only one can really be put down to a clear and obvious mistake. Yugoslavia had matched Scotland's tally of two within fourteen minutes in Gelsenkirchen. The first was created down the left from where Dzajic crossed and the giant Bajevic, unmarked, headed in to the top corner, while the second was a magnificent twenty-yard free kick curled into the same corner by Dzajic, an effort few, if any, goalkeepers would have got anywhere near. In between, Zaire had cut through the Yugoslav defence with a fine passing move, Kakoko denied only by a good save by Maric.

It was 3–0 within eighteen minutes. The ball was overrun by Kilasu Massamba some twenty-five yards from his goal, a clear mistake. But it then took a clinical and skilful four-man passing move to cut through the African rearguard before Surjak scored with a low-angled shot just inside the far post.

The tone for the remainder of the game was then set in the space of an utterly ridiculous sixty seconds. Kazadi had just pulled off a good diving save from a Bogicevic volley when the signal came from the Zaire coach that he was to be substituted by Tubilandu. As the bemused number one made his way round the touchline, his replacement took his position between the posts to defend a free kick from the right. When the ball was swung in, three Slavs found themselves clear in the penalty area, not one Zaire defender within twelve yards of their goal. Katalinski controlled the ball, then hammered it past the keeper. It looks bizarre, but that Zaire defence had previous – Scotland's second goal against them, the Joe Jordan header, had been scored from a near-identical situation. Their plight became even worse as top scorer Ndaye Mulamba, the hero of the Africa Cup of Nations victory, was sent off for his part in the mass protest that followed. The match was just a quarter through and Zaire were down to ten men.

On the half-hour mark it was 5–0, Bajevic again towering above two opponents to easily head home. Kakoko spurned another chance for Zaire, shooting wildly over the bar after a Maric fumble, and within minutes it was six. Tubilandu had just pulled off a decent save, but in the next attack went walkabout and, as he collided with one of his team-mates, Bogicevic looped a header into the unguarded net.

In the second half, Mayanga broke clear deep in the Yugoslav half, only to be denied by Maric handling well outside his box. These days the keeper would have instantly been sent off; that night he was not shown even a yellow card.

It was not until the hour mark that Yugoslavia added their seventh goal. Oblak drove in a twenty-five-yard angled free kick that Tubilandu had covered all the way, only to spill it inside his right post: an obvious error. Petkovic scored the eighth minutes later, running on to the ball after a superb defensive tackle by Tshimen succeeded only in setting up the Slav. He buried his shot in the bottom corner. Bajevic did likewise late on, completing his hat-trick with a back-post volley after again finding freedom in the box.

The last opportunity of the match fell to Zaire, a nicely worked move allowing Mayanga the chance to shoot from the edge of the area, but he was denied by a smart save by Maric.

As the final whistle sounds, the camera cuts to the Zaire bench, where their coach, the Yugoslav Vidinic, sits apparently stunned and stony-faced. He is motionless for a few moments, then gathers his shoulder bag and steps out of the dugout. He does not look like a man who has enjoyed the previous ninety minutes of football.

Having reviewed what footage I have been able to locate, I am left with the impression that what I watched was one vastly superior football team totally outclass a far less skilled, a far less experienced opposition. At no point was there the sense that Zaire were 'lying down' or not applying themselves; they simply were not good enough to prevent the scoring avalanche.

What made that game stand out is that Yugoslavia translated their dominance into goals. That does not always happen, the winning team often starts to coast when a match is clearly under control, but on occasion it does, and there have been far better teams than the Zaire of '74 that have suffered heavy beatings.

Peter Lorimer played every minute of Scotland's three matches at the World Cup finals. Like Blackley, he has heard different stories over the years, but does not share his old team-mate's lingering suspicions regarding that 9–0 encounter. Instead, he has some doubts over the Africans' final game, the 3–0 loss to Brazil: 'There were rumours at the time, I mean Brazil just beat them in the end, didn't they, by the amount of goals they needed . . . There were rumours that Brazil had agreed to go there and play friendly matches for them, which I could well believe because, in fairness, in those days football was a little bit . . .' – he searches for the correct word, then finds it – '. . . corrupt, to a degree. Referees were bribed, and we had two European finals with AC Milan and Bayern Munich and both referees got banned for life for being got at . . . but the game was a little bit like that at that particular time.'

Either side of the 1974 World Cup, Leeds United had lost those matches in controversial circumstances. In the '73 European Cup Winners' Cup final against Milan, Norman Hunter was contro-versially sent off and two cast-iron Leeds penalty claims were waved away by referee Christos Michas, who was later found guilty of match-fixing by the Greek FA and banned by UEFA. The Italians won the match 1–0. In the '75 European Cup final, French official

Michel Kitabdjian disallowed a perfectly good Lorimer goal and denied further penalty claims as Bayern won 2–0 to lift the trophy. There has been much misinformation since, but Kitabdjian was in fact never found guilty of corruption, or banned from refereeing. His reputation, despite what Lorimer believes, remains intact, although the Leeds man still has his suspicions: 'Nowadays the referee will have a UEFA or FIFA representative guarding them at all times at European or international games . . . Back then it wasn't anything like as tightly regulated, and there wasn't so much money around; for small sums of money they could organise anything. The truth is I think we knew the other teams would beat Zaire, but if they'd put the effort in they did against us, they certainly wouldn't have been beaten by nine . . . Maybe it was the anti-climax for them, getting beat in the first game, and they were feeling down or whatever, because against us they were a bit brutal, a bit naughty. They were up for it, and it seemed like after that they just turned it in, but it's hard to say . . . You always get rumours . . . But, if we'd have won one of those other two games we should have won, we'd have got through, that's top and bottom of it. The individual games we played, I didn't think there was any problem with them, it just didn't happen for us. We didn't get the luck, we didn't get the breaks.'

Aside from the conspiracy theories, other stories began to emerge during the tournament that have been elaborated on since. They may give a more credible reason why the Leopards disintegrated so badly.

Zaire was at that time run by its authoritarian leader Joseph Mobutu, who had taken power of the then Democratic Republic of Congo in a military coup in 1965. He changed the name of the country to Zaire in 1971. Mobutu saw football as a way of uniting the nation, of gaining international recognition, and he invested in the game. He brought in foreign coaches and barred the players from plying their trade abroad, ensuring the best talent was available for the domestic market. Having won the Africa Cup of

Nations for a second time in 1974, there was confidence – misplaced, as it turned out – that Zaire could make a positive impact at the World Cup finals.

To try to ensure that, Mobutu, by then a very wealthy individual, decided to offer incentives. Squad members were given cash bonuses, cars and houses just for qualifying, with the promise of more to follow should they succeed in West Germany.

Then, after losing to Scotland and before being humiliated by Yugoslavia, it seems the players discovered the riches on offer had instead been kept by one or more government representatives. There was nothing left to distribute to the team.

As outlined in chapter 9, the players threatened to go on strike; they wanted to return home before the final group game with Brazil. They were persuaded against taking such drastic action; perhaps the realisation of what repercussions there might be back home kicked in, but they were clearly in no mood to concentrate on football matters.

Ndaye Mulamba was the undoubted star of that side, top scorer during their Africa Cup triumph a few months before the finals. In a BBC interview in 2010 he explained why the heart and soul had been ripped out of that team: 'I cry when I think about those days . . .' he told reporter Andrew Harding, before going on to claim each member of the squad had been promised $45,000 but that before the Yugoslavia match an official had taken their money and fled Germany, leaving the players with nothing. 'So we decided not to play.' Mulamba was sent off during the mayhem in Gelsenkirchen.

Mulamba's team-mate Mwepu Ilunga would become a household name for the bizarre incident late on against Brazil when he rushed from a defensive wall and booted the ball up the pitch as the Brazilians waited to take a free kick. It is an undoubtedly humorous moment – one Ilunga even recreated years later in a 'Phoenix From the Flames' sketch for Baddiel and Skinner's *Fantasy Football League* television programme – but which has a more sinister background, as the defender outlined in a BBC interview in 2002: 'I was very

194

proud, and still am, to have represented Black and Central Africa at the World Cup. But we had the erroneous belief that we would return as millionaires. We got back home without a penny in our pockets.'

He went on to back up Mulamba's assertion that the team had been robbed of its bonuses: 'Before the Yugoslavia match we learned that we were not going to be paid, so we refused to play.'

Ilunga then went on to claim that Joseph Mobutu had intervened and that dire warnings had been issued against the players: 'After the Yugoslavia match he sent his presidential guards to threaten us. They closed the hotel to all journalists and said that if we lost 4–0 to Brazil, none of us would be able to return home.'

Which might explain why, with the score at 3–0 and with just a few minutes left on the clock, he rushed from his wall and lashed the ball up-field in a desperate attempt to waste a few precious seconds. There had been patronising suggestions in 1974 that Ilunga did not fully understand the rules of football, that he had thought he was allowed to kick the ball as the referee had blown his whistle. The player utterly dispelled those suggestions in a later interview: 'I did that deliberately. I was aware of football regulations, but I did that deliberately. I did not have a reason to keep on playing and getting injured while those who would benefit financially were seated on the terraces watching. It doesn't work like that. Why should I continue playing while other people are getting paid for it? I preferred to do that and get a red card, but the referee was quite lenient and only gave me a yellow card. I did that deliberately, I don't regret it at all.'

Ilunga admitted the players had been well rewarded for reaching the finals: 'Mobutu was like a father to us . . . He gave each of us a car and a house . . . But his generals were so jealous of us he had to give them a car each to keep them quiet.'

The defender does not elaborate further on whether he believes the president was directly behind the intimidation, or whether that jealousy drove Mobutu's men to take the matter into their own hands, but he does make it quite clear the frightened footballers were taking the threats seriously.

The Zaire players were allowed to return home, but not to the hero's welcome they had dreamed of. Instead, they became largely forgotten figures, shunned by the establishment, Ilunga pointing out in that interview almost three decades later, 'Look at me now, I'm living like a tramp.'

The true story of what happened in 1974 may never be fully uncovered, but the available evidence suggests there was no high-level collusion, no official conspiracy as such. Rather, it seems, Zaire's capitulation was down to corruption, the players' spirit sucked from them after learning their lives were not about to be altered thanks to the man, or men, who absconded with their riches. As Mulamba admitted, 'Of course, it is all about the money.'

Martin Buchan says he has no recollection of rumours of any kind and does not personally buy into the conspiracy theory anyway: 'No, I don't remember anything being said . . . But by then, it was too late in the day anyway, nothing we could do about it. As far as Zaire go, I think they'd possibly just given their all in the first game, Yugoslavia got them at the right time, and then they lifted themselves because Brazil was always going to be a big game for them . . . But I don't think you were looking for Zaire to create an upset, were you?'

Denis Law has heard the stories over the years, says there were some suggestions made at the time, but it is not something he has dwelt upon either: 'There were some rumours going around. Brazil to knock in the three they needed, Yugoslavia to score that many . . . but it was all over for us anyway.'

A familiar smile breaks across Denis's face as he pauses, before adding, 'We knew there was something . . . But you can't say it, can you . . . ?'

12

AFTERMATH

Three days after the squad had returned from the finals, and with euphoria still running high, Tennent Caledonian Breweries displayed excellent public-relations thinking when the company organised a photocall with Willie Ormond.

The brewers had struck a deal on the eve of the World Cup that had the potential to cost them a significant sum. As it was, with the team failing to progress beyond the initial group stage, the performance-related package attracted great publicity but cost them a relatively small amount.

Tapping into the mood of the nation, Tennent's upped the figure from £7,500 to a nice round £10,000 and photographs of a beaming 'Mr W.H. Finlay, sales director' handing the cheque over to Ormond appeared in all the national newspapers.

'We felt that we wanted to increase our negotiated fee because of the performance of the Scots,' he told reporters, before going on to praise, 'their tremendous dedication to the job, and of how they fought so magnificently'.

In the 1970s that fee was a respectable sum of money but not unaffordable for such a successful company, and it certainly paid off in terms of publicity. It was announced the cash would be divided equally between the players, the manager, and the trainers,

Hugh Allan and Ronnie McKenzie. Each would get the princely sum of £400.

A number of the men in that 1974 squad went on to make a very good living from the game, others would have been comfortably off in their retirement, but not one got rich purely as a result of being among that group in West Germany, despite the promises churned out by their extrovert business manager.

The players recall Bob Bain arriving out of nowhere and then vanishing just as quickly, rather like his pledge to make them all millionaires.

Davie Hay remembers him as a larger-than-life character and smiles at the thought of what Bain actually delivered: 'He was going to make us millions! What we got out of it was a sponsored car, a Vauxhall VX490, which you had for a year then you could buy at a discount price if you wanted to keep it. Then there was the record, so that was a night out in London with Rod Stewart, but not a lot of money. I think if we were lucky, counting the car, we wouldn't even have made a thousand pounds each.'

While the squad had no further dealings with the businessman, Hay very nearly had the chance to ask him a few questions later that year: 'After the World Cup I've signed for Chelsea and I'm driving round Piccadilly Circus. Who do I see but Bob Bain, and he recognised me . . . must have been the VX490! He waves to me and I'm thinking, "There's that Bob Bain, I'm going to stop and see him." I wasn't going to do anything, but I would have liked to speak to him. Before I can find somewhere to stop, he's disappeared. Again!'

None of the players expressed any jealousy about the sums the leading modern-day footballers can earn; they enjoyed playing when they did. But Davie Hay admits there is that lingering feeling that he and his contemporaries were victims of bad timing: 'That was just the start of it . . . There certainly wasn't the commercial side to the game that there is now.'

'Ah, the car . . .' laughs John Blackley. 'I remember the car. I don't know about the rest of the lads, I thought the car was ours, but it was only for a year. It was a lovely car, but I didn't buy it at the end. There were always contentious moments about what was in the big pot. We had ideas we were all going to get thousands, but it never quite worked out like that. There was a bit of money, but not a great deal.'

As a junior member of the squad, Jim Stewart had little input into such dealings, but vividly remembers Bain's promises and him arriving for showdown talks before the players flew off on their travels: 'He turned up on the morning of the England match to have a meeting with the committee, Billy Bremner and Denis Law and the other top guys. They were to do this deal and all of a sudden it came out that there was massive amounts of money to be earned here . . . Just my luck, it never materialised! I can't remember getting anything out of it. There was a big falling-out too over the arrangement with adidas and we ended up taking the stripes off the boots. There we were, all these players heading off to the World Cup finals, and we were sitting round the dinner table picking the stripes of these boots because they hadn't come up with the deal we wanted. If you look at the pictures from the games you'll see they're all wearing plain black boots: no stripes. They couldn't agree a fee, so we said, "OK we'll bin that" . . . and we ended up with nothing!'

That particular disagreement arose ahead of the opener against Zaire, when the players discovered adidas were paying the West Germans £3,000 each to wear their boots. The Scots demanded £1,000 a man; the company offered around £300. A rival firm tried to step in. Stylo Matchmaker – famous for their earlier tie-up with George Best – were keen to get involved, and prepared to fly negotiator Paul Ziff out to Germany to strike a deal. It was suggested they were ready to pay the squad a lump sum of £37,500 to wear their boots, but nothing seems to have come of it and the players took to the pitch with their doctored footwear.

'Nothing' was exactly what Danny McGrain recalls getting: 'I don't remember getting anything! Davie got a thousand pounds? Better off than me, I'll have to speak to him about that! Oh yeah,

Bob Bain . . .' He smiles and shakes his head. 'The millionaire! He was a big American guy, he made all these promises, and we were like wee dogs just waiting to be fed, "OK Bob, all right Bob . . ." My car was OK, it was fine, but it was too big and I needed to get something cheaper to run. I'm sure Sandy crashed about three of them! Bob Bain appeared like Aladdin out of the lamp . . . and disappeared just as fucking quick!'

Much like Bain, the '74 squad disintegrated rapidly in the wake of the finals. That group of players would never again be called together to represent their country. Some would go on to carve out glowing international careers; others would never again play for Scotland. For all of them, after a brief holiday, it was about getting back to club football.

The season 1974–75 would be a tumultuous one for goalkeeper David Harvey and his Leeds team-mates Billy Bremner, Peter Lorimer, Joe Jordan and Gordon McQueen. It began with the Charity Shield at Wembley, a game in which Bremner got himself sent off for fighting with Kevin Keegan, and he was subsequently fined £500 and banned for eleven matches. Brian Clough had been the shock choice to replace the new England boss Don Revie, and his tempestuous reign at Elland Road would last just forty-four days. The steadying hand of Jimmy Armfield led the Yorkshire club to the European Cup final, where they lost in that controversial match with Bayern Munich, but the defending champions could finish no higher than ninth in the English First Division. All five would remain with Leeds for a number of years; Bremner would go on to manage the club, Lorimer in later life becoming a director, then ambassador.

The four Celtic players returning to domestic duties would also experience mixed fortunes during that campaign. The team won both cup competitions up for grabs, but saw their record-breaking run of nine successive league titles ended by rivals Rangers, Celtic finishing in third place, behind runners-up Hibernian. Davie Hay had left long before then, joining Chelsea after a contractual dispute. Remarkably, he never played for his country again. Kenny Dalglish had three more years at Celtic Park before moving to Liverpool and becoming one of the most celebrated Scottish players of all time, while Jimmy Johnstone had that one final season with his beloved 'Hoops' before an itinerant four years brought his marvellous career to a close. Danny McGrain would remain with Celtic for a further thirteen years, and would later return to the club in a coaching capacity. He played almost fifty matches during that 1974–75 campaign, a remarkable statistic given what he had discovered on his return from West Germany: 'I went to the World Cup weighing eleven stone, four pounds and came home at nine stone. I'd been away six or seven weeks and when we got back to the hotel in Glasgow the first thing my wife, Laraine, said was, "What's wrong with you?" Nobody had said, "Danny, you're losing a lot of weight." I was drinking a lot of liquids, every game I had my head under the water tap filling up my system . . . I don't know how I got through it. Thankfully I didn't know, thankfully I didn't go into a coma. It sounds very dramatic now, but I could have died.'

McGrain struggled badly in his first few days back in Scotland: he felt lethargic and had an unquenchable thirst. A non-drinker, he even tried Mackeson Stout in a bid to alleviate the problem, but eventually realised he had to go to hospital, where he was diagnosed with diabetes. Thanks to the correct medication he was able to continue his career without interruption, finally retiring almost a decade and a half later.

For the Manchester United players in the squad it would be a season in the second tier of English football, but a highly successful one, as Tommy Docherty led his revamped side to promotion back to the top flight. It would be Willie Morgan's last with United, he then returned to former club Burnley, and Jim Holton also left soon after, for a brief spell with Sunderland. Martin Buchan's time at Old Trafford lasted considerably longer, extending until 1983, by which time he had made 456 appearances for the club. He collected a total of thirty-four Scotland caps, Holton gathered just one more, Morgan none at all.

Across Manchester, City had two players returning from international duty. Willie Donachie, who had not even made the bench in West Germany, was one of the young rising stars at Maine Road. He would play more than 350 times for the club, and didn't retire until 1990, having made thirty-five appearances for his country along the way. City finished the season in eighth place, but by then the legendary Denis Law had hung up his boots. Having been told he would only be likely to feature for the first team in the case of emergencies, Law had thought seriously about retiring. After two games in the pre-season Texaco Cup tournament, he had made up his mind and called a halt to his glittering career.

Hibernian were the only other club to have multiple Scottish representatives at the finals. John Blackley and Erich Schaedler were two of the stars of the thrilling Easter Road side of the early seventies, and enjoyed good seasons in 1974–75. Hibs lost out in the title race to eventual champions Rangers only in the closing weeks of the campaign, and reached the Scottish League Cup final, where they were beaten 6–3 by Celtic at Hampden. Blackley would play three more games for Scotland, while Schaedler would never add to the solitary cap he won before the finals.

The two back-up goalkeepers were Thomson Allan and Jim Stewart. Allan, an unused substitute for all three group matches, continued his career with Dundee, the Dens Park side finishing sixth in that campaign to easily secure a place in the following season's inaugural Premier Division. Stewart, the youngest member of the squad, had always known he was just going along for the experience, but was to have disappointments in the future: 'I was amazed to get the call-up because at that time Peter McCloy was playing with Rangers, Ally Hunter had moved to Celtic, there was Bobby Clark at Aberdeen. I had been taken along as the younger goalkeeper, one for the future, and I knew what to expect. By the time the next World Cup came round I was with Middlesbrough and had been in most of the squads but got left out for the finals, and then the first game after Argentina '78 we went to play Austria and I got called back into the squad, stayed in for another period of time, and then I was left out again, didn't make the '82 World Cup, and then came back in right after that. That was frustrating, there was the realism I suppose that I'd at least been to one . . . but it could have been three.'

Sandy Jardine, the only Rangers player at the finals, would be celebrating a first league title by the summer of 1975 and would go on to lift honours aplenty with the Ibrox side, before an impressive spell with Hearts saw him voted the Football Writers' Player of the Year more than a decade later.

Peter Cormack saw no action in West Germany, but played his part for Liverpool that season as they finished second in the English First Division, pipped to the title by two points by Derby County. Donald Ford went back to Hearts, serving the club for a further two years and becoming a Tynecastle legend, but, like Cormack, was never again called up by Scotland. Tommy Hutchison did remain part of the international set-up for another year or so, and had a lengthy career with Coventry, Manchester City and a host of other clubs before finally retiring in his mid-forties.

* * *

In the history of the Scottish national football team there have perhaps been better sides than that 1974 vintage, better individual players from different eras than some of those who shone in West Germany. But there is a very strong argument to be put for that team being the most successful this nation has ever produced. That group came closer than any other to making it through from the initial group stage at a World Cup finals, and did so without losing a match and having enhanced their reputations along the way.

Among that squad were players who made a huge impact in their careers at both club and international level, who performed alongside some excellent footballers and achieved great things. Who better than them, the men who were out there flying the flag for their country, to assess the true standing of that '74 side?

Among them was Joe Jordan, who would become one of the true legends of the Scottish game. In actual fact, he had all but guaranteed that the night his diving header buried deep into the Czechoslovakia net at Hampden Park to secure a long-overdue return for Scotland to the top table of world football. He would enjoy great success at club level, and personally with the national team, but still looks back at that squad of 1974 with a genuine fondness; he knows just how special that group of players was: 'What made it a special squad? Guys like Danny McGrain: Danny was a hard player, he would intimidate opponents just with his presence, his reputation. He was as hard as nails but still had all the qualities needed at the top level: he played the game on the front foot, he was your attacking full-back and, remember, he did it on both sides of the park. Billy Bremner typified for the supporters what it meant to play for Scotland; it meant an awful lot to him. He wanted to play against the best players because he wanted to prove he was one of the best players, he was a firebrand, but there was a lot more to him than that; he could change a game from midfield and he scored an incredible amount of important goals, particularly for Leeds. Then there was Kenny Dalglish and Denis Law . . . Kenny was cute, he'd get the ball with his back to goal, he could hold it in, or he could turn you and bend it into the top corner. Great player. Denis was the man – whether it was with Scotland or Manchester United, Denis was the man. You had Charlton, you had Best at Old Trafford, but Denis was 'The King'. He had an aura about him, he had a track record and he could score goals from anywhere. He was unique, a world-class striker.

'I was in three World Cup squads, but that was the first one, and the way I look at it – I wouldn't say we underachieved, but there were missed opportunities there. If things had been slightly different then I think Scotland could have progressed . . . If we could have got through that stage, maybe beaten Brazil or got those extra goals, we would have grown in stature, grown in confidence, grown into a team that would have maybe surprised a few countries there.'

Davie Hay acknowledges the previous generation of Scottish footballers, the sixties stars, were outstanding but makes the argument that in his era the big difference was that the team he was part of actually delivered, something his predecessors, despite all their talents, had failed to: 'You had Denis Law, Ian St John, Jim Baxter, Dave MacKay . . . Fantastic players . . . Probably you could almost say they might have been better than us, but they couldn't make it happen, couldn't reach the finals . . . I remember them losing that play-off to Czechoslovakia [in 1961] . . . but I think Willie Ormond got a group together and it gelled. He made it work, we made it work.'

Denis Law, of course, spanned the generations, at last taking his World Cup finals bow against Zaire, and although his role on the park was somewhat limited by then, he was still a huge inspiration to the rest of the class of '74, as Hay recalls: 'This was a guy I used to idolise as a kid. I called him the first of the Scottish superstars, and he always will be in my mind. Rather than be intimidated, you actually got a massive boost to your confidence knowing you were playing with a guy like him.'

Law himself rates that '74 squad very highly, and he is better placed than anyone else to make comparisons between it and the sides of the sixties: 'It was a good team . . . Good players . . . Led by Billy Bremner, who not only was a terrific player, he was a good captain as well, but we had a few players in those days who when you went on the field all had a great influence. Just think about the guys we had . . . Wee Jimmy Johnstone . . . If Jimmy was playing today, he would be another Messi. In fact, I think he added to my cartilage problems, because he'd have the ball and I'd think he was going to give it to me, but he'd jink, then I'd set myself, then he'd be off in another direction, and the whole time I'm spinning back and fore trying to get into position. What a fantastic player he was. We had some great, great players.'

So, was that team as good as those Denis had played in during the previous decade?

'Definitely! Oh, definitely, yes. It was like a production line of fantastic players. If you think that most English clubs had a number of Scottish lads in their team, and they weren't just run-of-the-mill squad members, they were the top men. We had a happy team. I don't know how it is today, but we were all pals – enemies when playing against each other for our clubs, but with Scotland we were pals. We liked to have a drink after the game, a few beers, there was a great team spirit, but not only that, we had players who could play football, really play football. These were special guys you could rely on to battle for you. I don't know if we could have gone on to win that World Cup had we got through, but we wouldn't have been far short.'

John Blackley is another who admits it was a childhood dream come true to line up alongside the 'Lawman', but points to the overall strength of the group as being the major factor in their success: 'It was a great time to be in a Scottish squad. When you look back at that World Cup, Davie Hay was unbelievable, he had an engine, with ability. What a player and what a combination in midfield with Bremner. You had one who could take the ball, dictate the play, and one who was back in the box, defending the one minute, driving forward the next. Peter Lorimer was a good player, a really good player ... and Danny was world class. Everywhere you looked in that squad there were just fantastic footballers. Willie Ormond knew that he had good players and we had a great leader in Billy Bremner. Willie saw sense in giving them the responsibility and in many ways just stood back, organised and let them get on with it. He could rely on us, on them. Bremner was a fantastic leader and, not only that, he was a great Scottish player. It was an incredible time and I'm just proud to have been part of that squad.'

Martin Buchan feels it was a group that quickly adapted to the demands of playing in the World Cup finals, largely down to the talent contained within it: 'It wasn't daunting in any way. We just got on with it ... It was a thoroughly enjoyable experience. I probably enjoyed '74 better than '78, that's for sure.'

Was that 1974 team the best he played with at international level?

'The '78 team that beat Holland wasn't bad, you know . . . weren't as good against Peru and Iran right enough . . . ! It's difficult to say, but it was certainly a very good team with very good players in those '74 finals. And I think we proved that.'

Peter Lorimer was among the most decorated of the players in that squad, boasting a haul of winner's medals as part of a Leeds United team that had dominated the English game in the years leading up to the finals. There was a healthy Scots contingent in that star-studded Elland Road line-up; at club level Lorimer was used to playing with the best against the best, but his time in that Scottish squad was, he says, even more rewarding: 'I got the buzz because I was playing for Scotland . . . The buzz when you walk down that tunnel onto the pitch at Hampden with 100,000 in those days was unbelievable. We didn't get the fortunes of money for playing, but you can't take that away from us, those experiences . . . playing in the World Cup, playing against England . . . It was a great time. In Germany we played bloody well, we had a good set of lads . . . I'm maybe biased, but in my opinion I don't think there's any question that's the best Scotland team that's ever gone to a competition like that. The quality, the number of quality players we had was unbelievable, and in all positions right through the team. We were a very strong outfit . . .'

At that point Peter starts to run through the squad from goalkeepers to strikers. Each time he pauses, he remembers another name, his smile broadening, the memories of individuals, of that team, flooding back.

'. . . And we had good substitutes as well, players who could come on and change a game for you. We were a right good team.'

As has been documented earlier in this book, and in countless other places over the years, they were also a difficult group to handle on occasion, and none more so than their leader, the late, great Billy Bremner. Peter Lorimer was closer to Billy than anyone else in that Scotland side and has countless tales to tell of the man who was his captain at both club and international level: 'Oh, he was brilliant. Brilliant. He was the most amazing person I know because he was a bad trainer, he liked a drink, he liked a smoke . . . but on a match day, Billy could do the ninety minutes. There were times down here when Vicki [Bremner's wife] went home for a few days and he would go out drinking and Don Revie would find out and give him a bollocking. He would say, "If I don't do it on Saturday, then you can have a go at me." And he'd go out and he'd be brilliant. When you'd go out and do cross-country runs – we used to train very hard with Revie – Billy would get tailed off, miles back, and the lads would be having a bit of a go at him and he'd say, "It's not about fucking cross-country runs, it's about what you do on the pitch on a Saturday," and to be fair, he had this in-built stamina, and he'd go out there and play fantastic. He was an amazing little character.'

He was also a problematic little character, regularly getting into scrapes. With Bremner there was, it seems, always a fine line and he crossed it more than most: 'Billy was a handful. When he was with Leeds he was usually OK because Revie was strong, but when he got up there and relaxed with the lads, he loved it and he was right in the middle of it. I used to always have to drive him up and drive him back when we were going to the matches because he wasn't capable of doing it himself. There was one game we went up and he was having his testimonial and after the match he had to go to Stirling to organise something with Alex Smith and Davie Cattenach [respectively the former Stirling Albion manager and player, and both lifelong friends of Bremner's]. Billy went off in my car and he said he'd pick me up at eleven o'clock the next morning. I'm sat there in the North British Hotel. Eleven o'clock, twelve o'clock, one o'clock . . . no Billy, so I rang Don Revie, because we were playing in London on the Saturday, and I told him Billy hadn't turned up. He liked bollocking me, so he says, "What have you done?" and I said, "Nothing." I explained he'd gone to Stirling, which is only half an hour from Glasgow, and that I'd lent him the car but that he hadn't shown up to collect me. So he told me to forget about Billy, to get the train back down and to come into Elland Road the following morning for training. So I'm sitting there and this fellow's walking around with the board as they did in hotels in them days, and it says "Phone call for Mr Lorimer". It was Billy. I says, "Where are you?" and he says, "I'm at Scotch Corner." He's nearly home! "I'm just sobering up," he says, "and I've only just realised it's your fucking car I'm driving." So, you can imagine the kind of situations I had with Billy. I had all the hassle with him . . . Not that I was an angel, but I knew when enough was enough . . . Billy just never knew when to stop.'

It was an era when alcohol was a big part of a professional footballer's life. It was accepted by the managers, indeed many joined in, but only as long as the drinking stopped a few days before the matches. The players back then trained hard, on many occasions it was how they worked through their hangovers, but the best of them, like Bremner, still performed when it mattered most: on the pitch on a Saturday, or a Wednesday night.

The sessions in the pub were seen as an important part of team bonding, and that 1974 squad certainly indulged enthusiastically. That played a part in forming a tightly knit unit, as did their whole-hearted approach to training sessions and to the games. But, according to goalkeeper Jim Stewart, there was an even more crucial aspect: a mutual respect shared by all in the group: 'When you think back to the players we had. Top, top players. Phenomenal really . . . a great squad and a good camaraderie . . . Nobody, not even the best of them, thought they were better than anyone else, they treated us all the same, and that was so, so important.'

That squad went to the World Cup finals having amassed 307 caps between them. They were, in the main, a relatively experienced bunch at club level, with a number of them in addition able to boast a significant international background, although, as has already been touched on, the finals were an entirely different experience for all.

Only fourteen of them got a taste of what it felt like to play in a World Cup that year. The starting eleven selected by Willie Ormond against Zaire had never previously lined up together for Scotland, and would never do so again. Similarly, the team chosen to face both Brazil and Yugoslavia – Buchan and Morgan replacing Blackley and Law from the opener – was an entirely new combination and only ever started those two matches. Tommy Hutchison, a substitute for Dalglish in the first and third games, was the only other player to see any action.

It is a squad that is fondly remembered by Scottish football fans of a certain age, revered perhaps, given what was achieved and the heartbreaking nature of the exit from the tournament. And yet, it was dismantled rapidly and ruthlessly.

Those twenty-two players earned, between them, a further 284 appearances for their country following their West German adventure. But eighty of those went to Kenny Dalglish, almost fifty to Danny McGrain and thirty-eight to Joe Jordan. Two of the younger squad members who were not utilised during the finals, Gordon McQueen and Willie Donachie, collected an additional twenty-nine and twenty-four caps respectively, while nineteen apiece were added by Martin Buchan and Sandy Jardine.

Eight of the players, among them legends such as Peter Lorimer, Billy Bremner and Jimmy Johnstone, earned only a handful of caps after the finals. Jim Holton picked up just one more, and seven – Thomson Allan, Donald Ford, Willie Morgan, Erich Schaedler, Peter Cormack, Denis Law and, incredibly, Davie Hay – never again played for Scotland.

Some were admittedly nearing the end of their playing careers and fell victim to the natural selection process that governs football at all levels; they were replaced by younger, fitter (although not necessarily better) men as the manager looked to the future, but others could rightly have expected to have had more time on the international stage, passing on their experience to the next generation.

As it turned out, that next generation, and those that followed, did not do at all badly. Having waited sixteen years to return to the World Cup, the Scots were about to embark on a glorious run, at least in terms of qualifying for the finals.

The 1978 tournament saw Scotland once again in a three-team group with old foes Czechoslovakia and near neighbours Wales. The campaign began with defeat in Prague, but back-to-back home wins set up a decider with the Welsh, which their FA chose, bizarrely, to stage at Anfield. The Tartan Army descended on the stadium en masse, creating a phenomenal atmosphere as Don Masson stroked home a late penalty – controversially awarded after it seemed Joe Jordan, rather than Joey Jones, had handled the ball – before two of the heroes of '74, Martin Buchan and Kenny Dalglish, linked up, the Liverpool forward heading in the clincher in a 2–0 success.

Ally MacLeod named just six of those who had been in West Germany for the ill-fated trip to Argentina: Buchan and Dalglish joined by Sandy Jardine, Willie Donachie, Gordon McQueen and Joe Jordan.

The striker scored the Scots' opening goal of the tournament, but MacLeod's men folded, losing 3–1 to Peru before an equally embarrassing 1–1 draw with Iran. The tournament ended with a stirring 3–2 win over Holland, Archie Gemmill netting one of the all-time classic goals, but the return home to Glasgow was in stark contrast to that of four years previously. There were no cheering throngs at the airport, no open-topped bus parade, no civic reception to honour their efforts.

It was to be three finals in a row in 1982, Scotland topping a five-country group that included Northern Ireland – who also made it as runners-up – Sweden, Portugal and Israel. With Jock Stein now in charge, the only defeat came in Lisbon at the end of the qualifying campaign, by which time the section had already been tied up.

The Scots again failed to emerge from the group stage in Spain, goal difference killing them off once more. A 5–2 win over New Zealand was followed by a 4–1 thumping by Brazil. Joe Jordan gave

Scotland the lead in the decider against the Soviet Union, but their opponents hit back and it took a late Graeme Souness goal to earn a 2–2 draw. By then the class of '74 had been stripped back to three: Danny McGrain, Joe Jordan and Kenny Dalglish the only survivors from Germany.

The 1986 World Cup finals were in Mexico and the sands of time had caught up with the previous generation. Kenny Dalglish almost made it but was a late call-off through injury. None of the others was included.

Alex Ferguson, then Aberdeen manager, took charge of the side for the tournament, the Scots having qualified via a two-legged play-off with Australia, but only after a night of high emotion in Cardiff. A 1–1 draw against Wales had kept Scottish hopes on track, Davie Cooper having equalised with a late penalty, but as the match drew to a close, Jock Stein collapsed near the dugout and died soon after.

As for the finals, in a tough group Scotland had lost narrowly to both West Germany and Denmark, but still had a chance to make progress by beating Uruguay in their final game. The South Americans had José Batista sent off in the first minute but managed to hold out for the 0–0 draw, which saw them, and not the Scots, qualify for the knockout stages.

1990 saw a fifth successive qualification, as runners-up behind Yugoslavia, and ahead of France, but Andy Roxburgh's men were to suffer crushing disappointment in Italy, losing their opening match 1–0 to Costa Rica. A 2–1 victory over Sweden revived hopes, but they were snuffed out in the last match, Brazil snatching the winner in the eighty-second minute.

The run set in motion by Tommy Docherty, Willie Ormond and their players two decades earlier finally ground to a halt with the Scots failing to reach USA '94. Craig Brown did lead his side to the 1998 finals in France, where they had the honour of kicking off the tournament against holders Brazil. They lost out only to a late Tom Boyd own goal, but that campaign ended in ignominy as Craig

Burley was sent off during a 3–0 humbling by Morocco to leave the side bottom of Group A, their only point gained in a 1–1 draw with Norway.

Since then, successive campaigns have ended in failure, some less gloriously than others.

Four finals have come and gone without Scotland. The nation's reputation – so high in 1974 that the managers of Brazil and West Germany were talking of the team as genuine contenders to win the World Cup – has plummeted as the country has slid down the world rankings.

Under Gordon Strachan there has been something of a revival; certainly there are encouraging signs as a crop of young talent emerges, but even reaching another finals seems to become more and more difficult as each tournament passes.

The break-up of Europe two decades ago has made competition for places at the top table yet more fierce. The 2018 finals will be staged in Russia, where more than fifty members of UEFA will be battling it out for nine or ten places. It will be a demanding task, a far cry from the much more straightforward route taken by those heroes of 1974.

Theirs might have been a less onerous campaign, certainly there were far fewer matches, but the pressures were the same, particularly after such a lengthy period of time and repeated failures to qualify.

The players who finally brought that run to an end have spoken in this book of the crushing weight of expectation, of the relief of finally reclaiming a place in the higher echelons of the world game. It was a pressure they had both the skills and temperament to handle, and they went on to prove that in the tournament itself, before creating history as they were eliminated in the cruellest way possible.

Those footballers revived interest in the national team at home and reinforced its reputation abroad; they inspired fans and future generations, and they will long be remembered for it.

After years of hurt, years of frustration, they achieved what others could not.

David Harvey. Danny McGrain and Sandy Jardine. John Blackley, Martin Buchan and 'six foot two, eyes of blue, big Jim Holton's after you'. Davie Hay and inspirational captain Billy Bremner. Peter Lorimer, Joe Jordan, Kenny Dalglish, Tommy Hutchison, Willie Morgan.

And the 'Lawman'. The legendary Denis Law, who eventually made it to the World Cup finals with Scotland just in time to call a halt to his glittering career. It was a fitting swansong for one of the game's greats, and it meant everything to him.

'It was just . . . it was just a dream. Playing for my country was special, playing for my country at a World Cup? Oh, dear! We had watched World Cups on television and seen these fantastic Brazilians and the rest . . . To be involved in it, it was like winning my first cap all over again, that tells you how much it meant to me. It was such a privilege to be part of it, to be part of that team. It's something I will never, ever forget.'

13

THE MANAGER

Falkirk-born Willie Ormond began his playing career with nearby Stenhousemuir, but after just a few appearances he was signed by Hibernian in November 1946 for the princely fee of £1,200. He would become an Easter Road legend, part of the celebrated 'Famous Five' forward line alongside Bobby Johnstone, Lawrie Reilly, Gordon Smith and Eddie Turnbull. All five scored in excess of 100 goals for the Edinburgh side, and despite recurring serious injuries – he suffered a broken leg on three separate occasions, in addition to a broken arm – Ormond collected three League Championship winner's medals during his decade and a half in the capital.

He finally left in 1961, seeing out his playing career with a year-long spell at home-town club Falkirk.

By then he had won six international caps, making his debut in a World Cup qualifier against England in April 1954. The Scots lost 4–2, but went to the finals in Switzerland as group runners-up. Ormond would play in both matches – despite it being a four-team group, each country played only two games – and having lost 1–0 to Austria in their opener, the Scots were destroyed 7–0 three days later by defending champions Uruguay. He would be in the international wilderness for almost five years before earning a surprise recall for a 1–0 defeat at Wembley, which was to prove to be his Scotland swansong, at least as a player.

Having spent a number of years as trainer with Falkirk, Ormond was unveiled as St Johnstone manager in 1967, and two years later led the Perth side to their first-ever League Cup final, which ended in a 1–0 defeat to the all-conquering Celtic side of that time. In 1970–71 St Johnstone achieved their highest-ever league placing, third in the First Division, qualifying for a debut in the UEFA Cup. Saints recorded memorable victories over SV Hamburg and Vasas Budapest, before going out to FK Zeljeznicar Sarajevo, a 1–0 win in the home leg well and truly wiped out by a 5–1 reverse in Yugoslavia.

Ormond's exploits and successes with St Johnstone had caught the eye of the Scottish Football Association, and after the flamboyant and controversial Tommy Docherty quit the national team to take over at Manchester United, Ormond – a well-respected and well-liked figure within the game – was seen as a much steadier and more reliable hand on the tiller. He was appointed on January 5th 1973, but just a month later suffered the worst possible start, a 5–0 thrashing by old enemy England at a snow-covered and frosty Hampden Park, the game held to 'celebrate' the centenary of the SFA.

The Home International Championship began with a 2–0 win in Wrexham, but there followed four straight defeats, to Northern Ireland and England in the same tournament, then against Switzerland and Brazil in friendlies.

Those matches were planned as warm-ups for the resumption of the World Cup qualifying campaign – Docherty having led the side to two victories over Denmark the previous autumn – and Ormond faced a winner-takes-all encounter with Czechoslovakia at Hampden Park. The 2–1 triumph sparked emotional scenes and clinched Scotland's place at West Germany '74, a World Cup finals from which they would emerge unbeaten – the only unbeaten side in the whole tournament – and yet still fall at the first hurdle.

The qualifying campaign for the 1976 European Championship finals got off to a poor start, a loss against Spain at Hampden followed by 1–1 draws in Valencia and away to Romania. When the

Scots finally secured their first victory, a 1–0 success in Denmark, it was quickly overshadowed by the 'Copenhagen nightclub incident', a late-night skirmish that saw five players – Joe Harper, Arthur Graham, Pat McCluskey, Willie Young and Billy Bremner – banned for life from the national team, a punishment that was later relaxed but left deep wounds and did Willie Ormond no favours.

The Scots failed to qualify for those finals, their only wins coming against the Danes, and with support for the manager apparently weakening within the corridors of power – Rankin Grimshaw, the Raith Rovers chairman and a Scottish FA board member, having pondered publicly 'perhaps another manager could do a better job with the players' – and after much speculation about his future, Ormond left Park Gardens in May 1977 to become Hearts boss.

His four and a half years in charge had certainly produced mixed results, but during that time Willie Ormond had done what no other Scotland manager had been able to. Not only did he return the nation to the top table of world football, but his team had also made a significant impact while there, and his players from that time have no doubts about the worth of his contribution.

Joe Jordan, the hero that October night in '73, believes Ormond was undervalued: 'I don't think he was given the credit that he should have been. He left me out of the first few squads; it was only when he saw me play in the European Cup final for Leeds against AC Milan that he took note of me and called me in. I was still a young man, on the bench that night at Hampden, but he had the wherewithal to bring me on to try to change the game. You make substitutions because things aren't quite clicking and that's what he did against Czechoslovakia. That was a big call, but those calls – they win you matches. He was a football man, he had football knowledge. He knew what he was doing. He wasn't a man who just picked the team and told them to go out and play, there was a thought process in everything he did. He had a bit of savvy about him, he knew how to read a game, he knew his players, and I think it showed in the success he had.'

Goalkeeper Jim Stewart agrees with that, pointing to Willie Ormond's man-management as being another factor in what he achieved: 'He was very relaxed, able to handle the big-name stars who were involved at that time, and he encouraged an attractive way of playing. We had good players, operating at the top level then, and the manager was able to integrate them into his team shape and get across his philosophy of how he wanted the side to play.'

There were strong characters in that Scotland set-up, young men who had amassed great experience at both club and international level, and had gained plaudits for their performances. Stewart believes Ormond was quick to realise he had to rely heavily on those players, that he had to get them working with him: 'He didn't dictate, he used dialogue, he spoke very closely with Billy Bremner, who was his captain, and I'm quite sure had an influence. In general he was pretty open-minded to suggestions from the players, but ultimately he was the manager and he certainly laid the tactics down.'

Davie Hay was one of the senior members of that squad. He had been 'capped' initially by Bobby Brown before being introduced to the very different managerial style of Tommy Docherty: 'I thought Docherty was geared for international football – I never worked with him at club level – The Doc had a way of lifting you, I enjoyed working with him, I definitely responded to his style of management. It was him who tarred me with the nickname the "Quiet Assassin" and I was sad to see him go to Manchester United.'

That meant Hay had a new boss to try to impress – he was fortunate to miss the 5–0 humiliation against England through injury, but when he did return to the national side he quickly discovered Ormond's strengths: 'You might think this is a daft thing to say, but he picked the best players and got the balance of the team right. You might say, "Well, that's a manager's job," but believe me, they can't all do it. Willie could. He struck the right blend, and it worked. Think about that Czechoslovakia game – he brought in

Tam Hutchison almost from nowhere, he put on Joe Jordan at just the right moment . . . A lot of good players around right enough, but he had the knack of choosing the right ones for the occasion. Wee Willie, in his quiet way, just picked the right team.'

Like Hay, Danny McGrain worked day to day with Jock Stein, an all-powerful manager, an intimidating presence. He found Willie Ormond to be an entirely different proposition: 'Willie was just a quiet wee guy,' he chuckles, before adding, 'I mean, how hard a job have you got when you're going to a World Cup with players like Billy Bremner and Denis Law, Peter Lorimer and Willie Morgan? I know Willie had got St Johnstone into Europe, but these guys had more experience at that level than he had, and he had the sense to use them. He certainly wouldn't have asked for advice on picking the team, but he didn't talk down to them, to any of us. If he had, he'd have lost their respect. He treated them like grown, experienced men. He was intelligent in how he handled the squad.'

Peter Lorimer recognises that side of the manager, but wonders now whether, given the strong characters who made up that squad, Willie Ormond's approach was not at least partly down to pragmatism: 'Willie was a lovely man, but I think in all honesty the job was maybe a bit too big for him. I think the pressure of the Scotland job and the kind of players . . . They were all a bit borderline, could go off the rails very easily and it was difficult. Willie was good, everything he did was good, but I think the job and the pressure, and the kind of players he took on was maybe too much for him, personally. Not only the pressure that was going on at the World Cup, but the pressure of the individuals that he was having to handle.'

One of the biggest decisions Ormond had to make was regarding Jimmy Johnstone. Having welcomed the winger back into the fold after his Largs escapade, the Celtic star had got involved in further trouble in Norway on the eve of the finals. The suspicion remains that Johnstone's non-appearance in West Germany was a form of punishment. It is a situation McGrain has long pondered: 'They were warm conditions, and Willie Morgan would work back the field more than wee Jimmy would, but I'd always thought Jimmy would play against Zaire. Even at two-nothing, struggling to get more goals, put Jimmy on for the last fifteen minutes and he might get you something. I think Willie had decided to put him on in the last game against Yugoslavia, wee Jimmy was warming up, but the ball never went out of play. I think he did want to let him be able to say he'd played in the finals. I just felt sorry for wee Jimmy, but as a manager at a World Cup you can't have feelings like that, you've got to do the right thing. Sensitivity doesn't come into it, you pick the right team for the right occasion, and at that time Willie Ormond did what he thought was best.'

It was not a decision Denis Law agreed with: 'I can't believe that he didn't play. My mind boggles . . . Can't believe it . . . That was a mistake by Willie. Jimmy Johnstone was, for me, one of the best players in the world. Ever.'

Had Jimmy played against Brazil or Yugoslavia, might Scotland have got the win that would have secured a place in the next phase? Law is unequivocal: 'Absolutely. Without any danger.'

John Blackley is another who believes leaving out 'Jinky' was perhaps the manager's one big fault in West Germany: 'I honestly look at the Brazil match, which was the vital one for us; if we get a result, that takes us through, and I feel Jimmy Johnstone would have been fouled relentlessly during the course of that game. The way he played he'd have got us free kicks, he'd have got guys sent off and he'd have taken us into dangerous areas. With Joe Jordan and big Jim Holton up there we'd have had a right few chances to score. For me, it was an error not to play Jimmy Johnstone in that game.'

If it was, Martin Buchan contends it was one of the few Ormond made during his time in charge of the national side: 'He generally picked the right team for the job. He wasn't particularly into tactics, and he was quieter than other managers I've had, but people demonstrate their football knowledge in different ways and he didn't get many of his judgement calls wrong. Tommy Docherty was laugh a minute, larger than life . . . Willie was shy and retiring when compared to The Doc, but he got the job done. We didn't really need a lot of coaching, not when you're playing at that level. As a back four you worked on set pieces with him, for and against, rehearsing. We all had to know who we were marking. The teams he picked would dictate the formation you played . . . and generally he made the right calls.'

Despite disagreeing with the manager over Jimmy Johnstone, Law is another who to this day holds Ormond in high regard: 'He was fantastic, a great football man. He was lovely. And he wanted the players to play attacking football, to give the crowd enjoyment. I did enjoy playing for him. There wasn't much discussion about the team or tactics, he realised we all had great experience; he just sent us out to play our football. He trusted us on the park.'

After leaving the Scotland job, Willie Ormond endured an unsuccessful three years at Tynecastle before crossing the capital to rejoin Hibernian, initially as assistant to former team-mate Eddie Turnbull, and then as manager. That lasted just a few months, ill health forcing Ormond to walk away from the pressures of the game, and he retired to help run the family pub in Musselburgh.

He died on May 5th 1984, aged just fifty-seven.

The sports writer Jim Reynolds penned a moving tribute to Willie in the next day's *Glasgow Herald*. Naturally, he listed Ormond's many achievements as player and manager, but he also offered more personal reflections, an insight into why the former national team boss would be missed by the many people he had encountered throughout his life in the game:

> The death of Willie Ormond will cast a giant shadow over Scottish football this morning. He was a nice man who contributed so much to our national sport, a man who, to my knowledge, did not have an enemy in the game. Who else could earn a living with both Hibernian

and Hearts and still be loved and respected by both sides? He helped both clubs until he decided his little public house in Musselburgh was the place he really wanted to be. I remember, when he was manager of Hearts and things were not going so well at Tynecastle I phoned the wee man and asked him if he had any problems. Willie said: 'Plenty, Jim, the beer delivery hasn't arrived yet.'

It was that kind of humour which made Willie so popular. When there were problems he would say: 'Let's have a wee wet.' It was his Navy jargon for having a couple of drinks to soothe whatever lay ahead. Willie Ormond was one of the best. Everyone in the game will miss him sadly.

GROUP 8 QUALIFYING CAMPAIGN: 1974 WORLD CUP

1972
Oct 18   Idraetsparken, Copenhagen   Attendance: 31,200

DENMARK   1–4 **SCOTLAND**
F. Laudrup (28)   Macari (17), Bone (19),
                                    Harper (83), Morgan (85)

Clark; Brownlie, Colquhoun, Buchan, Forsyth; Lorimer,
Bremner, Graham, Morgan; Macari (Dalglish 87), Bone
(Harper 64)

Nov 15   Hampden Park, Glasgow   Attendance: 47,109

SCOTLAND   2–0 **DENMARK**
Dalglish (2), Lorimer (48)

Harvey; Brownlie, Colquhoun, Buchan, Donachie;
Lorimer, Bremner, Graham, Morgan; Dalglish (Carr 70),
Harper

1973

May 2   Idraetsparken, Copenhagen   Attendance: 19,942

DENMARK   1–1 **CZECHOSLOVAKIA**
Bjornemose (15)   Petras (32)

June 2   Letna Stadion, Prague   Attendance: 17,432

CZECHOSLOVAKIA   6–0 **DENMARK**
Nehoda (46),
Vesely (56, 65, 80),
Bicovsky (57), Hagara (60)

Sept 26   Hampden Park, Glasgow   Attendance: 95, 786

SCOTLAND   2–1 **CZECHOSLOVAKIA**
Holton (40), Jordan (74)   Nehoda (32)

Hunter; Jardine, Holton, Connelly, McGrain; Morgan,
Bremner, Hay, Hutchison; Dalglish (Jordan 63), Law

Oct 17   Tehelne Pole, Bratislava   Attendance: 13,668

CZECHOSLOVAKIA   1–0 **SCOTLAND**
Nehoda (pen 15)

Harvey; Jardine, T. Forsyth, Blackley, McGrain; Morgan,
Dalglish, Hay, Hutchison; Jordan, Law (Ford 58)

	P	W	D	L	F/A	Pts
SCOTLAND	4	3	0	1	8–3	6
CZECHOSLOVAKIA	4	2	1	1	9–3	5
DENMARK	4	0	1	3	2–13	1

SQUAD DETAILS AT THE START
OF THE 1974 WORLD CUP FINALS

1   DAVID HARVEY   Leeds United   **Age 26   7 caps**
Signed for Leeds by Don Revie in February 1965, he replaced club legend Gary Sprake as regular first-choice keeper in 1972. Harvey joined Vancouver Whitecaps in 1980, before returning to Elland Road three years later, by which time Leeds had been relegated to the Second Division. He later had very brief spells with both Partick Thistle and Morton before retiring in 1987. He later moved to Sanday, one of the Orkney Islands, with his family and worked as a postman. David suffered a heart attack, from which he recovered, on Christmas Eve 2009.

Born in Leeds, he qualified for Scotland through his father, and made his debut in a 2–0 win over Denmark at the start of the '74 qualification campaign. He won sixteen caps, the last of which was against Finland in a 6–0 friendly win in September 1976. Harvey played in all three matches in West Germany.

2   SANDY JARDINE   Rangers   **Age 25   16 caps**
Signed for Rangers in 1965, making his debut a week after the club's most shocking defeat, against Berwick Rangers in the Scottish Cup in February 1967. After a success-laden Ibrox career, he moved to Hearts in 1982, later becoming player–assistant manager to Alex MacDonald. Sandy also had a spell as joint manager of the

Tynecastle club. He worked in broadcasting, and with Rangers in various positions, playing a major role in rallying the support in the wake of the Craig Whyte affair that led to the club being liquidated. In November 2012 it was revealed he had been diagnosed as suffering from throat and liver cancer.

He made his Scotland debut as a substitute for Davie Hay in a 2–0 European Championship qualifying win over Denmark in November 1970. His first start came eleven months later in the same competition, a 2–1 win over Portugal. He played all three matches in West Germany, and also in the 1–1 draw against Iran in the 1978 World Cup finals. He won thirty-eight caps, finishing off in a 3–1 home defeat to Belgium in a European Championship qualifier in December 1979.

3 DANNY McGRAIN Celtic　　　　　**Age 24**　　**12 caps**

His twenty-year playing career with Celtic began in 1967, with his debut coming in a League Cup tie against Dundee United in 1970. Danny made well over 600 appearances before retiring after a final season, 1987–88, with Hamilton. He fractured his skull in a game against Falkirk in 1972, and was diagnosed as suffering from diabetes after returning from the '74 finals. McGrain was manager of Arbroath from 1992–94 and later returned to Celtic, eventually becoming an important part of Neil Lennon's coaching team.

He made his Scotland debut in a Home International Championship 2–0 defeat to Wales in May 1973 at right-back, but won many caps at left-back, including all three matches in West Germany. Danny made two further appearances at the World Cup finals, against New Zealand and the USSR in 1982, winning his sixty-second and last cap in the latter match.

4 BILLY BREMNER Leeds United　　　　**Age 31**　　**48 caps**

Born in Stirling, Bremner enjoyed a stellar seventeen-year career with Leeds United, his contribution recognised by a statue being erected outside Elland Road. An inductee of both the Scottish and

English Football Halls of Fame, he wound down his playing career with Hull City and Doncaster Rovers. Billy became player–manager with Rovers before taking over at Leeds, but he failed to get the club promoted and was sacked in September 1988. He returned for another spell with Doncaster, leaving in 1991. Billy Bremner died on December 7th 1997 after suffering a heart attack, two days before his fifty-fifth birthday.

He made his Scotland debut in a 0–0 friendly draw with Spain in May 1965 and played all three games in West Germany, winning his fiftieth cap in the 0–0 draw with Brazil. His fifty-fourth and final appearance came in a 1–0 win in Denmark in a European Championship qualifier in September 1975, after which he was banned by the SFA as part of the 'Copenhagen Five' who had become embroiled in a nightclub incident. The ban was lifted in '76, but Bremner never played for Scotland again.

5   JIM HOLTON   Manchester United   Age 23   11 caps

Holton spent his entire playing career in England, coming to the fore after joining Manchester United from Shrewsbury in 1972. He had two spells in the North American Soccer League, as well as later stints with Sunderland and Coventry City, before injury forced him to retire at the age of thirty. He died after suffering a heart attack while at the wheel of his car on October 5th 1993. He was just forty-two.

Jim made his Scotland debut in May 1973 in a Home International Championship defeat in Wales, and six months later scored the equaliser against Czechoslovakia while winning just his sixth cap. He played all three games in West Germany. His international career lasted fewer than eighteen months, his fifteenth cap coming in a 3–0 friendly win over East Germany in October 1974.

6   JOHN BLACKLEY   Hibernian   Age 26   3 caps

John spent over a decade with Hibernian before leaving in 1978 for a year with Newcastle United. There followed spells with Preston and Hamilton (where he was player–manager), before a return to Easter Road to wind down his career in 1984. He combined coaching there with playing, taking over as manager until 1986. He was also boss at Cowdenbeath and has worked in coaching alongside Paul Sturrock at a number of clubs.

'Sloop' made his international debut in the 1–0 defeat in Czechoslovakia in October 1973 and earned just his fourth cap in his only appearance in West Germany, the 2–0 win over Zaire. He collected his last cap – making a total of seven – in a 3–1 friendly win over Sweden in April 1977.

7 JIMMY JOHNSTONE Celtic   Age 29   21 caps

In a fourteen-year spell with Celtic, 'Jinky' became a world-renowned player, his crowning glory coming as part of the Lisbon Lions team that won the European Cup in 1967. After leaving Celtic Park, the final four years of his playing career were spent in such diverse places as San Jose and Elgin. Voted Celtic's best-ever player in 2002, Jimmy died four years later after a battle with motor neurone disease.

The first of his remarkably small total of twenty-three caps was won in a 3–2 defeat to Wales in the Home International Championships in October 1964. His last appearance was in a European Championship qualifying 2–1 loss to Spain at Hampden in November 1974. Having been embroiled in the 'Largs rowing boat' incident prior to the '74 World Cup finals, he failed to feature in West Germany.

8 KENNY DALGLISH Celtic   Age 23   19 caps

Having emerged in the wake of the Lisbon Lions, Kenny spent eight years with Celtic until 1977, when Liverpool paid a British record transfer fee of £440,000 to entice him to Anfield. After a trophy-laden spell, he became player–manager in 1985. He enjoyed great success before resigning in 1991, only to re-emerge at Blackburn, where he won promotion, then the Premier League in

1995. He had later spells with Newcastle United and Celtic, as director of football then manager, before resuming managerial duties at Liverpool, winning the League Cup and reaching the FA Cup final in 2011–12.

Kenny made his international debut as a substitute in a 1–0 win over Belgium at Pittodrie in a European Championship qualifier in October 1971. He played all three games in West Germany and in Argentina 1978, and appeared twice in the '82 finals, against New Zealand and Brazil. Left out of the 1986 squad, a decision that sparked controversy at the time, but which was blamed on a knee-injury, he made his final appearance against Luxembourg, a 3–0 European Championship success at Hampden on November 12th 1986. His total of 102 caps is a Scottish record, and he is joint top-scorer for his country with Denis Law on thirty international goals.

9   JOE JORDAN   Leeds United   Age 22   11 caps

After a brief spell at Morton, Joe's entire playing career was away from home, most notably with Leeds, and after a £350,000 move – a record fee at the time between two English clubs – Manchester United, who he joined in 1978. He moved to Italy, becoming an AC Milan legend, before winding down his career with Southampton and Bristol City, where he was briefly player–manager. He has also taken charge of Hearts and Stoke City, was assistant to Liam Brady at Celtic and to Lawrie McMenemy at Northern Ireland, and has worked alongside Harry Redknapp at Portsmouth, Tottenham and QPR.

He made his international debut in a 1–0 Home International Championship defeat to England at Wembley in May 1973. His first goal was the famous winner against Czechoslovakia, a match in which he was collecting just his fourth cap. He played in all three games in West Germany and at Argentina '78, and in the 2–2 draw with the Soviet Union in '82, a match in which he won the last of his fifty-two international caps. He is the only Scot to have scored in three separate World Cup finals tournaments.

10   DAVIE HAY   Celtic   Age 26   24 caps

Having come through as part of the 'Quality Street Kids' alongside the likes of Dalglish and McGrain, Davie went on to play more than 200 games for Celtic before joining Chelsea in 1974. A detached retina, suffered during a match, left him blind in his right eye and he eventually retired in 1979 following a serious knee injury. Appointed Motherwell manager in 1981, Davie led them to an impressive promotion back to the Premier Division, before winning League and Cup honours as Celtic manager between 1983 and '87. After a spell in Sweden with Lillestrøm, he managed St Mirren, Livingston – where he won the League Cup – and Dunfermline.

Davie made his international debut in a Home International Championship encounter with Northern Ireland, a 1–0 victory in April 1970, and played all three games in West Germany, winning his final cap, his twenty-seventh, in the 1–1 draw with Yugoslavia.

11   PETER LORIMER   Leeds United   Age 27   14 caps

Dundee-born Peter made his Leeds debut at just fifteen, although it would be a further two years before he began to play regularly. Renowned for his powerful shooting, he was a major part of the Don Revie side of the sixties and seventies. Having left in '79, Lorimer returned to Elland Road between 1984 and '85, playing more than 700 games for Leeds and scoring a club record of 238 goals. In between he played for Toronto and Vancouver in the North American Soccer League and had a spell with York City. At the end of his playing days he became a pundit and columnist with the local media, and the fans' representative on the club's board of directors.

Lorimer made his Scotland debut in a 2–0 World Cup qualifying defeat in Austria in November 1969 but had to wait until May '71 before returning to the international side. He played in all three matches in West Germany, scoring the opening goal against Zaire with a trademark shot. He won twenty-one caps in total, the last of which was earned in a 1–1 draw with Romania in a European Championship qualifier in December 1975.

12 THOMSON ALLAN **Dundee** **Age 27** **2 caps**
After beginning his career with Hibernian, Thomson moved to
Dundee in 1971, helping the club win the Scottish League Cup in
'73. He had later stints with Hearts and Falkirk, among others,
before retiring in 1983.

He made his international debut in a 2–1 friendly defeat to West
Germany in Frankfurt in March 1974 and also played in the 2–1 win
in Norway in June, a World Cup warm-up. He never featured at the
World Cup finals, or again for his country.

13 JIM STEWART **Kilmarnock** **Age 20** **0 caps**
Five years with Kilmarnock was followed by a spell at
Middlesbrough, then a four-year period with Rangers. He also had
brief spells with Dumbarton, St Mirren and Partick Thistle before
announcing his retirement in 1986. He went on to become a highly
successful goalkeeping coach with various clubs, most recently
Rangers, and also holds that position with the Scottish international
team.

The only uncapped player in the squad, Jim was third-choice
keeper and had to wait three years before earning the first of his
two international appearances, as a substitute for Alan Rough in a
4–2 friendly win in Chile in 1977. His only start came in a European
Championship qualifier the following October, in a 3–2 win over
Norway.

14 MARTIN BUCHAN **Manchester United Age 25** **13 caps**
Appointed Aberdeen's youngest-ever captain, he led the club to
Scottish Cup success in 1970, before signing for Manchester United
two years later. He spent over a decade at Old Trafford, playing
more than 450 games and winning the FA Cup in 1977. He wound
down his career with Oldham, before retiring in 1985. He was
appointed Burnley manager that year but resigned after just four
months in the job, his last involvement in club football. He now
works with the Professional Footballers' Association in Manchester.

The first of his thirty-four caps was won as a late substitute in a 2–1 European Championship win over Portugal in October 1971, and he made his full debut against Belgium at Pittodrie the following month. He played against Brazil and Yugoslavia in the 1974 finals and in all three group matches in Argentina '78. He won just three more caps, in European Championship qualifiers the following season, the last of which came in a 1–0 loss in Portugal in November 1978.

15   PETER CORMACK   Liverpool   Age 27   9 caps
Peter spent seven years with Hibernian before moving south for successful spells with Nottingham Forest, Liverpool – where he won League, Cup and UEFA Cup honours – and Bristol City. In 1980 he returned to Easter Road and also played briefly for Partick Thistle, where he took over as manager until 1984. He also had a spell as assistant manager to Alex Miller at Hibernian, and managed Cowdenbeath – where he was sacked without playing a game – and Morton, leaving Cappielow in 2002.

Peter made his Scotland debut in a 1–1 friendly draw with Brazil in June 1966 and won his final cap in a 2–1 friendly defeat in Holland in December 1971. Despite his long absence from the team, he was called up for West Germany, but did not feature.

16   WILLIE DONACHIE   Manchester City   Age 22   11 caps
Born in Glasgow, Willie never played in his homeland, kicking off his long career with Manchester City in 1968. After more than a decade at Maine Road, and two periods in the North American Soccer League with Portland, he had stints with Norwich and Burnley, before seeing out his career with a successful six-year spell at Oldham. He retired in 1990. Donachie coached at various clubs and had a year in charge of Millwall, before taking up a post at the Newcastle United academy in December 2009.

Willie's first game for Scotland was a 2–0 friendly win over Peru in April 1972. He didn't play in West Germany but featured in two games at Argentina '78, the 1–1 draw with Iran and the 3–2 win over Holland. His last cap, his thirty-fifth, came in a 1–0 European Championship qualifying defeat in Portugal in November 1978.

17   DONALD FORD   Hearts   Age 29   3 caps

A Hearts legend, Ford played more than 250 games and scored almost 100 goals between 1964 and '76, when he left for a final season with Falkirk, a knee injury ending his playing career at the age of thirty-two. He was involved in persuading Wallace Mercer to buy Hearts in the early 1980s and was a renowned cricketer, representing his country in that sport too.

The first of his three caps came in the 1–0 defeat in Czechoslovakia in October 1973 as a substitute for Denis Law. He also replaced Law in the 2–1 friendly defeat in West Germany the following March and made his first and only start in a 2–0 win against Wales in the Home International Championship in the May of 1974. He did not feature during the World Cup finals.

18   TOMMY HUTCHISON   Coventry City   Age 26   8 caps

Tommy began his career with Alloa, before moving south for successful spells with Blackpool (1967–72) and Coventry City (1972–81). He spent a year at Manchester City – scoring for both sides in the 1981 FA Cup final, a 1–1 draw with Tottenham – and later in Hong Kong and for Burnley. He then revitalised his career with Swansea City, making his European debut in the European Cup Winners' Cup in September 1989 at the age of forty-one. He finally retired five years later, winding down his career in the Southern League with Merthyr Tydfil.

Hutchison made his Scotland debut in the memorable 2–1 win over Czechoslovakia in September 1973 and played as a substitute against Zaire and Yugoslavia at the World Cup finals. The last of his seventeen caps was won against Denmark in a European Championship qualifier in September '75, a 1–0 win. He was tipped for inclusion in the 1978 World Cup finals squad but did not get the call-up.

19   DENIS LAW   Manchester City   Age 34   54 caps

Aberdeen-born Law's stellar career – often blighted by injury – began at the age of just sixteen with Huddersfield. He was sold to Manchester City for £55,000 and then, after just one season, to Torino for a record fee of £110,000. Denis spent only one year in Italy before Manchester United bought him for £115,000, paving the way for the Lawman to become an Old Trafford legend. He is the only Scot to have been named European Footballer of the Year, collecting the award in 1964. After almost a decade with United, he saw out his career with a final season back at City, retiring in the summer of 1974.

Law made his international debut on October 18th 1958, scoring against Wales in Cardiff in a 3–0 win in the Home International Championships. He played just once in Germany, his only appearance at a World Cup final, in the 2–0 win over Zaire, winning his fifty-fifth and final Scotland cap. His tally of thirty international goals has been matched only by Kenny Dalglish.

20   WILLIE MORGAN   Manchester United   Age 29   19 caps

Morgan's career began in 1960 with Burnley, and after eight years at Turf Moor he moved to Manchester United, ending his career there by helping United to promotion back to the top flight in 1975. There followed a season back at Burnley and four years at Bolton, two spells in the North American Soccer League, and a final season with Blackpool before he retired in 1981.

Willie won his first cap in a 1–0 defeat to Northern Ireland in a European Championship qualifier in October 1967, but had to wait almost five years before his recall in a 2–0 friendly win over Peru. He played in all four World Cup qualifiers, scoring in the 4–1 win in Denmark in October '72, and started the games against Brazil and

Yugoslavia at the finals. The latter was the winger's last for his country, in which he won his twenty-first cap.

21   GORDON McQUEEN   Leeds United   Age 21   1 cap
Having begun his career with St Mirren, Gordon went on to enjoy long and successful spells with both Leeds United and Manchester United before retiring in 1985. He had a brief spell as manager of Airdrie, and coached at St Mirren and Middlesbrough, where he later joined the scouting staff.

Gordon's international debut came in a friendly defeat in Belgium just before the '74 World Cup finals, at which he was an unused squad member. He went on to score five goals in thirty games for Scotland, the last of which was a 2–0 defeat in Wales in the Home International Championships in May 1981.

22   ERICH SCHAEDLER   Hibernian   Age 24   1 cap
The son of a German prisoner of war, Biggar-born Schaedler began his career with Stirling Albion before becoming a key component of the exciting and successful Hibernian side of the early 1970s. Two spells with Hibs sandwiched a four-year stay at Dundee. He joined his last club, Dumbarton, in 1985 and took his own life in the Cardrona Forest on Christmas Eve that year, aged just thirty-six.

Erich played his one and only Scotland game in a 2–1 friendly defeat in West Germany in March 1974.

GROUP 2: 1974 WORLD CUP FINALS

June 13 5 p.m. Waldstadion, Frankfurt   Attendance: 62,000

BRAZIL   0–0 YUGOSLAVIA

June 14 7.30 p.m. Westfalenstadion, Dortmund Attendance: 25,000

ZAIRE   0–2 **SCOTLAND**
                                 Lorimer (26), Jordan (34)

Harvey; Jardine, Holton, Blackley, McGrain; Lorimer,
Bremner, Hay, Dalglish (Hutchison 75); Law, Jordan

June 18 7.30 p.m. Parkstadion, Gelsenkirchen   Attendance: 20,000

YUGOSLAVIA   9–0 **ZAIRE**
Bajevic (8, 30, 81),
Dzajic (14), Surjak (18),
Katalinski (22),
Bogicevic (35), Oblak (61),
Petkovic 65)

June 18 7.30 p.m. Waldstadion, Frankfurt   Attendance: 50,000

SCOTLAND   **0–0 BRAZIL**

Harvey; Jardine, Holton, Buchan, McGrain; Lorimer, Bremner, Hay, Morgan; Dalglish, Jordan

June 22 4 p.m. Waldstadion, Frankfurt   Attendance: 60,000

SCOTLAND ·   **1–1 YUGOSLAVIA**
Jordan (88)   Karasi (81)

Harvey; Jardine, Holton, Buchan, McGrain; Lorimer, Bremner, Hay, Morgan; Dalglish (Hutchison 65), Jordan

June 22 4 p.m. Parkstadion, Gelsenkirchen   Attendance: 35,000

ZAIRE   **0–3 BRAZIL**
                      Jairzinho (12),
                      Rivelino (66),
                      Valdomiro (79)

	P	W	D	L	F/A	Pts
YUGOSLAVIA	3	1	2	0	10–1	4
BRAZIL	3	1	2	0	3–0	4
SCOTLAND	3	1	2	0	3–1	4
ZAIRE	3	0	0	3	0–14	0

ACKNOWLEDGEMENTS

I have some recollection of the 1970 World Cup. They revolve mainly around watching grainy images on the small black and white television set in our family home as my dad enthused about the magical football being played by Brazil. Those finals came just after my beloved Aberdeen had won the Scottish Cup and helped to reinforce my love for the game.

In November '71 my old man took me along to my first Scotland match, the 1–0 win over Belgium at Pittodrie under Tommy Docherty, and I was hooked by the national team. Less than two years later we sat watching the unfolding drama of the qualifier against Czechoslovakia – we had gone to a friend's house, presumably because they had a colour TV – and I still recall the excitement, the disbelief of that astonishing night. Little did I know then that for a Scotland fan, as I have been ever since, nights like those were to be few and far between. Much more frequent have been the gut-wrenching disappointments, the glorious failures, like the exit from the 1974 finals following the 1–1 draw with Yugoslavia, played out on the day of my fourteenth birthday. My father died years ago, but I still hold him personally responsible every time football either rips my heart out or fills me with joy. Cheers, Dad!

More currently, thanks have to go to my agent, Kevin Pocklington, who was enthused by the idea for this book right from the start, and to all at Black & White Publishing for their support and encouragement, particularly my editor, Karyn Millar, and Janne Møller, who sourced some superb photographs.

It was a huge thrill recalling the dim and distant days of the early 1970s with some of those who had been talented enough to be called up to represent their country. In the end I collected contributions from eight of the squad, men who had different experiences to relate, given the varying contributions they made on and off the pitch. My sincere gratitude goes to Davie Hay, Danny McGrain, Jim Stewart, Martin Buchan, Peter Lorimer, John Blackley and 'The King' Denis Law. Also to my colleague, Kenny Macintyre, who interviewed Joe Jordan for me while compiling a 'Team Talk' for BBC Radio Scotland. Those guys gave willingly of their time and went to some lengths to recall incidents from four decades previously. Without their help, this project would have been impossible.

Of the twenty-two-man squad that travelled to West Germany, four – Billy Bremner, Jim Holton, Jimmy Johnstone and Erich Schaedler – are no longer with us. Neither is their manager, Willie Ormond. All feature in the tale I have told; none will ever be forgotten.

A number of the journalists who covered football at that time have also died in the subsequent years. I thank them for their hard work and diligence. Their recording of events all those years ago made the task not only easier but also more enjoyable, as I relived some of the most notable moments in the history of the Scottish game. I have used quotations from contemporary news reports, mainly from the *Herald*, throughout the book to add colour and drama but have not given individual sources so not to interrupt the flow.

My thanks must also go to staff at the Mitchell Library in Glasgow, where I spent many hours researching the archives, using microfilm and age-old newsprint, as I trawled through copies of the *Glasgow Herald*, the *Evening Times*, the *Scottish Daily Express* and the *Scottish Daily Record*.

Beyond that, countless (and I mean countless!) hours were

devoted to online research, where the following websites were, in particular, most useful:

http://scottish-football-historical-archive.com/drybroughcup.htm
http://news.google.com/newspapers
http://www.scottishfa.co.uk/football.cfm?page=2867
http://en.wikipedia.org/wiki/1974_FIFA_World_Cup_squads#Scotland
http://en.wikipedia.org/wiki/1974_FIFA_World_Cup_qualification_(UEFA)
http://www.hibshistoricaltrust.org.uk/player-profiles/item/44-willie-ormond
http://historicwarriors.comuv.com/index_files/page0043.htm
http://homepage.ntlworld.com/carousel/ITV/WorldCup74.html
http://www.youtube.com/watch?NR=1&feature=endscreen&v=kvxziVzAZsk
http://www.londonhearts.com/scotland/games/19721018.html
http://inbedwithmaradona.com/journal/2011/7/25/that-joke-isnt-funny-anymore-zaire-at-the-1974-world-cup.html
http://www.bbc.co.uk/blogs/thereporters/andrewharding/2010/06/africas_abandoned_football_leg.html
http://news.bbc.co.uk/sport3/worldcup2002/hi/history/newsid_1993000/1993333.stm
http://www.sfu.ca/~maxwell/scot_cl.htm

Various people offered help, information and advice along the way. As ever, in a situation like this, some names will be missed out, but among those deserving of a mention are George Yule, Paul Kiddie, Michael Grant, Darryl Broadfoot and Shaughan McGuigan. Apologies if you should have been included but weren't.

Finally, sincere thanks to one of my all-time football heroes, Gordon Strachan, for agreeing to write the foreword to this book.

ACKNOWLEDGEMENTS

As I sat on the sofa or bounced around the sitting room in the late autumn of 1973 watching that crucial qualifier against Czechoslovakia, I could never have imagined I would, decades later, be chronicling those events and the team's subsequent adventures in West Germany. It has been, in equal measure, a hugely rewarding and intensely frustrating process – but, in the main, great fun.